THE COLLECTED WORKS OF

F. A. Hayek

VOLUME XI

CAPITAL AND INTEREST

PLAN OF THE COLLECTED WORKS
Edited by Bruce Caldwell

Volume I	The Fatal Conceit: The Errors of Socialism (1988)
Volume II	The Road to Serfdom: Text and Documents—The Definitive Edition (2007)
Volume III	The Trend of Economic Thinking: Essays on Political Economists and Economic History (1991)
Volume IV	The Fortunes of Liberalism: Essays on Austrian Economics and the Ideal of Freedom (1992)
Volume V	Good Money, Part I: The New World (1999)
Volume VI	Good Money, Part II: The Standard (1999)
Volume VII	Business Cycles, Part I (2012)
Volume VIII	Business Cycles, Part II (2012)
Volume IX	Contra Keynes and Cambridge: Essays, Correspondence (1995)
Volume X	Socialism and War: Essays, Documents, Reviews (1997)
Volume XI	Capital and Interest (2015)
Volume XII	The Pure Theory of Capital (2007)
Volume XIII	Studies on the Abuse and Decline of Reason: Text and Documents (2010)
Volume XIV	The Sensory Order and Other Essays
Volume XV	The Market and Other Orders (2014)
Volume XVI	Hayek on Mill: The Mill-Taylor Friendship and Related Writings (2015)
Volume XVII	The Constitution of Liberty: The Definitive Edition (2011)
Volume XVIII	Essays on Liberty and Economics
Volume XIX	Law, Legislation and Liberty
Supplement	Hayek on Hayek: An Autobiographical Dialogue (1994)

The plan is provisional. Minor alterations may occur in titles of individual books, and additional volumes may be added.

THE COLLECTED WORKS OF

F. A. Hayek

VOLUME XI

CAPITAL AND INTEREST

EDITED BY

LAWRENCE H. WHITE

Routledge
Taylor & Francis Group
LONDON AND NEW YORK

F. A. HAYEK (1899–1992), recipient of the Presidential Medal of Freedom in 1991 and cowinner of the Nobel Memorial Prize in Economics in 1974, was a pioneer in monetary theory and a leading proponent of classical liberalism in the twentieth century.

LAWRENCE H. WHITE is professor of economics at George Mason University.

First published 2016 by Routledge

2 Park Square, Milton Park, Abingdon, Oxfordshire OX14 4RN
52 Vanderbilt Avenue, New York, NY 10017

Routledge is an imprint of the Taylor & Francis Group, an informa business

First issued in paperback 2020

British Library Cataloguing in Publication Data
A catalogue record for this book is available from the British Library

ISBN: 978-1-138-92327-0 (hbk)
ISBN: 978-0-367-66848-8 (pbk)

THE COLLECTED WORKS OF F. A. HAYEK

Founding Editor: W. W. Bartley III
General Editor: Bruce Caldwell

Published with the support of

The Hoover Institution on War, Revolution, and Peace
Stanford University

The Cato Institute

The Earhart Foundation

The Pierre F. and Enid Goodrich Foundation

The Heritage Foundation

The Morris Foundation, Little Rock

CONTENTS

Editor's Introduction ix

One Some Observations on the Imputation Problem (1926) 1

Two On the Problem of Interest Theory (1927) 20

Three Utility Analysis and Interest (1936) 32

Four Capital Consumption (1932) 47

Five Saving (1934) 67

Six On the Relationship between Investment and Output (1934) 75

Seven Professor Hayek and the Theory of Investment by Frank H. Knight (1935) 100

Eight The Mythology of Capital (1936) 118

Nine Technical Progress and Excess Capacity (1936) 141

Ten The Maintenance of Capital (1935) 156

Eleven Maintaining Capital Intact by A. C. Pigou (1941) 190

Twelve Maintaining Capital Intact: A Reply (1941) 194

Index 199

EDITOR'S INTRODUCTION

Hayek on Capital and Interest before The Pure Theory of Capital

The present collection of articles spans the first fifteen years of Friedrich A. Hayek's professional career, a period almost entirely devoted to technical work in economic theory. Regarding the difficult issues of capital and interest theory, the period can be divided into two unequal sub-periods. The first two articles represent the young Hayek's Vienna period, during which he had been most importantly influenced by his distinguished University of Vienna teacher Friedrich von Wieser.[1] The later articles represent the more mature Hayek's London period, during which he was teaching at the London School of Economics, and had been most importantly influenced by his post-university mentor Ludwig von Mises. The second period followed his 1931 lectures published as *Prices and Production* and culminated in his 1941 book *The Pure Theory of Capital*.[2] In these later articles, as in *The Pure Theory of Capital*, Hayek developed in his own distinctive way a perspective on capital and interest not grounded on the work of Wieser but rather on the work of Wieser's Viennese contemporary Eugen von Böhm-Bawerk. Additional influences were the work of the Swedish economist Knut Wicksell, who had developed Böhm-Bawerk's theory more rigorously, and the business cycle theory of Mises, who built on Böhm-Bawerk and Wicksell.

[1] On Hayek's turn away from his early Wieserian thinking in connection with the socialist calculation debate, see Laurence S. Moss, "Hayek's Borderless Economy: His Escape from the Household Model," in *F. A. Hayek as a Political Economist: Economic Analysis and Values*, ed. Jack Birner, Pierre Garrouste, and Thierry Aimar (London: Routledge, 2002).

[2] F. A. Hayek, *Prices and Production* (London: Routledge, 1931); 2nd rev. ed. (1935); reprinted in *Business Cycles: Part I*, ed. Hansjoerg Klausinger, vol. 7 of *The Collected Works of F. A. Hayek* (Chicago: University of Chicago Press, 2012); Hayek, *The Pure Theory of Capital* (Chicago: University of Chicago Press, 1941); reprinted as vol. 12 of *The Collected Works of F. A. Hayek*, ed. Lawrence H. White (Chicago: University of Chicago Press, 2007).

The Problem of Imputation

Recalling his studies in economics, psychology, and law at the University of Vienna between 1918 and 1921, a period during which Wieser returned from government service to the university, Hayek wrote: "In economics it was my teacher Friedrich von Wieser who directed my interest to the intricacies of the subjective theory of value, on one particular problem of which, the theory of 'imputation,' I wrote during the following year and a half a doctoral dissertation while employed in a temporary government office."[3] With his first degree (*doctor juris*) in hand, the twenty-two-year-old Hayek landed the government job in October 1921 by presenting a letter of recommendation from Wieser to one of the directors of the office, the prominent economist Ludwig von Mises, who was then forty years old. While working in the office, Hayek wrote a thesis for his second degree (*doctor rerum politicarum*). He then took a leave of absence to spend the period from March 1923 to May 1924 as a non-degree graduate student and research assistant at New York University. In autobiographical notes, Hayek continued the story, linking his thesis to a journal article on imputation published in 1926:

> I continued to register at the university [the University of Vienna] for the degree of *doctor rerum politicarum*, and in the summer of 1922 started work on a thesis on the theory of imputation, for which I got my second degree in February or March 1923, just before I went to America. Though I learnt a great deal in the work and the article on *Zurechnung* [imputation] which later emerged from it is a fairly respectable performance, I rather hope that no copies of the thesis have survived.
>
> . . . During the first six months in New York, I used my spare time . . . to turn my Vienna thesis on imputation of value into an article which Wieser had given me to understand might be used for the *Handwörtenbuch der Staatswissenschaften* but which ultimately appeared in Conrad's *Jahrbücher*. On the

[3] F. A. Hayek, introduction to *Money, Capital & Fluctuations: Early Essays*, by Hayek, ed. Roy McCloughry (Chicago: University of Chicago Press; London: Routledge and Kegan Paul, 1984), p. 1. On the Vienna period of Hayek's career, see Bruce Caldwell, *Hayek's Challenge* (Chicago: University of Chicago Press, 2004), ch. 6. Jörg Guido Hülsmann, in *Mises: The Last Knight of Liberalism* (Auburn, AL: Ludwig von Mises Institute, 2007), p. 472, following a working paper by Shigeki Tomo ("1922: A Watershed Year for Mises and Hayek," Kyoto-Sangyo University working paper, September 2003), stated that Hayek's dissertation was written "under the direction of Hans Kelsen and Othmar Spann." But Tomo corrected this claim in a later paper (Susumu Egashira and Shigeki Tomo, "Spann's Influence on Hayek: Dissertation and After," unpublished ms., n.d.). Spann and Kelsen were examiners who signed off on the dissertation. Wieser was the supervisor. Eugen-Maria Schulak and Herbert Unterköfler, *The Viennese School of Economics*, trans. Robert Grözinger (Auburn, AL: Ludwig von Mises Institute, 2010), p. 96. They noted that Wieser also supervised Hayek's post doctoral *Habilitationschrift* of 1929.

> whole I felt somewhat tired of the subjects which had chiefly occupied me in Vienna during the preceding year or so, such as the theory of subjective value or the problem of economic calculation under socialism.[4]

The absence of Mises' name from the 1926 article calls for explanation. Hayek wrote his 1923 thesis for Wieser, on the Wieserian approach to imputation. Although he wrote it while working in a government office where Mises also worked, they were not yet closely connected. Hayek reworked the thesis at Wieser's behest, into the shorter article included here, while away in New York. Hayek did not join Mises' private seminar until after he had returned from the United States in May 1924. It is therefore not surprising to find that the article reflects the influence of Wieser and not that of Mises. Mises' direct influence on Hayek could only barely have begun when the article was completed in late 1923, although that influence was evident in Hayek's newer work by the time the article finally appeared in print in 1926.

Hayek was, however, already aware of Mises' argument—which first appeared in a famous 1920 article—that a socialist planning board, in an economy without competitive entrepreneurial bidding for the services of factors of production, could not assign appropriate prices to those factors (labor, land, machines, materials, and so on). Mises wrote in his 1922 book *Socialism*: "To suppose that a socialist community could substitute calculations in kind for calculations in terms of money is an illusion. In a community that does not practice exchange, calculations in kind can never cover more than consumption goods. They break down completely where goods of higher order are concerned. Once society abandons free pricing of production goods rational production becomes impossible."[5] Hayek seems to have been challenging this argument in his 1926 article when he wrote: "If one holds the view that

[4] F. A. Hayek, *Hayek on Hayek: An Autobiographical Dialogue*, ed. Stephen Kresge and Leif Wenar (Chicago: University of Chicago Press, 1994), pp. 64–66. The dates indicate that although Hayek spent about a year and a half in the Vienna office job before his trip to New York, he spent only the second nine months of that period writing his dissertation. The first part of Hayek's unpublished dissertation, contrary to his expressed hope, survives in the Hoover Institution's Hayek archive. The journal article, "Bemerkungen zum Zurechnungsproblem," *Jahrbücher für Nationalökonomie und Statistik*, vol. 124, series III, no. 69, 1926, pp. 1–18, included in the present volume as "Some Observations on the Imputation Problem," would not have been appropriate for the *Handwörtenbuch der Staatswissenschaften*, in which the articles had the character of encyclopedia entries. Ludwig Elster, Adolf Weber, and Friedrich Wieser, eds., *Handwörterbuch der Staatswissenschaften*, 4th ed., 8 vols. (Jena, Ger.: Gustav Fischer, 1923–1928). The article "Zurechnung," written by Hans Mayer, that did appear in the *Handwörtenbuch*, vol. 8, 1928, pp. 1206–28, cited Hayek's 1926 article.

[5] Ludwig von Mises, *Die Gemeinwirtschaft: Untersuchungen uber den Sozialismus* (Jena, Ger.: Gustav Fischer, 1922); English translation, *Socialism: An Economic and Sociological Analysis* [1922], trans. J. Kahane (Indianapolis, IN: Liberty Fund, 1981), part 2, ch. 5, para. 22.

no fully satisfactory solution to the [imputation] problem has yet been found, it cannot be excluded—as several younger authors claim—that the determinants for the prices of the factors of production exist only in an exchange economy and that for this reason an imputation of value is not possible. Yet this admission would be tantamount to abandoning subjective value theory as a satisfactory explanation for economic processes and would deprive these authors of the very basis for many of their analyses."[6]

If Mises (who was thirty years younger than Wieser) was one of the "younger authors" to whom Hayek referred, then the claim in the second sentence above—that to deem non-market imputation of factor values impossible is to reject subjective value theory in the explanation of economic processes—signals that Hayek was siding with the methodological position of his teacher Wieser and opposing what he took to be the methodological position of Mises.

Such opposition may seem inconsistent with Hayek's well-known later arguments supporting Mises' critique of socialism. In the 1945 essay "The Use of Knowledge in Society," Hayek pointedly rejected Joseph Schumpeter's proposition "that consumers in evaluating ('demanding') consumers' goods *ipso facto* also evaluate the means of production which enter into the production of these goods." Hayek argued that to impute appropriate factor values, an observer would need to know not only all consumer demand curves for outputs, but also all producer supply and demand curves for inputs for all potential combinations of prices, which amounts to needing to know every potentially relevant bit of information about production techniques and local circumstances held by any of the myriad producers or potential producers in the market. He then took Schumpeter (and by implication other economists who thought "market socialism" feasible) to task for conflating an abstract model with reality:

> To assume all the knowledge to be given to a single mind in the same manner in which we assume it to be given to us as the explaining economists is to assume the problem away and to disregard everything that is important and significant in the real world. . . . I am far from denying that in our system equilibrium analysis has a useful function to perform. But . . . it is high time that we remember that it does not deal with the social process at all and that it is no more than a useful preliminary to the study of the main problem.[7]

[6] Hayek, "Some Observations on the Imputation Problem," this volume, p. 3.

[7] F. A. Hayek, "The Use of Knowledge in Society," in *Individualism and Economic Order* (Chicago: University of Chicago Press, 1948), pp. 90–91; reprinted in *The Market and Other Orders*, ed. Bruce Caldwell, vol. 15 of *The Collected Works of F. A. Hayek* (Chicago: University of Chicago Press, 2014), 103–4.

The 1926 article does not in fact conflict with this 1945 statement regarding the infeasibility of socialist central planning, however, because in the earlier article Hayek was not talking about socialism. Its subject was not the feasibility of correct pricing by a real-world central planner, but rather imputation by the explaining economist who has *by construction* all the knowledge necessary to solve a model that he himself builds. Hayek's 1926 claim is that an analyst who has *stipulated* the tastes, technologies, and resources of a model economy might in principle impute prices to its factors of production while abstracting from decentralized market exchange. In other words, in principle the economist might solve a general-equilibrium (GE) model for input prices, simultaneously with solving for consumer prices and for all input and output quantities. That Hayek was proposing such an approach to the factor-pricing problem is apparent in his remark toward the end of the article that "under Walras' leadership, the mathematical school of economics has already tackled successfully a similar set of tasks."[8]

In a pure exchange economy without production, given a set of consumer goods endowments, the consumers' subjective values are the sole cause of exchange and the sole determinant of equilibrium prices. In the simplest case of two consumers and two goods, the explaining economist can, to put matters in standard terms, draw a two-dimensional Edgeworth-Bowley box and thereby illustrate the simultaneous determination of the equilibrium range of mutually beneficial prices and quantities traded (or the single equilibrium price and associated quantities traded, if we assume that perfectly competitive behavior prevails in the bilateral exchange). In the case of a pure exchange economy of many consumers and many goods, an economist who knew all preferences and endowments could likewise determine equilibrium prices and quantities traded. Hayek in his 1926 article proposed that economists could extend the subjective value theory of the pure-exchange-economy model to a production-economy model although, as he noted, "altogether different conditions apply" to factors of production, and thus their prices "require a separate explanation" from consumer goods prices.[9] In 1926 it remained to be rigorously established that a GE model of a production economy with variable factor proportions could indeed be solved for the prices of the factors of production.

Mises and Hayek differed from their opponents in the socialist calculation debate of the 1930s and 1940s over how much relevance the solution of a GE model would have for guiding factor pricing in a real-world non-market economy. Their opponents, the "market socialists" led by H. D. Dickinson, Oskar Lange, and Abba Lerner, offered the solving of a simultaneous-

[8] Hayek, "Some Observations on the Imputation Problem," this volume, p. 19.
[9] *Ibid.*, p. 3.

equation GE model, together with trial-and-error adjustment of prices toward equilibrium, as practical techniques for real-world planning.[10] Hayek in 1926 made it clear that he was *not* asserting the feasibility of socialist planning in a complex real-world economy, because complete information about endowments and tastes could not be taken for granted in the real world. He cautioned: "Each solution of the imputation problem must take into account the totality of all the complementary goods used in an economic system and all the needs for whose satisfaction products are employed. This necessity may render impossible the practical application of imputation to any comprehensive economic system."[11] In 1945 he emphasized the additional necessity for taking into account the totality of relevant possibilities for productive transformation of goods, and—in place of 1926's cautious "may"—insisted against Lange and Lerner that the inescapable dispersion of knowledge *does indeed* render impossible the practical application of the GE-model-solving approach to directing any complex real-world national economy.

The 1926 article does, however, take a different view from the 1945 article with regard to the explanatory sufficiency of equilibrium theory. The two sides of the socialist calculation debate differed on how much relevance the GE approach has for understanding the factor pricing of a real-world market economy. In 1926 Hayek in Wieserian fashion offered "subjective value theory as a satisfactory explanation for economic processes." But in 1945, Hayek cautioned that a GE model "does not deal with the social process at all."

If GE theory is insufficient for understanding the market process, then it needs to be supplemented (or partly replaced) by a theory of price and quantity adjustment through entrepreneurial competition or something like it. Hayek would contribute to such a theory in his later essays "The Meaning of Competition" (1946) and "Competition as a Discovery Procedure" (1968). Israel Kirzner, in *Competition and Entrepreneurship* (1973) and later works, has further developed the Mises-Hayek entrepreneur-driven approach to the market process. Franklin Fisher has been the most important developer of a neoclassical mathematical analysis of equilibrating price adjustment.[12]

[10] For surveys of the debate, see Trygve J. B. Hoff, *Economic Calculation in the Socialist Society* [1938] (Indianapolis, IN: Liberty Fund, 1981); Don Lavoie, *Rivalry and Central Planning: The Socialist Calculation Debate Reconsidered* (Cambridge: Cambridge University Press, 1985); Bruce Caldwell, introduction to *Socialism and War: Essays, Documents, Reviews*, ed. Caldwell, vol. 10 of *The Collected Works of F. A. Hayek* (Chicago: University of Chicago Press, 1997), pp. 10–30; Lawrence H. White, *The Clash of Economic Ideas* (Cambridge: Cambridge University Press, 2012), ch. 2.

[11] Hayek, "Some Observations on the Imputation Problem," this volume, p. 19.

[12] F. A. Hayek, "The Meaning of Competition," in *Individualism and Economic Order*, and Hayek, "Competition as a Discovery Procedure" in *New Studies in Philosophy, Politics, Economics and the History of Ideas* (London: Routledge & Kegan Paul, 1978); both essays are now included in *The Market and Other Orders*, *op. cit.* Israel M. Kirzner, *Competition and Entrepreneurship* (Chicago: University of

Hayek continued to consider Wieser's omniscient-planner framework analytically useful for understanding and expositing the equilibrium conditions of a production economy, even though it did not illuminate the dynamics of the market process. Hayek used the "simple economy" device—exposition in terms of the optimizing principles to be observed by an omniscient and benevolent planner of a non-exchange economy—through much of *The Pure Theory of Capital* of 1941.

A puzzle remains. If Hayek's position in 1926 was that a GE approach to value imputation was appropriate—or even obligatory—for subjective value theorists developing *a model* of a production economy, why did he think that his position clashed with that of marginal productivity theorists who stressed a need for competitive markets to price inputs appropriately *in the real world*? The 1926 Hayek was talking about a purely logical construct with production techniques assumed by the modeler, a Wieserian one-mind omniscient-planner "simple economy."[13] The non-Wieserian marginal productivity theorists such as Mises, and the 1945 Hayek, were talking about an economy of many entrepreneurial minds containing various bits of knowledge and conjectures about efficient production techniques. One could hold both positions, as indeed Hayek did in 1945 when he said that GE analysis was a "useful preliminary" for theoretical understanding although it disregarded "everything that is important and significant in the real world" for the economy's guidance. When Hayek in 1926 declared it a mistake—"tantamount to abandoning subjective value theory as a satisfactory explanation for economic processes"—to claim that "the determinants for the prices of the factors of production exist only in an exchange economy and that for this reason an imputation of value is not possible," he was mistakenly viewing Wieser's logical construct as the only factor-pricing theory consistent with subjective value theory. Mises, in rejecting the usefulness of Wieser's one-mind given-techniques approach for pricing factors in the real world of competitive bidding for factors, did not reject equilibrium constructs *per se* and certainly did not reject subjective value theory.

Could Hayek have had some other critic of Wieser in mind besides Mises? Joseph Schumpeter is a candidate. R. C. McCrea argued that Schumpeter in his *Theorie der wirtschaftlichen Entwicklung* [*Theory of Economic Development*] held the

Chicago Press, 1973). Franklin M. Fisher, *Disequilbrium Foundations of Equilibrium Economics* (Cambridge: Cambridge University Press, 1983).

[13] Expositions of Walrasian GE theory also advance the proposition, based on the first and second fundamental welfare theorems, that one can solve for an economy's equilibrium allocation by solving the maximization problem of a benevolent social planner. For a critical perspective on this approach, see Kevin D. Hoover, *The Methodology of Empirical Macroeconomics* (Cambridge: Cambridge University Press, 2001), pp. 83–85.

position that, in McCrea's words, the problem of determining factor incomes "cannot be solved by an explanation of value phenomena, for income phenomena are price phenomena."[14] That is, *values* in Wieser's sense inhabit economic theories, whereas factor *prices* inhabit markets. But Hayek discussed Schumpeter by name elsewhere in the article, so it would have been odd not to identify him in these passages if Schumpeter's was the position under criticism. For Hayek not to wish to criticize his new job supervisor Mises by name in print, on the other hand, would have been understandable. So it seems likely that Mises and not Schumpeter was the object of Hayek's criticism.

Although Hayek's position in the 1926 article can be partly reconciled with his position in the more famous 1945 article, it clashes with another of his well-known later articles—namely, "Economics and Knowledge" of 1937.[15] In the 1937 article, Hayek insisted that the observation of how people gather and communicate information through markets is a crucial empirical element to understanding market processes. Hayek later characterized the article as a criticism of Misesian apriorism, a demonstration that there are sharp limits to the range of phenomena explainable by "the pure logic of choice" alone. But Mises' position on socialism—that without actual market exchange by private owners an economy cannot appropriately price factors of production—is in an important sense more empirical and *less* aprioristic than Hayek's 1926 position that factor pricing and optimal allocation can be understood by Wieser's "simple economy" construct of a single decision-maker. Wieser's construct is after all based on nothing but the pure logic of choice. Hayek in 1937 was thus also implicitly criticizing the Wieserian apriorism that he himself had embraced just over a decade earlier.

In what respects Hayek's well-known later critique of socialist calculation (found in his book chapters and journal articles of the 1930s and 1940s, collected in *Individualism and Economic Order*) was complementary to Mises' critique, and in what respects they were at odds, is a thorny question beyond the scope of our discussion here.[16] However, it should be clear that Hayek's 1926

[14] R. C. McCrea, review of *Theorie der wirtschaftlichen Entwicklung* by Joseph A. Schumpeter, *Quarterly Journal of Economics*, vol. 27, no. 3, May 1913, p. 523.

[15] F. A. Hayek, "Economics and Knowledge," *Economica*, n.s., vol. 4, no. 13, February 1937, pp. 33–54; reprinted in *The Market and Other Orders, op. cit.*, 57–77.

[16] Hayek, *Individualism and Economic Order*. For discussion of the issue, see Israel M. Kirzner, "Reflections on the Misesian Legacy in Economics," *Review of Austrian Economics*, vol. 9, no. 2, 1996, pp. 143–54; Bruce J. Caldwell, "Wieser, Hayek, and Equilibrium Theory," *Journal des Economistes et Etudes Humaines*, vol. 12, no. 1, March 2002, pp. 47–66; Joseph T. Salerno, "Friedrich von Wieser and Friedrich A. Hayek: The General Equilibrium Tradition in Austrian Economics," *Journal des Economistes et Etudes Humaines*, vol. 12, no. 2, June/September 2002, pp. 357–77; Odd J. Stalebrink, "The Hayek and Mises Controversy: Bridging Differences," *Quarterly Journal of Austrian Economics*, vol. 7, no. 1, Spring 2004, pp. 27–38; and Steven Horwitz, "Mone-

article on imputation does not show that Hayek's *later* writings on socialism are Wieserian rather than Misesian. It was written in 1923 before Hayek became more fully exposed to Mises' thinking. And as we have just seen, Hayek in his later writings had clearly moved away from his 1926 position in crucial respects.[17]

If Wieser, and Hayek in 1926, wanted to impute values to factors of production in a model without market exchange, and therefore without market prices, in what units are the values to be measured? Samuel Bostaph has raised the units question with regard to Wieser's equations, commenting: "Assuming that they are subjective value units begs the question of how such subjective values have been objectified."[18] Hayek in 1926, following Wieser, clearly regarded them as subjective value units, what other economists have called "utils," objectified by the analyzing economist and assumed to be measurable and interpersonally addible.

Since Lionel Robbins' 1932 book *The Nature and Significance of Economic Science*—heavily influenced by Mises' methodological subjectivism—economists have commonly recognized that choice-theoretic utility does *not* require measurability or interpersonal comparability in order for the theorist to derive demand curves and explain market prices, and so those properties can be excluded by the principle of Occam's razor. But Wieser clearly conceived of utility as something measurable and interpersonally comparable when he spoke of maximizing total social utility and when he endorsed progressive taxation on the grounds that a poor man values the marginal dollar of his income more than a rich man.[19] Hayek acknowledged that Wieser "considers the calculability of utility as basic for dealing with the whole problem, as can be hardly avoided."[20] If we follow Robbins in excluding "calculability" (measurability or interpersonal comparability) from choice-theoretic utility, then the need to assume calculability is a fatal flaw in Wieser's concept of imputation without market prices. It is not surprising then that Hayek in his later writings would have moved away from Wieser's concept.

tary Calculation and the Unintended Extended Order: The Misesian Microfoundations of the Hayekian Great Society," *Review of Austrian Economics*, vol. 17, no. 4, 2004, pp. 307–21.

[17] Thus although I agree with Jörg Guido Hülsmann, *op. cit.*, pp. 473–74, that Hayek in the 1926 article was criticizing Mises' position on imputation, I do not agree that "this fact is crucial to understanding the later stages of the debate on economic calculation under socialism" or that "the paper on imputation already indicated the future course of his argument" on socialism.

[18] Samuel Bostaph, "Wieser on Economic Calculation under Socialism," *Quarterly Journal of Austrian Economics*, vol. 6, no. 2, Summer 2003, p. 19.

[19] Friedrich von Wieser, *Social Economics*, trans. A. Ford Hinrichs (New York: Adelphi, 1927), pp. 433–34.

[20] Hayek, "Some Observations on the Imputation Problem," this volume, p. 18.

The Problem of Interest Theory

Hayek's 1927 essay "On the Problem of Interest Theory" is notable for the contrast between its critique of time-preference-based interest theory and Hayek's own later position, represented in this volume by his 1936 essay "Utility Analysis and Interest." In an appendix to *The Pure Theory of Capital*, Hayek essentially repudiated his 1927 article, commenting that in it he had used a particular approach "without being aware of the illegitimate assumptions which it involves."[21]

Hayek in 1927 criticized what he called the "*ad hoc* assumption that future needs are invariably valued lower compared to the same needs at the present time."[22] In 1936 Hayek took note of "the progress which has been achieved by Professor Irving Fisher's application of the modern apparatus of utility analysis."[23] In *The Pure Theory of Capital*, he would declare that the interest theory exposited by Fisher in *The Theory of Interest* (1930) was "formally unimpugnable."[24] The consumer in Fisher's theory has intertemporal preferences that, in an ordinary equilibrium, imply the subjective discounting of marginal future consumption relative to marginal current consumption. That an individual ordinarily (not invariably) values future satisfaction of "needs" below the present satisfaction of "the same needs" then becomes an implication of equilibrium and not an "*ad hoc* assumption." Subjective or "psychical" (as Hayek called it in 1936) discounting by consumers is the same concept that Hayek in 1927 characterized as "systematic under-valuation of future needs," but without the connotation (found also in Böhm-Bawerk's exposition) that the consumers are committing an error.[25]

Hayek in 1927 lamented the way in which Böhm-Bawerk's approach had excluded productivity explanations of interest. Fisher's theory, alongside subjective discounting, incorporates productivity in the form of an intertemporal production possibilities frontier. Hayek in 1927 also criticized what he characterized as "Böhm-Bawerk's approach, in which the structure of production generally did not constitute an object of analysis but was taken as given."[26] This was an uncharitable view of Böhm-Bawerk's approach. Böhm-Bawerk's model establishes an equilibrium in which the degree of roundaboutness in production—a scalar measure of the time period that will elapse between the first application of input and the arrival of output under the chosen produc-

[21] Hayek, *The Pure Theory of Capital*, *op. cit.*, p. 374 n. 4.
[22] Hayek, "On the Problem of Interest Theory," this volume, p. 20.
[23] Hayek, "Utility Analysis and Interest," this volume, p. 32.
[24] Hayek, *The Pure Theory of Capital*, *op. cit.*, p. 64.
[25] Hayek, "Utility Analysis and Interest," this volume, p. 33.
[26] Hayek, "On the Problem of Interest Theory," this volume, p. 22.

tion plan—is endogenously determined along with the equilibrium interest rate. The equilibrium interest rate equates the marginal subjective discount rate to the marginal physical rate of return from extending the degree of roundaboutness (for example, the marginal percentage increase in lumber yield from delaying the harvest of a growing tree). Thus the length of the structure of production *was* an object of analysis. Böhm-Bawerk offered a pair of diagrams that depicted longer and shorter structures of production as larger and smaller sets of concentric rings. Hayek used triangular diagrams for the same illustrative purpose. Hayek's diagrams were more readily adapted to other uses, particularly to illustrate the progress of a business cycle in which credit expansion fuels an investment boom.

In a footnote, Hayek offered an interesting rationale for the thesis that more roundabout production processes yield a greater physical output from given inputs: "The longer the time period in question, the greater the number of methods available for roundabout production, so that now production methods with a higher yield *may* become feasible, which previously have not been available."[27] Hayek's rationale is best understood as an alternative way of stating the general proposition that the greater productivity of more roundabout production processes is a logically implied characteristic of the frontier of non-dominated choices. Any positive discount rate implies that a process taking longer to bear fruit must produce *more* fruit to be potentially preferred to a shorter process.

In his 1936 article "Utility Analysis and Interest," Hayek used Fisherian diagrams to analyze an economy without "psychical discount," but instead exhibiting Schumpeter's assumption that, when anticipated future income equals present income, marginal future consumption is *not* discounted relative to marginal current consumption. Combining Schumpeter's assumption with the assumptions that capital accumulation is the only source of higher future incomes (technical progress being assumed absent) and that the returns to capital diminish toward zero with a growing capital stock, Hayek not surprisingly found that the economy's net saving, economic growth, and interest rate must all converge to zero. Hayek's analysis of the convergence to equilibrium persuaded him that the marginal rate of return to capital accumulation (intertemporal transformation or "productivity") was the dominant determinant of the equilibrium interest rate, with time-preference relegated to the minor role of determining the rate of saving along the path to stationary equilibrium.

Hayek drew heavily on his 1936 analysis in appendix 1 to 1941's *The Pure Theory of Capital*, titled "Time Preference and Productivity." But he had second thoughts about the dominance of intertemporal transformation over time-

[27] *Ibid.*, p. 23 n. 8.

preference in determining the interest rate in "Time Preference and Productivity: A Reconsideration" (1945), reprinted as appendix 5 to the latest edition of *The Pure Theory of Capital*.[28]

Capital Consumption and Saving

In his essays on "Capital Consumption" (1932) and "Saving" (1934), Hayek developed some long-run implications of his version of Austrian capital theory, the short-run (cyclical) implications of which he had sketched in *Prices and Production*.

In "Capital Consumption," Hayek expressed concerns about the evident shrinkage of the capital stock in Austria. Such concerns were shared by other Austrian School economists, especially Ludwig von Mises, Fritz Machlup, and Oskar Morgenstern. Hayek cited Morgenstern's statistical study of the problem for the Austrian Institut für Konjunkturforschung, published in 1931. Although he did not cite them, Hayek was probably aware of some of the other efforts, in Vienna and elsewhere, to diagnose and quantify the extent of Austria's capital consumption. Ludwig von Mises collaborated with Engelbert Dollfuss and Edmund Palla on an official report analyzing the sources of weakness of the Austrian economy, anonymously published in December 1930, and Mises devoted his university seminar in winter 1931 to the topic of capital formation, maintenance, and consumption.[29] Nicholas Kaldor, who at the time was a Hayekian (or Robbinsian—he had graduated from the London School of Economics the year before Hayek arrived there), discussed Austria's capital consumption in an article published in the *Harvard Business Review* in October 1932. Machlup would publish his research on the topic in the *Review of Economic Statistics* in 1935.[30]

[28] Hayek, *The Pure Theory of Capital*, *op. cit.*, pp. 396–402.

[29] [Ludwig von Mises, Engelbert Dollfuss, and Edmund Palla], *Bericht über die Ursachen der Wirtschaftlichen Schwierigkeiten österreichs* [Report on the causes of the economic difficulties in Austria] (Vienna: Staatsdruckerei, 1930); Hülsmann, *op. cit.*, pp. 614–15.

[30] Nicholas Kaldor, "The Economic Situation of Austria," *Harvard Business Review*, vol. 11, no. 1, October 1932, pp. 23–34; Fritz Machlup, "The Consumption of Capital in Austria," *Review of Economic Statistics*, vol. 17, no. 1, January 1935, pp. 13–19. These three works are cited by Richard Ebeling, "The Economist as the Historian of Decline: Ludwig von Mises and Austria between the Two World Wars," in *Political Economy, Public Policy and Monetary Economics: Ludwig von Mises and the Austrian Tradition* (New York: Routledge, 2010), pp. 133–34 nn. 40 and 41. Ebeling added that the findings of the Mises, Dollfuss, and Palla study are summarized in English by Frederick Hertz, *The Economic Problem of the Danubian States: A Study in Economic Nationalism* (London: Victor Gollancz, 1947), pp. 145–68, and that Mises had discussed the problem of capital consumption due to the distortion of accounting profits by inflation in his 1919 book *Nation, State and Economy*, ed. Bettina Bien Greaves, trans. Leland B. Yeager (Indianapolis, IN: Liberty Fund,

Hayek emphasized the trade-off between consumption today and consumption tomorrow (via saving and investment today): "The physical quantity of consumer goods per capita can only be increased by consistently devoting a larger part of productive resources to capitalistic investment rather than to immediate consumption."[31] One can illustrate the trade-off by drawing a production possibilities frontier between consumption and investment, as Roger Garrison has done in his important work developing Hayekian macroeconomics, particularly in the book *Time and Money*.[32] Although the trade-off derives directly from the assumption of scarcity, and is today taken for granted by economists in the context of growth theory, Hayek noted that it is implicitly denied by all those economists who "assume that the demand for capital goods changes in proportion to the demand for consumer goods."[33] The most prominent such economists in 1932 were the "underconsumption" theorists of economic depressions, including John Maynard Keynes in his *Treatise on Money* of 1930, which Hayek cited in this connection. Keynes amplified the underconsumption theme in his *General Theory* of 1936.[34] The assumption that consumption and investment move in the same direction over the business cycle (by contrast to the trade-off acknowledged in the analysis of long-run growth) has been fundamental to Keynesian macroeconomics up to the present day.

The business cycle theory of Hayek's *Prices and Production*, as Garrison has emphasized, is a theory of an unsustainable investment boom. The boom is unsustainable because an unwarranted credit expansion finances the investment of inputs into processes too roundabout to be completed by the available voluntary savings (resources made available by voluntary abstention from consumption by income-earners). Hayek labeled the misallocation "forced saving." As Garrison has pointed out, such a label unfortunately suggests that investors are compelling an immediate reduction in consumption by bidding resources away from consumers, or in other words that the economy remains on the same consumption-investment frontier even during the expansion phase of the business cycle. But an immediate reduction in consumption is difficult to reconcile with the fact that the interest rate, which represents the reward for saving rather than consuming, *falls* at the outset of the credit expansion.

2006), pp. 161–63. See also Hansjoerg Klausinger, "From Mises to Morgenstern: The Austrian School of Economics during the *Ständestaat*," *Quarterly Journal of Austrian Economics*, vol. 9, Fall 2006, pp. 25–43.

[31] Hayek, "Capital Consumption," this volume, p. 52.

[32] Roger Garrison, *Time and Money: The Macroeconomics of Capital Structure* (London: Routledge, 2001).

[33] Hayek, "Capital Consumption," this volume, p. 53.

[34] John Maynard Keynes, *A Treatise on Money*, 2 vols. (London: Macmillan, 1930); Keynes, *The General Theory of Employment, Interest, and Money* (London: Macmillan, 1936).

Garrison's own development of the Mises-Hayek cycle theory, building on Mises' identification of "overconsumption" during the early boom, provides greater coherence. It recognizes explicitly that credit expansion can temporarily push the economy beyond its sustainable frontier by financing overfull employment of labor and machines. The employment rates of laborers and machines (capacity utilization) rise above what economists today call their natural rates. During such a credit boom total investment can for a time increase somewhat (an increase that will later be regretted) without any reduction of current consumption.[35]

In 1932 Hayek had published a "Note on the Development of 'Forced Saving'" that traced the history of the concept among earlier economists. In his 1934 encyclopedia article on "Saving," included in this volume, he expanded his categorization of types of saving. Interestingly, the encyclopedia article criticized the use of the label "forced saving" for the case that Hayek himself had used it, calling such usage "an instance of the misleading practice of treating the term [saving] as equivalent to 'capital formation.'"[36]

The Debate with Frank Knight over Interest, Investment, and Capital

In a valuable 1970 restatement of neoclassical capital theory, Jack Hirshleifer formalized the three leading approaches to the relationship between capital goods and output.[37]

(1) The simplest approach is Frank Knight's "Crusonia-plant" model, in which capital consists of a single good that is physically homogenous with (and thus always "trades" 1:1 against) the consumption good. Imagine a huge fungus that can be eaten or left to grow. The single labor-using production process is the removal of pieces of fungus for immediate consumption. Production is instantaneous and simultaneous with consumption. The unconsumed remainder of the fungus grows naturally by itself (no labor required) at a known rate. The representative agent faces a single trade-off: higher consumption today versus a permanently higher flow of future consumption. Every future period's sustainable consumption, consistent with neither consuming nor accumulating capital, is exactly equal to one period's natural expansion of the remaining fungus.

(2) In the more complex second approach, the capital good is distinct from the consumption good. The price of the capital good relative to the consump-

[35] Roger W. Garrison, "Overconsumption and Forced Saving in the Mises-Hayek Theory of the Business Cycle," *History of Political Economy*, vol. 36, no. 2, Summer 2004, pp. 323–49.

[36] Hayek, "Saving," this volume, p. 69.

[37] J. Hirshleifer, *Interest, Investment, and Capital* (Englewood Cliffs, NJ: Prentice-Hall, 1970).

tion good can now vary. Production is not instantaneous but proceeds in two steps. In the current period, some share of inherited capital and labor are combined to produce the current consumption good, while the remaining share is used for investment—that is, to produce the end-of-period capital stock to be carried forward to the next period. In the next period the choice repeats with the carried-forward capital stock becoming the new inherited capital stock.

(3) In the most complex (Austrian) approach, the capital stock is not one good but a time-phased chain of intermediate goods—that is, goods-in-process at different distances from the dates at which they will mature into the consumable output good. The relative price of any particular capital good can vary against that of the consumption good, and also against prices of the earlier and further-along capital goods. There are arbitrarily many production stages, in the limit a continuous temporal stream of inputs, leading to consumption.

Hirshleifer treated the alternative approaches as employing different but equally legitimate sets of abstractions, making them useful for tackling different but equally legitimate analytical questions. Knight did not see it that way. The Crusonia-plant theory of capital he favored was "correct" and "sound," whereas the Austrian capital theory, particularly as represented by Hayek's 1931 book *Prices and Production*, was "incorrect" and useless, lacking "the essentials of a sound theory" of capital. In freeing economics from the "incubus" of Austrian capital theory, "the doctrines to be eliminated include all notions of any definite relation between quantity of capital and the 'length of the production process,' or 'time' in any form except the basic one of a dimension in summating any process, and include also the notion that the production process, under the ordinary conditions of capitalistic industry, has any determinate time length."[38]

Hayek defended the Austrian theory against Knight in his 1934 article "On the Relationship between Investment and Output," and counter-attacked in his 1936 article "The Mythology of Capital." Hayek did not entirely reject the usefulness of Knight's theory for certain basic questions, and agreed with some of Knight's criticisms of the model that Hayek had used in *Prices and Production*. But Hayek stressed the limitations of Knight's simple model for addressing the topics that Hayek wanted to address, particularly investment in a world where capital goods are not homogeneous, so that the capitalist-entrepreneur must choose among non-interchangeable types of capital goods that he might produce or use. Knight's model could have nothing to say, for example, about changes in the types of the capital goods that look most profitable to produce when the interest rate falls due to increased genuine saving

[38] Frank H. Knight, "Capital, Time, and the Interest Rate," *Economica*, n.s., vol. 1, no. 3, August 1934, pp. 257–58.

or due to central-bank credit expansion. It could have nothing to say about capital goods reallocations in propagating business cycle fluctuations. Such topics lie beyond the Knight model's simple analytics of a choice between a higher level of current consumption and a permanently higher level of future consumption.

Focusing on the concept of a permanent level flow of future consumption, Knight insisted that "all using up [of specific machines and materials] is a technical detail; all capital is normally conceptually, perpetual."[39] Thinking exclusively in terms of a perpetual capital good with instantaneous production, Knight was unable to make sense of the Austrians' concept of a choice among prospective investment periods—that is, a choice between investing for a near future date or for a more distant future date. Knight's perspective implied, as Avi J. Cohen has explained in a useful account of the Hayek-Knight controversy, that "specific periods of production are irrelevant and unmeasurable concepts."[40] In Knight's own words the concept of a period of production is "without theoretical significance for the nature and rôle of capital."[41]

Cohen noted that from Hayek's standpoint in "The Mythology of Capital," conversely, "Knight's homogeneous, permanent fund of capital purges any analysis of processes in time."[42] Hayek at one point accused Knight of trying "to expel the idea of time from capital theory altogether,"[43] but elsewhere he more accurately noted that Knight's aim was to reduce the time element in capital theory to the choice between a higher level of present consumption and a higher level of perpetual future consumption. To address the important questions that interested Hayek, a capital theory must include a theory of *intertemporal production choices* and not just a theory of intertemporal consumption choice treating production as automatic.

Knight in an earlier article had rejected Böhm-Bawerk's distinction between "original" (unproduced) and produced factors of production,[44] a distinction that Hayek had used in *Prices and Production.* Hayek in "The Mythology of Capital," and later in *The Pure Theory of Capital,* agreed that to be useful for the economic analysis of production decisions, such a distinction cannot be backward-looking.

[39] *Ibid.*, p. 259.

[40] Avi J. Cohen, "The Hayek/Knight Capital Controversy: The Irrelevance of Roundaboutness, or Purging Processes in Time?," *History of Political Economy*, vol. 35, no. 3, Fall 2003, p. 470.

[41] Frank H. Knight, "Professor Hayek and the Theory of Investment," *Economic Journal* vol. 45, no. 177 (March 1935), pp. 77–94; this article is reprinted in the present volume.

[42] Cohen, "The Hayek/Knight Capital Controversy," p. 470.

[43] Hayek, "The Mythology of Capital," this volume, p. 124.

[44] Frank H. Knight, "Capitalistic Production, Time, and the Rate of Return," in *Essays in Honour of Gustav Cassel* (London: George Allen and Unwin, 1933), pp. 327–42.

For Hayek's model there are two important distinctions among factors of production. The first distinction is between (*a*) *inherited* capital goods, or goods already existing at the moment that a production plan is being made, and (*b*) intermediate goods, or capital goods (of greater or lesser permanence) *to be produced* as part of a sequence of production steps leading to final output. Hayek's exposition in *Prices and Production* neglected inherited capital goods. It depicted the first production stage as involving only land and labor, which create intermediate goods that then progress through subsequent production stages toward final sales. Knight's model, by abstracting from roundabout production, abstracts entirely from intermediate goods. It offers only undifferentiated capital (the inherited Crusonia plant), which instantly yields consumption.

The second important distinction is between (*a*) factors that yield fixed streams of service each period—namely, simple labor and *permanent* non-labor input sources—and (*b*) factors whose use today diminishes their future usefulness and raises the problem of maintenance. The first group of factors, apart from labor, can be called economic "land" goods, whether given by nature (David Ricardo's "original and indestructible powers of the soil") or man-made (Hayek's example in *The Pure Theory of Capital* was a railroad tunnel that will need no maintenance once excavated). The second group encompasses all *impermanent* capital goods, from one-use blasting caps to depletable natural resource deposits to imperfectly durable machines. The simplified production model of *Prices and Production* treated all value-adding inputs, being applied in consecutive stages to advance intermediate goods toward final consumption, as coming from type (*a*) factors. The model reduced type (*b*) factors, impermanent capital goods, to intermediate goods. Knight's model neglected impermanent capital goods in a different way. Its construct of a perpetual capital stock implied that the maintenance or replacement of any impermanent tools is automatic, embodied in the decision about the permanent level of future consumption.

Hayek in "The Mythology of Capital" declared his "full sympathy with those who see in the concept of a single or average period of production a meaningless abstraction which has little if any relationship to anything in the real world."[45] But he rejected Knight's statement that "there is no productive cycle, or length of production period, which has determinate length or meaning."[46] The length of a production period in the backward-looking sense (applied to capital goods already at hand) is indeed meaningless, but prospective time-to-completion cannot be meaningless when choosing among various production processes that involve intermediate goods. Such choices lie out-

[45] Hayek, "The Mythology of Capital," this volume, pp. 119–20.
[46] Cohen, "The Hayek/Knight Capital Controversy," p. 471.

side the scope of the Crusonia-plant model with its single process and instantaneous production.

In the standard neoclassical theory of factor pricing, an hour's labor or machine service paid for today is priced under competition at the present *discounted* value of the input's marginal contribution to *future* revenue. To estimate discounted marginal revenue, an entrepreneur must estimate how many months will elapse until revenue accrues from the input—that is, must estimate the forward-looking (downstream) length of the investment period. The same information is necessary to estimate how the price of a capital good used in roundabout production, say a specialized lathe or a river barge, will change relative to the price of consumption goods in response to a change in the interest rate. Knight's Crusonia-plant model cannot analyze such a relative price change because, by the construction of a single capital good that is homogeneous with the consumption good, no such relative price change is possible.

Knight, as Cohen has pointed out, saw no role for capital theory in the explanation of business cycles. For Knight, recessions essentially originated from price stickiness in the face of monetary contraction (a fall in the stock or the velocity of money), a position that has been labeled both Old Monetarism (when associated with pre-1980 works by Clark Warburton, Milton Friedman and Anna J. Schwartz, and Leland Yeager) and New Keynesianism (in more recent works that attribute business cycles to demand shocks in an environment of sticky prices).[47] Without sticky-price frictions in the equilibrating process, growth would be smooth. Knight's capital theory can contribute little to business cycle theory because it was built entirely for other purposes. As already noted, it abstracts from any heterogeneity among capital goods, and even further assumes that the single capital good is homogeneous with the economy's consumption good. This approach makes it impossible to understand how the existing configuration of heterogeneous capital goods, in Hayek's words, "limits the possibility of current investment."[48]

The timelessness of production in the Crusonia-plant model—the feature that production and consumption are simultaneous—is innocuous enough in a stationary state, an equilibrium setting where economic agents simply go through the same motions every period, and no decisions about intertemporal production remain to be made. But the abstraction of timelessness will

[47] See Clark Warburton, *Depression, Inflation, and Monetary Policy: Selected Papers, 1945–1953* (Baltimore: Johns Hopkins University Press, 1966); Milton Friedman and Anna J. Schwartz, *Monetary Trends in the United States and the United Kingdom: Their Relation to Income, Prices, and Interest Rates* (Chicago: University of Chicago Press, 1982); Leland B. Yeager, *The Fluttering Veil: Essays on Monetary Disequilibrium*, ed. George Selgin (Indianapolis, IN: Liberty Fund, 1997); N. Gregory Mankiw. "New Keynesian Economics," in *The Concise Encyclopedia of Economics*, ed. David R. Henderson (Indianapolis, IN: Liberty Fund, 2008).

[48] Hayek, "The Mythology of Capital," this volume, p. 136.

not do, Hayek pointed out, for analysis of the non-stationary conditions represented by changes in the path of economic growth or by periods of adjustment in response to a shock to supply or demand for loanable funds (which may be monetary or real in origin). Knight's concept of perpetual homogeneous capital, Hayek argued in his 1936 essay, "prevents him from seeing at all how the choice of particular methods of production is dependent on the supply of capital, and from explaining the process by which capital is being maintained or transformed."[49] In Knight's model an increase in real saving will increase the quantity of capital (reduced consumption means more of the Crusonia plant is left to continue growing), but it *will not generally decrease the equilibrium interest rate* (unless an increase in the plant reduces the marginal rate at which the Crusonia plant grows, contrary to the usual assumption of a fixed percentage growth rate), and it cannot lengthen periods of production (production remains instantaneous). Hayek emphasized that "the concept of a definite time-structure of investment is even more important for the understanding of the dynamic processes of the accumulation and consumption of capital than for the mere description of the conditions of a stationary equilibrium."[50]

Abba Lerner in a 1953 article clearly explained how the Austrian concept of an anticipated *period of production* or *investment period* separating the date of a marginal input and the anticipated date of its output—for example, between the planting of a tree and the harvesting and sale of its lumber—necessarily eludes the grasp of Knight's perennial Crusonia-plant model of capital:

> An increase in the quantity of the perennial plant, brought about by failing to consume the whole of its growth, does not change the manner of production in any way whatever. Nothing is changed but the scale. The growth of the perennial plant being at a constant (geometric) rate, proportional to the quantity of it in existence, and the only input (in the stationary state) consisting of a decision not to consume more than the current accretion, the period of production is completely arbitrary. The current growth may just as well be considered as due to the stock not being consumed five years ago as to its not being consumed a hundred years ago or to its not being consumed one second ago, so that the period of production concept is quite meaningless.
>
> . . . It is as though we had a forest in which it made no difference what was the age of the trees cut down. Whether we cut down seedlings or mature trees or trees thousands of years old, as long as we did not remove more than a certain number of tons of timber each year, the forest would continue to give the same yield forever.
>
> . . . But as soon as we leave Knight's perennial and consider forests where

[49] *Ibid.*, p. 122.

[50] Hayek, "On the Relationship between Investment and Output," this volume, p. 76.

> it *does* make a difference at what age trees are cut, the period of production does become relevant. And the same kind of thing, that is, the existence of many methods of production with different time dimensions and having different efficiencies, is true of all production outside of "Crusonia."[51]

In Knight's analysis, capital is regarded as a single homogenous good. The theorist can talk about the growth or stationarity or shrinkage of capital *en masse*, but not of decisions made by any entrepreneur about whether to maintain or replace a particular capital good with its earnings, or instead to invest the earnings in something else. Capital accumulation is "permanent" in the sense that the single capital good, the aggregate Crusonia plant, does not shrink in a stationary or growing economy. In Hayek's analysis, by contrast, savings may be used to construct the wrong mix of various capital goods. An economy-wide cluster of malinvestments, associated with a disturbance of the market interest rate away from the equilibrium rate, ends in a period of reduced and possibly negative growth, and results in capital shrinkage. A characteristic feature of a business cycle recession, the idleness of some machines and not others, cannot be explained under the assumption that all capital goods are homogeneous and interchangeable.

In an account of Knight's career, George Stigler declared that in the Hayek-Knight capital theory controversy, "it is fair to claim victory for Knight over his adversaries (including Hayek, Machlup, Lange, and Kaldor) on this score: the period of production concept, which had never been fertile in real applications of capital theory, has virtually vanished from the literature."[52] It is true that today the "period of production" concept receives little discussion by that name, outside of studies in history of economic thought. But that is equally true of the Crusonia-plant concept and other distinctive features of Knight's theory of capital. It is therefore unwarranted to claim victory for Knight today on that score. The nucleus of the period of production concept does live on in "time-to-build" models of cyclical investment dynamics.[53]

Hayek's criticism of Knight was complementary to his critique of market socialism, as Peter Boettke and Karen Vaughn have noted. In Hayek's view

[51] Abba P. Lerner, "On the Marginal Product of Capital and the Marginal Efficiency of Investment," *Journal of Political Economy*, vol. 61, no. 1, February 1953, pp. 4–5.

[52] George Stigler, "Frank Hyneman Knight" (working paper 37, Center for the Study of the Economy and the State, University of Chicago, December 1985), p. 8.

[53] Finn E. Kydland and Edward C. Prescott, "Time to Build and Aggregate Fluctuations," *Econometrica*, vol. 50, no. 6, November 1982, pp. 1345–70; Michael R. Montgomery, "Capital Complementarity, Time-To-Build, and the Persistence of Investment Starts," *Journal of Macroeconomics*, vol. 17, no. 2, Spring 1995, pp. 187–205; Montgomery, "Austrian Persistence? Capital-Based Business Cycle Theory and the Dynamics of Investment Spending," *Review of Austrian Economics*, vol. 19, no. 1, March 2006, pp. 17–45.

both Knight and the market socialists made the mistake of thinking that their perfect-foresight general-equilibrium models, which by construction abstract from the problem of adjusting capital combinations in response to unforeseen shocks, were the only form of economic analysis available. Accordingly Knight—in sharp contrast to Mises and Hayek—thought that socialism was questionable only on political and not on economic grounds.[54]

Maintenance, Technical Progress, and Excess Capacity

In "The Maintenance of Capital," Hayek criticized A. C. Pigou's attempt to provide a workable definition of the concept of "maintaining capital intact." Pigou's concern was to guide business accountants and tax authorities in identifying net income (after capital maintenance has been subtracted) as distinct from gross income. Following Carl Menger's insight that the market values of capital goods derive from the values of the consumer goods they are expected to produce, Hayek observed that the economist's baseline should not be the requirements for constancy of the capital stock along some arbitrarily specified dimension but the requirements for constancy of final income. These are different things: "the stock of capital required to keep income from any moment onwards constant cannot in any sense be defined as a constant magnitude." And the economist's even more general goal should be to understand the requirements for equilibrium between "the decision of the consumers as to the distribution of consumption over time," which need not favor constant income, and "the decisions of the entrepreneur-capitalist[s] as regards what quantities of consumers' goods to provide for different moments of time," decisions that will not mesh if the set of market interest rates is not right.[55]

Hayek also made a point against Pigou similar to one he would make against Knight: when an economist limits his attention to stationary states, he cannot analyze how the structure of capital responds to shifts in time preference or technology. When a structure of capital, "which is the result of the equilibrating process, is treated as if it were a datum"—that is, the set of capital goods is treated as "given"—the result is a blindness to capital adjustment issues.[56] Treatment of the capital structure as a datum is implied whenever an economist focuses exclusively on "the quantity of capital," and whenever said "quantity" is held constant.

Pigou did not reply to Hayek in the pages of *Economica* until 1941, when he

[54] Peter Boettke and Karen Vaughn, "Knight and the Austrians on Capital, and the Problem of Socialism," *History of Political Economy*, vol. 34, no. 1, Spring 2002, pp. 155–76.

[55] Hayek, "The Maintenance of Capital," this volume, pp. 181–82.

[56] *Ibid.*, p. 157.

commented critically on *The Pure Theory of Capital*'s restatement of Hayek's argument. Hayek provided a brief rejoinder in the same issue. Because Pigou had not changed his position, Hayek restated his critique with an explicit example showing where Pigou's way of measuring capital, not taking anticipated obsolescence into account, clearly goes astray. In a 1942 contribution to the debate, J. R. Hicks judged that Pigou's "carefully constructed method of measuring capital," which did not account for obsolescence, "has (I think) been torpedoed by Professor Hayek." Hayek's argument, particularly the example given in the rejoinder, "establishes conclusively that there are instances where the physical maintenance of capital would not suffice to ensure the maintenance of capital in an economic sense." To achieve whatever income stream he desires, the capital owner must take into account the anticipated technical obsolescence of his machines (their reduced economic value once better machines become available) and not merely their physical wear and tear. Hicks noted correctly that the purpose for which Pigou (and Hicks) sought to measure capital was "the measurement of the Net Social Income," whereas Hayek may have been "thinking of a different problem," so that the argument between Pigou and Hayek was "to some extent at cross-purposes."[57]

Hayek's purpose in criticizing Pigou was indeed not the better measurement of aggregate social income. At the essay's end, he called his effort a "preliminary clearing up of the fundamental concepts."[58] It extended his efforts to develop Austrian capital theory. As he did in his criticisms of the Knightian model of capital and interest, Hayek sought to point out the analytical limitations imposed by treating the stock of capital goods as a homogenous mass. Such an approach cannot be used to study how mismatched intertemporal plans can bring about an unsustainable configuration of capital goods, which for Hayek was the key to understanding business cycles. The essay thereby reinforced the central message of Hayek's 1933 Copenhagen lecture "Price Expectations, Monetary Disturbances, and Malinvestments," namely, that monetary forces can create a business cycle (investment boom followed by a bust) by disturbing the matching of intertemporal plans.[59] To treat capital

[57] J. R. Hicks, "Maintaining Capital Intact: A Further Suggestion," *Economica*, n.s., vol. 9, no. 34, May 1942, p. 174. Note also Hicks' comment (p. 175n.): "When I wrote *Value and Capital*, Chapter XIV, I was myself an adherent of the Hayekian school on this matter, so I can appreciate the qualities of Professor Hayek's definition. I can also appreciate what Professor Hayek must feel about the quite unfounded accusation by Professor Pigou that the definition by constant income stream is a definition of gross income." For a critical retrospective on the Pigou-Hayek-Hicks discussion, see Maurice Scott, "Maintaining Capital Intact," *Oxford Economic Papers*, n.s., vol. 36, *Supplement: Economic Theory and Hicksian Themes*, November 1984, pp. 59–73.

[58] Hayek, "The Maintenance of Capital," this volume, p. 187.

[59] F. A. Hayek, "Preiserwartungen, Monetäre Störungen und Fehlinvestitionen," *Nationalökonomisk Tidsskrift*, 3rd series, no. 43, 1935, pp. 176–91; translated as "Price Expectations, Monetary Disturbances, and Malinvestments," in *Profits, Interest, and Investment*, by Hayek (London: Routledge, 1939); reprinted in *Good Money, Part I: The New World*, ed. Stephen Kresge, vol. 5 of

purely as a homogenous aggregate may be useful for other purposes, such as interest rate theory à la Fisher. But because it rules out consideration of how a variety of capital goods is configured, it excludes capital theory from helping to explain business cycles.

Hayek's 1936 lecture "Technical Progress and Excess Capacity" is a lively discussion of the practical policy question—still extremely relevant—of whether an economy is likely to grow faster when its investments (particularly in new technologies) are steered by government planning or by unrestricted entrepreneurial competition. Hayek emphasized that competition in this context is not an equilibrium state of affairs in which all plans are consistent and all returns equalized, but instead a process of rivalry in which firms test their various and not-mutually-consistent hunches about which investments in new technologies will prove most profitable. A central planning of investment will place the job of judging which investments are to be pursued "more or less arbitrarily in the hands of a few people," a job that market competition leaves open to a wide range of investors who are risking their own money. "It seems clear to me," Hayek wrote, "that there is no reason at all to assume that a central planning authority would have more knowledge or foresight than individual entrepreneurs" who know that their success will be determined ex post by the profits or losses.[60]

Hayek was concerned to rebut the argument, which he considered to have "enormous influence" on policy despite being "totally fallacious," that unrestricted competition in technology squanders resources when it "forces an entrepreneur to discard [or idle] machines that might still serve many years and replace them with new ones."[61] Thus again, as in "The Maintenance of Capital," Hayek addressed the implications of obsolescence. He showed that an imagined benevolent economic dictator, with the same information, would make the same decisions about new technology as would a profit-seeking entrepreneur. Both for society and for the entrepreneur, it pays to idle old machines when, but only when, the total costs of producing with new machines (including purchase and installation) are lower than the "running costs" of producing with the old machines (writing off sunk purchase and installation costs entirely). To be worth introducing, in other words, the new process has to save resources of greater value than the capital losses felt by the owners of now-

The Collected Works of F. A. Hayek (Chicago: University of Chicago Press, 1999), pp. 232–44. In the 1939 publication of the lecture (p. 153), Hayek added a footnote citing "The Maintenance of Capital" as the execution of his intent to "show more fully on another occasion" that "even if we could assume that entrepreneurs possessed full knowledge of all relevant future events there would be no reason to expect that they would act in such a manner as to keep the value of their capital (or any other measurable dimension of this capital itself—as distinguished from the income derived from it) at any particular figure."

[60] Hayek, "Technical Progress and Excess Capacity," this volume, p. 143.

[61] *Ibid.*, p. 145 (italics omitted from the first two quoted phrases).

obsolete equipment. The resource savings come from the reduced use of other inputs—labor, raw materials, land, energy, non-specific capital goods—which Hayek noted "can now be employed elsewhere."[62]

The lecture also complements the article "The Maintenance of Capital" in re-emphasizing in another context the point that maintaining the value of capital is only a means to satisfying consumer wants, not an end in itself. To maintain the value of *particular* capital goods by artificially impeding the introduction of better machines is contrary to the fundamental end of satisfying consumer wants to the greatest extent possible. Therefore, Hayek warned, "Individual capitalists serve the interest of the whole economy best by applying their intelligence and foresight to the discovery of the most profitable investment opportunities. They assume a nefarious role when they invoke *state protection against technical progress* that threatens the value of their capital investments."[63]

In the very interesting eighth section of the lecture, Hayek seemingly digressed to defend competitive product differentiation against the view that compulsory standardization would increase economic efficiency wherever it would lower average production cost through economies of scale. If consumers really would prefer a generic product at a lower price, he noted, there are profits to be made by those "standardization fanatics" willing to invest their own money in testing the proposition. This section is not really a digression, because it reinforces Hayek's point that "underutilized capacity is not always tantamount to wastefulness."[64]

The lecture grapples more directly with economic policy questions than any other piece in the present volume. We can appropriately close this introduction to the volume by quoting Hayek's concluding remarks on the role of the academic economist in public policy discussions when popular opinion fails to share the economist's appreciation for the benefits of free markets:

> I do consider it the task of academic economists, however, to represent the claims of reason, no matter what their short-run effectiveness. Public opinion, which today may in truth hamper a reasonable policy, is not set in stone, and I am afraid that our predecessors, the previous generation of economists, bear some blame for the current state of affairs. If all hope is forlorn, one hope still remains: that we academic teachers, through our influence on the thinking of the next generation, will undo at least in part the great harm inflicted by some of our predecessors.[65]

[62] *Ibid.*, p. 147.
[63] *Ibid.*, p. 149.
[64] *Ibid.*, p. 151 (italics omitted).
[65] *Ibid.*, p. 155 (italics omitted).

ONE

SOME OBSERVATIONS ON THE IMPUTATION PROBLEM[1]

1. The Concept of Economic Imputation and Its Origins

Whenever an economic good yields utility directly and in isolation, the theory of marginal utility enables us to establish a well-defined correspondence between its utility and its subjective value.[2] Under these conditions, as is well-known, the value of a given amount of the good is determined by the smallest amount of utility that can be obtained from its use without foregoing a greater amount of utility that can be obtained elsewhere.[3] However, this principle does not apply directly to goods that do not satisfy certain needs on their own, but can do so only in conjunction with other economic goods.[4] According to Menger, these are called complementary goods. Under these circumstances, the utility obtained in each case is brought about and depends on several goods. Thus, several values must be derived from this utility, if value is still

[1] [Hayek later recalled that his teacher Friedrich von Wieser at the University of Vienna "directed my interest to the intricacies of the subjective theory of value, on one particular problem of which, the theory of 'imputation,' I wrote . . . a doctoral dissertation." F. A. Hayek, introduction to *Money, Capital & Fluctuations: Early Essays*, by Hayek, ed. Roy McCloughry (Chicago: University of Chicago Press; London: Routledge and Kegan Paul, 1984), p. 1. Hayek then reworked the dissertation into the present article: "Bemerkungen zum Zurechnungsproblem," *Jahrbücher für Nationalökonomie und Statistik*, vol. 124, series III, no. 69, 1926, pp. 1–18; translated by Grete Heinz as "Some Remarks on the Problem of Imputation," in Hayek, *Money, Capital & Fluctuations*, pp. 33–54; translation revised by Hansjoerg Klausinger.—Ed.]

[2] [Note that Hayek here distinguishes "utility" from subjective value. "Utility" means "use" and not a subjective value-ranking indicator as became common in later Anglophone economics. On the confusion caused by the common translation of *Grenzwert* (marginal value) as "marginal utility," see J. Huston McCulloch, "The Austrian Theory of the Marginal Use and of Ordinal Marginal Utility," *Zeitschrift für Nationalökonomie*, vol. 37, nos. 3–4, December 1977, pp. 249–80; and Jack High and Howard Bloch, "On the History of Ordinal Utility Theory: 1900–1932," *History of Political Economy*, vol. 21, no. 2, Summer 1989, pp. 351–65.—Ed.]

[3] [For example, if Robinson Crusoe has twelve sacks of grain, the subjective value to him of one sack of grain—what he would lose in value if he were to lose one sack of grain—is the importance he assigns to his twelfth-most important use for a sack of grain.—Ed.]

[4] [For example, a teapot may satisfy no want without tea, and likewise the tea without a teapot.—Ed.]

to be explained by utility. This raises a highly important issue, since the underlying relationship between value and utility is not limited to those cases where needs require several consumer goods for their satisfaction but includes those in which needs are met by a *product* and thus indirectly require a multiplicity of (producer) goods for their satisfaction. While the former case is usually disregarded as trivial, considerable attention has been paid in the literature to the problem of deriving the value of the individual producer goods from the utility jointly created by them. This problem, for which Wieser introduced the term *Zurechnung* (English: imputation; French: *imputation*; Italian: *imputazione*) in analogy to its use in jurisprudence,[5] has been dealt with extensively by the so-called Austrian School in its elaboration of the theory of subjective value.

2. *The Position of the Doctrine of Imputation in Modern Economic Theory*

According to the modern theory of subjective value, the determination of prices is basically explained by individual valuation. At the same time, since Ricardo, it has been widely agreed that the objective of economic theory is to discover the determinants of income, primarily by investigating what determines the prices of the factors of production. Consequently, all economic theory rests on the explanation of the value of producer goods and hence on the theory of imputation. A satisfactory solution of the imputation problem is thus a precondition for a distribution theory based on the theory of subjective value. As subjective value, to be explained by this theory, is itself the cause of exchange and the determinant of price, the solution must proceed without recourse to exchange. It must therefore be based on that type of an economy guided by a single will that Wieser has called a simple economy. Unless otherwise specified, we will refer to the conditions of such a simple economy in our subsequent observations.

For a theory of distribution based on subjective value theory, the importance individuals attribute, under given conditions, to each of the factors of production must derive from the valuation of the utility of the product. As remains to be shown, this issue is intimately related to the question to what extent the production which requires the use of the good in question is to be economically expanded. It thus implies a question about man's use of goods as circumstances demand. In seeking to determine the value of a given quan-

[5] [The imputation principle of jurisprudence apportions legal liability for an act among the responsible actors. Hayek's teacher Friedrich von Wieser had discussed the parallels between economic and legal imputation in the course of his seminal discussion of the imputation problem in Wieser, *Natural Value*, ed. William Smart, trans. Christian A. Malloch (London: Macmillan, 1893), book 3, ch. 2, pp. 75–76.—Ed.]

tity of consumer goods, although the answer found overcame the spurious contradiction between value and utility and simultaneously laid the groundwork for all value theory, the problem thus solved constitutes only a part of the problems of theoretical economics. The foundations for answering the question of the structure of the economy as a whole and hence for the problem of distribution are only addressed by the theory of imputation. If the imputation problem has not received due attention and has been ignored altogether in some systems of subjective economic theory, which moved directly from the explanation of the value of consumer goods to the explanation of prices and the forms of income, this is due to the mistaken belief that, by explaining the value of consumer goods, the problem of economic value as a whole has been solved. It thus has been overlooked that producer goods, to which altogether different conditions apply, require a separate explanation. It is not true that imputation theory is merely a special application of the general rules for determining value, as was believed in the early days of the marginal utility theory. In truth, it is the next and decisive step in the development of economic theory based on subjective value. We shall attempt to show in subsequent sections what strides have been made in that direction. If one holds the view that no fully satisfactory solution to the problem has yet been found, it cannot be excluded—as several younger authors claim—that the determinants for the prices of the factors of production exist only in an exchange economy and that for this reason an imputation of value is not possible.[6] Yet this admission would be tantamount to abandoning subjective value theory as a satisfactory explanation for economic processes and would deprive these authors of the very basis for many of their analyses.

[6] [Here the claim that "the determinants for the prices of the factors of production exist only in an exchange economy" probably refers to Mises' argument that a socialist planning board, in an economy without markets for factors of production, could not assign meaningful prices to those factors. Ludwig von Mises, "Economic Calculation in the Socialist Commonwealth" [1920], trans. S. Adler, in *Collectivist Economic Planning*, ed. F. A. Hayek (London: Routledge, 1935), pp. 87–130; Mises, *Socialism: An Economic and Sociological Analysis* [1922], trans. J. Kahane (Indianapolis, IN: Liberty Fund, 1981). In the next sentence the young Hayek objects that the claim in question rejects subjective value theory, by which Hayek appears to mean the Wieserian pure logic of choice. But Mises argued that central planning was unable to price factors of production in an *actual economy*, not that a *model* of benign central allocation of factors of production has no explanatory value. In an economy with production, a Wieserian or Walrasian economist can derive specific general-equilibrium prices (including factor prices) from consumer tastes and factor endowments only by *assuming* (hence fully knowing) a specific set of efficient production methods. A more mature Hayek would later emphasize, following Mises, that in the real world we must rely on markets to provide prices to factors of production because no planner can come close to fully knowing the set of efficient production methods. No single mind, but only rivalrous bidding by entrepreneurial producers in markets, can price factors to reflect all the relevant knowledge about production possibilities because that knowledge is dispersed among various producers.—Ed.]

3. Older Formulations of the Problem

The imputation problem has often been formulated—not quite correctly—as asking which share of the utility attained by a product is attributable to specific producer goods used in its production. In this formulation, the problem coincides with a perennial problem of economics, namely, the relative productivity of the factors of production. In a wider sense, all attempts to answer this question, unclear as is its meaning, could be classified as imputation theories. There have always been some, J. St. Mill among them, who have insisted that the problem is inherently insoluble because each factor is an indispensable condition for the outcome as a whole, but over the years various efforts have also been made to solve the problem. Most of these efforts were doomed from the start, however, because of their underlying materialistic concept of productivity, based on ideas from physics, and the corresponding objective interpretation of value. In addition to the endeavors of the Physiocrats and the classical and socialist schools, which ascribe productivity exclusively to the "value-creating power" of land or human labor, the best-known attempt is J. B. Say's theory of productive services. However, these cannot be counted as imputation theories in the narrower sense, if for no other reason than that the systems of thought embodying them had not developed an independent measure of the economic outcome to be imputed, other than the actual expenses for producer goods.

As long as no adequate explanation for the expression of economic outcome, that is, value, had been found, all attempts to determine the participation of the factors of production in this outcome were bound to fail. Explanations had to be shifted to the field of technology until the relationship between the usefulness and the scarcity of goods became the point of departure for explaining all economic actions. It is true that Ricardo, as well as his predecessors and his successors, in the specific case of land rent correctly described one element in the relationship between the value of products and the value of one factor of production in their theory of differential rent. They thereby introduced into economic theory the idea of imputing part of the value of a product determined independently of the participation of the producer good.[7] However, this idea could not be generalized because it lacked a theoretic framework for deriving a measure of economic outcome and for divorcing its magnitude from its physical causes. H. v. Thünen's more elaborate version of the rent theory came closest to being interpreted as a theory of imputation—its basic features were in fact subsequently developed specifically by American

[7] [That is, in Ricardian rent theory the value of a plot of land derives from the value of its output. Elsewhere in classical economics—namely, in the cost-of-production or labor theory of value—the value of an output derives from the value of the inputs that go into it.—Ed.]

scholars along these lines (see Section 5).[8] It too failed, however, for lack of an appropriate concept of value. Once the subjective value theory showed that the outcome of economic activity could be expressed in terms of value, independently of the activity itself, the problem of determining the participation of the individual production factors in this outcome could be tackled with some hope for success. The long neglected scholar H. H. Gossen, who first developed this theory, already fully recognized this fact and attempted to solve the problem in a way that is in principle analogous to Menger's and Böhm-Bawerk's later attempts.[9] The systematic treatment of the theory of imputation, however, must be dated from the publication of Menger's *Grundsätze der Volkswirtschaftslehre* in 1871.[10]

4. *The Development of the Imputation Theory by the Marginal Utility School*

The so-called principle of substitution, which had already been used successfully in explaining the value of consumer goods, underlay the first attempts at solving the imputation problem. Menger, like Gossen before him, made some tentative attempts in that direction, while Böhm-Bawerk later constructed a self-contained imputation theory on this foundation. The principle of substitution states that the value of a good disposed to a specific use equals the smallest utility to be attained not in this use but the smallest utility in any use whatsoever. According to Menger value is explained by the dependent utility of the good in question. His reasoning goes as follows: If a good originally disposed to a use with a higher utility ceases to be available, it will be replaced by the good that until that time was in the use with the lowest util-

[8] [Johann Heinrich von Thünen, *Der isolierte Staat in Beziehung auf Landwirtschaft und Nationalökonomie*, 3 vols. (Berlin: Biegandt, Hempel, and Parey, 1875); English translation, *Von Thunen's Isolated State: An English Edition of "Der isolierte Staat,"* ed. Peter Hill, trans. Carla M. Wartenberg (Oxford: Pergamon Press, 1966).—Ed.]

[9] [Hermann Heinrich Gossen, *Die Entwickelung der Gesetze des menschlichen Verkehrs, und der daraus fließenden Regeln für menschliches Handeln* (Brunswick, Ger.: Vieweg und Sohn, 1854). Hayek wrote an introduction for the third edition of this work (Berlin: Prager, 1927). English translation, *The Laws of Human Relations and the Rules of Human Action Derived Therefrom*, trans. Rudolph C. Blitz, with an introduction by Nicholas Georgescu-Roegen (Cambridge, MA: MIT Press, 1983). Hayek commented in a letter to Georgescu-Roegen in May 1982 on his own 1927 effort: "Wholly inexperienced in the job of editing as I then was (at 27 years of age) I did my best to collect all available information, but did not even have time to re-read the book whose importance I had recognized but which I had never really closely studied." As quoted by Paola Tubaro, "Personal Drama or Theory-Building? Georgescu-Roegen on Gossen" (working paper, University of Greenwich, 2011), p. 6.—Ed.]

[10] [Carl Menger, *Grundsätze der Volkswirtschaftslehre* (Vienna: Wilhelm Braumüller, 1871); English translation, *Principles of Economics*, trans. James Dingwall and Bert F. Hoselitz (New York: New York University Press, 1976).—Ed.]

ity. Thus the loss of utility caused by the unavailability of the original good would ultimately manifest itself at the position vacated after this substitution. Menger applies the same reasoning to replaceable goods of higher order. For irreplaceable producer goods he supplemented it by the further consideration that the loss of utility due to the unavailability of such a producer good and the prevention of production caused by it is partially compensated by the utility achieved by the complementary goods in new uses. The final loss thus amounts only to the difference between the utility originally expected and that finally attained. However, if none of the complementary goods required for a specific purpose can be used elsewhere or replaced, the entire utility attained by the combination will be lost if any one of the goods is unavailable. Böhm-Bawerk summarizes the resulting rules for the imputation of value in the following three cases[11]

1. If none of the required complementary goods can be replaced or used elsewhere, then considering the loss or acquisition of these goods the entire utility of the product can be imputed alternatively to each of the goods.
2. If a producer good can be used elsewhere, its value must correspond at least to the utility attainable in the alternative use and the difference between the total utility of the product and this value constitutes the upper limit to the value of the remaining complementary goods.
3. The value of replaceable goods must never exceed the utility that can be attained in their alternative use.

Within these limits, which may be quite narrow in the case of goods that have multiple uses, the value imputed to the individual goods will depend on the specific situation in which valuation takes place. When the acquisition or loss of a "final unit" is involved, whereas the availability of the remaining complementary goods is taken for granted, it should be attributed all that remains after deducting the minimal values for the other goods from the value of the product; on the other hand, according to the above rules, when the provision of the necessary complementary goods is not yet ensured, only the minimal value will then be imputed to the good, which has to be viewed as an isolated "splinter." In other words, if we are to apply the latter method to the valuation of all complementary goods, the undistributed residual will be attributed to the value of that good the lack of which would make production impos-

[11] Eugen von Böhm-Bawerk, "Grundzüge der Theorie des wirtschaftlichen Güterwerths," in *Jahrbücher für Nationalökonomie und Statistik*, n.s., vol. 13 (1886). [Böhm-Bawerk's long article appeared in two parts, "I. Die Theorie des Subjektiven Werthes," pp. 1–82, and "II. Die Theorie des Objektiven Werthes," pp. 477–541. English translation, *Basic Principles of Economic Value*, trans. Hans F. Sennholz (Grove City, PA: Libertarian Press, 2005).—Ed.]

sible. Generally speaking, to irreplaceable factors therefore the entire remaining amount over and above the minimum values of the other goods will be imputed, while goods that have no alternative uses only obtain the amount of value left over after the maximal value attainable by the complementary goods has been deducted. Therefore the results of the imputation will differ according to the stipulated situation. As a consequence, the sum of the various values ascribed to the individual factors may well either not exhaust or exceed the value of the product. This outcome is nevertheless consistent with the general theory of value held by the authors adhering to this interpretation, for whom the principle of marginal utility is only of alternating effectiveness in determining the value of the units of a given quantity of goods. It is also an unavoidable consequence of their defining value in terms of dependent utility. The method, however, fails in determining the values of a set of producer goods which must be used jointly to generate utility. Invoking substitutability or alternative uses of these goods only refers to cases which are as much in need of an explanation as the one in question. It is for cases like these that Wieser's attempted solution was intended.

Wieser's *Ursprung und Hauptgesetze des wirtschaftlichen Wertes* had closely examined the conditions relating to the value of producer goods even prior to the publication of Böhm-Bawerk's above-mentioned treatise. After offering a critique of Menger's and Böhm-Bawerk's attempted solutions, he presented his own fully developed solution to the imputation problem in a second work, published in 1889 under the title *Der natürliche Wert.*[12] Wieser's second work remains the basic and most thorough treatment of the problem even today and can be viewed as the classical account of the theory of imputation as such, although it has been superseded and complemented to some extent by his comprehensive treatise on economic theory.[13] Menger's and Böhm-Bawerk's attempts mainly consisted in extending to producer goods their successful explanation of the value of consumer goods by dependent utility. Wieser's solution, however, takes into account in a broader sense the specific conditions of production, which he has incorporated into the system of subjective value theory by his fundamental inquiry into the law of costs. At least at the outset of his inquiry he concentrates on the value of the products as the primary problem the solution of which will result in the solution of the problem of imputation. Just as the economic principle requires for consumer goods used for different

[12] [Friedrich von Wieser, *Über den Ursprung und Hauptgesetze des wirtschaftlichen Wertes* [On the nature and essence of economic values] (Vienna: Alfred Hölder, 1884); and Wieser, *Der natürliche Werth* (Vienna: Alfred Hölder, 1889); English translation, *Natural Value*, trans. Christian A. Malloch, ed. William Smart (London: Macmillan, 1893).—Ed.]

[13] [Hayek refers here to Friedrich von Wieser, *Theorie der gesellschaftlichen Wirtschaft* (Tübingen, Ger.: J. C. B. Mohr, 1914); English translation, *Social Economics*, trans. A. Ford Hinrichs, with a preface by Wesley Clair Mitchell (New York: Adelphi, 1927).—Ed.]

purposes that the same margin of use is maintained in all these uses, producer goods, accordingly, should also be used in such a way that their share of the value of the product in none of its uses be smaller than the greatest value that might have been attained in any other use, but could not be accomplished for lack of a sufficient provision of these goods in arranging the production process. It follows that in a simple economy, production will be extended to the point where the individual producer goods have the same valuation in the various lines of production and the utility attained in each production is distributed fully among the various production factors. Only if this condition is fulfilled, will the available producer goods be put to the most advantageous use. Then it will be impossible to achieve a more advantageous use by shifting individual units of producer goods to the production of goods the utility of which exceeds the sum of the values of these producer goods or by withdrawing them from the production of goods where the reverse is true. The only exception is where a product's utility scale is discontinuous and thus prevents the extension of production up to this point. In this case the value of the product is determined by its "cost utility," that is, the sum of the values to be imputed to its factors in their marginal uses (law of costs).

Since the value of a given means of production is equal in its various uses, the mutual relation between the values of products from the same factors on the one hand and their relation to the values of the production factors on the other hand can be expressed in the form of equations. The same factors of production will appear as values of equal magnitude on one side of these equations, which are thus mutually dependent. Inserting specific values either for the products or for the producer goods therefore allows the calculation of the values of the other items, respectively. Wieser makes use of this equivalence by inserting the values of the products on one side of the equations and deducing from them the values of the producer goods. He considers this the basic form of value imputation, which he denotes as "common imputation." In a partial adoption of Böhm-Bawerk's analysis, Wieser complements this basic form of value imputation in his *Theorie der gesellschaftlichen Wirtschaft* with a sort of remainder imputation denoted as "specific imputation" for certain goods. The distinction between these goods, which justifies the different methods of imputation, is based on the different diversity in the uses of different goods of higher order. Producer goods with multiple uses are thus classified as "cost goods" and those with relatively limited uses as "specific producer goods," a classification, which by its very nature is not absolute but applies perfectly only in extreme cases, while in the intermediate cases it is of only relative significance. Cost goods, which can be used in almost all lines of production, exert a certain leveling influence on the margin of use of all their products, so that the marginal utilities of products requiring only cost goods in their production will generally stay within relatively narrow limits and will therefore differ from each other only in terms of the number of productive groups required for their production. The fewer the lines of production in which a good can be used, the narrower the scope within which such a leveling can take place and, for this reason, the more will its specific relative scarcity make itself felt with the respective products in a deviation from the general level of the marginal utility of products. Its products will display a margin of use relatively narrower or wider than the average of cost products. This narrower margin of use should not be confused with the one occasioned by the discontinuity in the utility scales of individual products. Wieser actually has stopped short of carrying his analysis of this question to its conclusion; at any rate, he does not clearly formulate that even within the "products of a general margin of use" the margins of use will necessarily differ due to differences in their relative composition. The particular influence of "specific producer goods" on the margins of use of the products in the production of which they are employed is also decisive for the method of imputation applicable for these producer goods. While the "cost goods" involved in the production are to be computed with the value imputed to them from cost products, the deviation from the general margin of use and the resulting unusually high or low value must be credited to the specific producer good. The entire difference between the given value of the cost goods and the value of the product must be thus imputed to the specific producer good. In the absence of the leveling tendency of cost goods, its value is therefore much more highly dependent on the value of specific products and on its fluctuations. Consequently the types of income that are largely dependent on the value of these specific production goods show distinctive movements for which they are described as rents and thereby as subject to distinctive laws of their own. Whenever several specific factors are combined in production, whichever factor is more versatile and therefore is closer to a cost good, is to be viewed as a cost element in relation to the other factors: the value it could achieve in alternative uses is to be deducted from the total value of the product and the remainder imputed to the specific factor.

Wieser's analysis is grounded on a conception of the principle of marginal utility that is at odds with the one held by most of the other proponents of the marginal utility school, namely, the cumulative computation of the value of all units of a given quantity of goods according to their marginal utility.[14]

[14] On this topic, see the articles on "Wert" and "Grenznutzen" in J. Conrad et al. (eds.) *Handbuch für Staatswissenschaften*, 3rd ed., Jena, Fischer, 1909–1911; see also H. Mayer, "Untersuchungen zu dem Grundgesetz der wirtschaftlichen Wertrechnung," *Zeitschrift für Volkswirtschaft und Sozialpolitik*, n.s., v. 1 (1921) [pp. 431–58] and v. 2 (1922) [pp. 1–23]. [In citing these two "Handbuch" articles by Wieser, Hayek presumably refers to Wieser's entries in Conrad et al., eds., *Handwörterbuch der Staatswissenschaften*, 3rd ed., 8 vols. (Jena, Ger.: Gustav Fischer, 1909–1911). The second-named article, "Grenznutzen," appeared in the second and third editions

However, following Wieser, this conception constitutes an essential element of the theory of subjective value, and in its absence the marginal utility principle could not provide a satisfactory explanation of economic phenomena. In Wieser's eyes, value is the calculation form of utility. This conception alone leads to an unambiguous and complete partitioning of the utility derived from the product and allows us to put the same value on several units of a good involved in a production process. On the other hand, only this solution provides a definitive answer to the question how to impute the shares of the value of the product to the individual factors of production in a stable simple economy. This imputation is a precondition for the rational organization of production in an economy without exchange.

J. Schumpeter is the only one aside from Böhm-Bawerk and Wieser, whose contributions we have discussed, to have attempted to solve the problem of imputation within a closed system of economic theory. Schumpeter's solution in its main points agrees with that of Böhm-Bawerk and deviates from it only to the extent required by the particular mathematical methods employed, which we shall not discuss here.[15]

5. A Second Approach: The Marginal Productivity Theory

How the physical magnitude of the product depends on the quantitative proportion in which the individual factors are combined in the production process is purely a matter of technology and therefore serves only as a "datum" in the derivation of economic laws. Nevertheless, the observation of how men react to this phenomenon gave rise to a method for imputing to each of the factors a share in the value of the product which essentially coincides with the solutions derived from the basic concept of the theory of subjective value. It appears, however, that its field of application is narrower and the theoretical edifice erected on it less coherent. Around 1890, quite independently of the efforts of the Austrian School, St. Wood and especially J. B. Clark in America used this phenomenon to create a comprehensive theory of distribution resting on the concept of marginal productivity, as H. v. Thünen had done in Germany sixty years earlier. A number of American scholars, notably T. N.

of Conrad's *Handwörterbuch*. The first-named article presumably refers to Wieser's entry "Gut," which was Wieser's only other entry in the *Handwörterbuch* (according to the detailed list of Wieser's publications at www.mises.de). It appeared in the first, second, and third editions and is reprinted in Kurt Leube, ed., *Die Österreichische Schule der Nationalökonomie*, vol. 1, *Von Menger bis Mises* (Vienna: Manz-Verlag, 1995).—Ed.].

[15] Cf. on this point Schönfeld's excellent critique "Über Josef Schumpeters Lösung des ökonomischen Zurechnungsproblems," *Zeitschrift für Volkswirtschaft und Sozialpolitik*, n.s., 4 [no. 8] (1924) [pp. 432–77].

Carver, as well as F. A. Fetter, H. R. Seager and F. W. Taylor, contributed to the development of this theory; in Europe, K. Wicksell, Ph. H. Wicksteed, and E. Barone dealt with it in mathematical terms. A large number of modern theorists have incorporated it in their systems, mostly without dwelling in any way on its relation to the imputation principles developed by the Austrian School.

The theory of marginal productivity rests on the insight that the law of diminishing returns (cf. the related article in the *Handwörterbuch der Staatswissenschaften*, 4th ed., vol. 1, p. 11ff), which was first noted in agriculture, has a general range of applications. It has long been a commonplace of economic theory that beyond a certain point an increase of individual factors of production given a constant quantity of the remaining factors induces an expansion of the product which is relatively smaller than the increase in those factors of production. T. N. Carver has succeeded in explaining this finding to full satisfaction on the basis of the principle of probability and the generally valid "law of variable proportions" derived from it.[16] Wherever the quantity of the individual production factors can be varied independently of the quantity of the remaining factors, it is possible to determine, for any given combination of the factors, the share in the quantity of the product that depends on the cooperation of a unit of each factor of production. For practical purposes, this share can be viewed as the product of each unit of the production factor in question. In this manner the total product can be split proportionately among its factors by the use of differential calculus. But the imputation problem is by no means resolved thereby. For what does now determine the choice of the combination of production factors in each individual case? In the usual presentation of this theory within the framework of an exchange economy, competition is assigned the task of ensuring that the shares of the product depending on the cooperation of each unit of the producer good in different lines of production obtain the same price or, in other words, that the price of the imputable share must correspond to the costs.

However, to understand the significance of the theory of marginal productivity as an imputation theory, that is, as a derivation of the subjective valuation of producer goods by individuals, which could serve as a basis for explaining the price formation of these goods, we must divest the theory of the cloak of the exchange economy in which it is usually presented, and, in particular, we must disregard the social concept of value with which it was associated by J. B. Clark and several of his students. Only then can the theory serve directly to explain income distribution, without the intermediate step of

[16] Cf. T[homas] N[ixon] Carver, *Principles of National Economy* [Boston: Ginn], 1921, and his student J[ulius] Davidson's article "On the physical foundations of economics," *Quarterly Journal of Economics*, v. 33, [no. 4,] August 1919 [pp. 717–24].

price formation. As long as one argues that objective phenomena of value are the result of individual valuations, logic requires that the latter be explained without recourse to exchange. If we now apply the theory of marginal productivity to a "simple" economy guided by a single will, one is forced to conclude that in each line of production factors of production must be combined in such a way that the *value* of that part of the quantity of the product depending on the cooperation of the last unit of a producer good will be equal in each production. It becomes immediately obvious that mere quantitative proportionality of the increases induced by the application of the same factors in different lines of production is not sufficient. Consider the common case where the same factors, even when used in the same combination, make proportionally different marginal contributions in the production of different consumer goods, or where the same proportion in the marginal contributions requires unequal combinations in different productions. It is obvious that in all these cases the economic principle requires the equalization of the value of these dependent shares in the product. That is another way of saying that producer goods are to be combined in such a way in each line of production that, once the dependent values are equalized in each production, the values of the producer goods will fully exhaust the values of the products. Since this is the basis of the imputation of value according to the marginal utility school (in Wieser's formulation), one might say that the value of the dependent shares will match the value imputed to the production factors by the direct method of value imputation. The theory of marginal productivity requires that the value contributed by the last unit of each factor to the quantity of the product equals the value imputed to this unit. It thereby complements the simpler imputation theory built solely on the basic principles of value theory by taking account of the further complication arising from the variability of the combinations of factors in many lines of production. If the scope of its underlying principle were the same as that of the direct value imputation of the marginal utility school, it would hardly be possible to decide which of the two principles should be assigned primary validity. In actuality, however, in a not inconsiderable number of cases, variability in the proportions of the production factors—a prerequisite for the applicability of the method of marginal productivity—is lacking. Whenever a change in the combination of factors is excluded by the nature of the production process or where for other reasons (such as the transitory character of the current situation) no adaptation of the proportion in which the factors are combined is undertaken, only the direct imputation method of the marginal utility school can be applied.

Nevertheless, quite apart from its value in the extremely numerous instances in which it is applicable, the theory of marginal productivity is of principal, and not merely casuistic, importance for determining the value of producer goods. If the combinations in which producer goods could be used in different lines of production were completely rigid and permitted no changes, it would be only in exceptional cases that all units of each good could find enough complementary goods to make them usable in production. Hence those goods for which not enough complementary goods could be found would drop out of the class of economic goods altogether for lack of other uses. It must therefore be assumed that there will always be a number of cases where the proportions in which the factors of production are combined can be varied. For this reason the theory of marginal productivity will be relevant to an understanding of the proportions chosen in these cases. Yet on the basis of the above discussion it is justifiable to say that the marginal productivity theory cannot be viewed as a self-contained, independent principle for the solution of the imputation problem and that in the final analysis it rests on the assumption that the problem can be solved by the method of the direct imputation of value. We can therefore hardly go wrong by focusing on the direct imputation of value in our assessment of imputation theory and can assume that our conclusions, with certain modifications, will also apply to the marginal productivity theory.

6. *Various Misunderstandings and Objections*

There are few economic concepts that have been exposed to as many fundamental misunderstandings as the concept of imputation. It is hardly necessary any longer to reject the view that imputation represents a moral judgment on the merits of those who are direct participants in the production process or who participate by their ownership of goods. Neither should it be necessary to emphasize that imputation makes no claims that it establishes a causal nexus between an individual production factor and a specific quantity of the product—inasmuch as the originators of the theory themselves have denied this claim from the very start. Even if this interpretation rarely appears any longer in its crassest form, a related one is widely held and underlies most of the presumed demonstrations that imputation is impossible. What we have in mind is the notion that value imputation is grounded on some sort of technical imputation which establishes a connection between certain quantities of the product and individual production factors, independent of the value relationship. As we have shown in the preceding section, the proponents of the marginal productivity school did in fact attempt to do just that for a special class of cases. But this misinterpretation is fostered above all by the leading proponents of imputation theory who carelessly speak of "productive contribution" and "the share depending on participation" without explicitly pointing out that these are shares in the value of the product. Thus an interpretation became possible according to which the imputation theory of the marginal utility school was considered as the search for a special type of economic causality whereby a specified physical quantity could be marked off as the economic share in the product. The imputation theory of the marginal utility school, on the contrary, despite occasional seemingly contradicting formulations, deals exclusively with a direct determination of the value shares imputed to the individual factors, without prior determination of any physical shares. Apart from the value relation there is no necessary connection between the individual production factors and their share in the product. For this reason the share of a production factor in the value of the product will change in response to a change in the determinants of value, even if the technical composition in this particular line of production remains unaltered. The misunderstandings with respect to this point are largely due to the neglect of one of the essential preconditions of the imputation theory: that the productive combinations from which the value of producer goods is to be derived, must at the same time be economically admissible. All attempts to determine imputable shares by investigating the yield from different combinations of production factors for a firm in isolation from the economy as a whole, are doomed to failure. The different combinations could certainly never co-exist under the same economic preconditions and therefore there will be no connection between the valuations of the different combinations. Misunderstood in this way, the imputation theory was bound to be criticized as absurd, but such criticism is completely beside the point.

However, not all objections, notably those by Wicksell, Birk, Taylor and others, can be dismissed as misunderstandings of the imputation theory. Their objections are not directed primarily against the correctness of its results but rather against the failure of the various attempted solutions to offer anything beyond what is already implicit in the formulation of the problem. We will consider the importance of these objections in the next section.

7. *Critique of Attempted Solutions and Suggested Reformulation of the Problem*

Economic value is the general expression for the determination of the use of a particular kind of good in an economic system. In this capacity it gives direct information about the minimum level of utility the good must yield for its use to be appropriate from an economic viewpoint, and this applies as much to producer as to consumer goods. Hence there is a direct connection between the reasons for adopting a specific line of production and for expanding it up to a certain point and the determinants of the value of the goods used in it. Imputation theory in its present form has severed this connection by starting from an independently given value of the product and thus a given structure of production when determining the value of producer goods. That may well be the reason for its failure to find a satisfactory solution to the problem up to now. The assumption that the value of consumer goods could simply be derived from the marginal utility principle shifted to a later explanatory stage the problem arising for the value of products when their quantity cannot be taken as fixed. At that later stage the question could not be answered meaningfully, since it was divorced from that of their appropriate use, for which the solution had been previously assumed.

The various proponents of the imputation theory of the marginal utility school differed in the degree to which they recognized the above-mentioned difficulty and tried to cope with it. The mental leap in treating this problem is particularly obvious in Böhm-Bawerk's case, in that he disregards the explanation of the value of products as a logically indispensable link between the explanation of the value of goods existing in fixed quantities and the explanation of the relationship between the value of the producer goods and that of their products. Both in his exposition of the law of costs (*Positive Theorie des Kapitals*, 3rd ed., pp. 205f)[17] and his analysis of the value of complementary goods (*ibid.*, p. 277),[18] he presumes that the individual means of production must always be used in the same combinations, in fixed "productive groups." In his eyes, determining the value of products therefore raises no other problems than does the value of a given quantity of consumer goods. According to him, the quantities produced in the various lines of production are regulated in such a way that "needs of approximately equal intensity relate to the last unit (of the product), so that the marginal utility of each unit is approximately of the same magnitude" (*ibid.*, p. 295).[19] No special solution is given for the much more significant case in which producer goods can be combined in varying proportions in different lines of production. He considers the conclusion derived from his assumption to be generally valid and believes that it offers an adequate explanation for the value of all products. The only case of differences in marginal utility in the different lines of production acknowledged by Böhm-Bawerk concerns inequalities in the satisfaction of individual needs arising from discontinuities in the scales of needs.

Böhm-Bawerk's lack of insight into the special problem of the use of several goods for a single purpose leads him to search for an imputation problem where no multiplicity of goods exists in a strictly economic sense. In his

[17] [Eugen von Böhm-Bawerk, *Kapital und Kapitalzins*, 3rd ed., vol. 2, *Positive Theorie des Kapitales* (Innsbruck, Austria: Wagner, 1912). The fourth edition (1921) was translated into English as Eugen von Böhm-Bawerk, *Capital and Interest*, vol. 2, *The Positive Theory of Capital*, trans. George D. Huncke and Hans F. Sennholz (South Holland, IL: Libertarian Press, 1959). The material on the law of costs that Hayek cites appears in *Capital and Interest*, vol. 2, pp. 173–74.—Ed.]

[18] [Böhm-Bawerk, *Capital and Interest*, vol. 2, pp.161–62.—Ed.]

[19] [*Ibid.*, p. 173. In this quotation from Böhm-Bawerk, the parenthetical remark "(of the product)" is Hayek's. That is, Hayek inserted "(des Produktes)" when quoting it in the German original of the present article.—Ed.]

exposition of the well-known "first" case (*ibid.*, p. 295),[20] concerning a product made from several goods, none of which is either replaceable or has an alternative use, there is actually only a single economic good, namely that very product, as its components must be present simultaneously, in rigid proportions, to be useful. For this reason, they constitute mere components of a single good; they have utility and, hence, value, only in this combination. Here it makes no sense to impute value to these factors, as each individual factor has no separable influence on the marginal utility of the product. It is therefore legitimate to treat each of these parts—each of which is essential for the product's having the quality of an economic good—in the same way as the whole product, as long as all the other parts are available. That means that the whole value of the product can be imputed to each part. The same procedure is not justified in cases of true imputation, however. Even in the "second" and "third" cases, which deal with true imputation, Böhm-Bawerk's interpretation leads him to erroneous conclusions. In these cases, the individual elements, or at least all the goods used with them, have alternative uses or are replaceable; hence they independently possess the quality of economic goods. Had Böhm-Bawerk not lost sight of the connection between the value of the producer goods and the question whether their use in the production in question is admissible, he would have had to accept the basic validity of Wieser's "partitioning concept." The latter question—for which he had little interest because he was only looking for "dependent utility"—cannot be answered otherwise than by stating that each production must be expanded to the point where the sum of the values attainable elsewhere by the production factors may be no lower than the value of the product in question. Böhm-Bawerk, however, who unquestioningly accepted the state of equilibrium as his starting point and who insisted that the current use of the good must be taken as a datum (*ibid.*, Exkurs VII, p. 209),[21] could answer the question about its value only by introducing a perturbation into the system and by having recourse to the so-called principle of "loss." It is true that for goods that are not in a complementary relationship with other goods, this principle identifies the smallest yield directly generated by goods of the same kind in a condition of undisturbed equilibrium. However, the loss of one production factor induces a multiplicity of displacements that change the efficacy of various production factors. For this reason it is wrong to assume that the difference in the total product under the two distinct preconditions can be regarded to determine in the same way the efficacy of the withdrawn factors. At a later point (Exkurs VII, *op. cit.*, p. 200), which, incidentally, contradicts his exposition in the main

[20] [*Ibid.*, p. 152.—Ed.]

[21] [Eugen von Böhm-Bawerk, *Capital and Interest*, vol. 3, *Further Essays on Capital and Interest*, trans. Hans F. Sennholz (South Holland, IL: Libertarian Press, 1959), p. 92.—Ed.]

text (*ibid.*, p. 285–6),[22] Böhm-Bawerk—mistakenly—tried to trivialize the difference between the sum of the values of the individual factors of production, as these values have been identified by their withdrawal, and the value of the product. His justification is that income distribution can be understood only by a two-stage explanation, whose first element is imputation theory and whose second element the theory of price formation, which is based on the subjective valuations as determined in the first stage. Yet, it is not obvious how according to his method of imputation the formation of prices will result in a partitioning of the product among its production factors that exhausts the product, as will actually be the case.

In contrast to Böhm-Bawerk, Wieser starts out, as a matter of principle, from the assumption that the same producer goods will be used in varying combinations. In his attempted solution of the imputation problem, Wieser thus recognizes that the value of complementary producer goods can be derived only by taking these varying combinations into account. He realizes that the independent nature of the individual producer goods as well as their differing relative scarcity inevitably express themselves in the differing values of the products, caused by the variations in the combination of these factors. Wieser deserves recognition as having been the first to have taken the basic concept of the marginal utility theory—that the last, actually attained satisfaction of needs depends on the available quantity of the good—and to have applied it consistently to producer goods by introducing his concept of differing margins of use. Furthermore, his imputation formula is superior to Böhm-Bawerk's in that it complies with the requirement to partition the entire product among the factors and can thus serve directly as the basis for a theory of distribution. Wieser's equations are undeniably a correct expression of the relationships between the value of the producer goods and the value of the product, all the more so since they merely represent the converse of the law of costs in a form that is adapted to the theory of subjective value. On the other hand his equations are unable to match the achievement of the marginal utility principle in the way of determining the value of consumer goods from a given quantity. The equations are incapable of deriving the value of producer goods from "the data," that is, scales of needs and the available quantities of producer goods. They do not show us the necessity of the uses in which those utilities are realized from which the value of producer goods is derived. As shown earlier, Wieser first tackled the problem of the value of producer goods and only after he had resolved it by means of the law of costs did he attempt to solve the imputation problem. However, he constructed his law of costs on the assumption that the value of producer goods was determinate, thus deriving the value of producer goods from the value of their products where, at

22 [Böhm-Bawerk, *op. cit.*, vol. 3, p. 88, and vol. 2, p.166, respectively.—Ed.]

the same time, in his analysis the value of the products could be determined only by recourse to the value of the producer goods. Thus his solution, too, cannot be traced back to extra-economic elements. The unsatisfactory nature of his solution is less apparent because of his implicit claim that the structure of production is arranged as required by the criterion of maximizing utility, and hence the underlying problem is resolved. Böhm-Bawerk makes this same claim explicitly. In the usual interpretation of the concept of maximizing utility, however, this means strictly to observe the hierarchy of needs and accordingly to prefer one need over another (cf. J. Schumpeter, *Das Wesen und der Hauptinhalt der theoretischen Nationalökonomie*, p. 132).[23] Yet, the complementary relationship of the goods rules out the direct choice between the satisfaction of two needs and makes the solution inapplicable. If, like Wieser, one considers the calculability of utility as basic for dealing with the whole problem, as can be hardly avoided, this means that the state of maximum utility cannot be determined without partitioning the utility of the products among the production factors, and thus without the prior solution of the imputation problem.

There is no way in which a one-sided derivation of the value of producer goods from the value of the products can succeed. This is because the value of the products cannot be determined without taking into account the degree of resistance against expanding production to the largest possible physical magnitude—which differs for each of the means of production used in the production process. As long as the factor can be used alternatively, as is true in most cases, this limitation depends on the value that must be imputed to it in its alternative use. This in turn depends on the value of other products and on its imputation to the factors of production. Deriving the value of either the product or the producer goods in terms of its factors or, respectively, their products, via the relationship established between them by the law of costs, is possible, but it is meaningless as a theoretical explanation of the way in which value is based on "economic data," that is, quantities of goods and needs, since neither of the two values can be ascertained independently of the other. This difficulty stems from the fact that neither producer goods nor products independently elicit both of the data needed to determine their value. For products only the utility attained is elicited, while for producer goods only the second element, the limitation of the available supply, can be ascertained absolutely.

This analysis does nothing to eliminate the problem of imputation, but only

[23] [Joseph Schumpeter, *Das Wesen und der Hauptinhalt der theoretischen Nationalökonomie* (Leipzig, Ger.: Drucker and Humboldt, 1908); English translation, Joseph A. Schumpeter, *The Nature and Essence of Economic Theory*, ed. Bruce A McDaniel (New Brunswick, NJ: Transaction Publishers, 2010).—Ed.]

offers a different formulation of the problem. What then becomes problematic is not the derivation of the value of producer goods from the value of the product, taken as given, but the influence of the relative scarcity of a producer good with given potential uses and complementary goods on the admissible expansion of each individual production of goods. The imputation problem becomes identical with the question of how available producer goods should be used in different lines of production, given the quantity of producer goods and the prevailing scales of needs. Each answer to this question and hence each solution of the imputation problem must take into account the totality of all the complementary goods used in an economic system and all the needs for whose satisfaction products are employed. This necessity may render impossible the practical application of imputation to any comprehensive economic system. However, it should be possible to demonstrate the applicability of the subjective value theory in principle in a simplified case and thus to prove that the imputation problem is theoretically solvable. Under Walras' leadership, the mathematical school of economics has already tackled successfully a similar set of tasks, but it too has failed to solve the imputation problem so far. At present there is nothing more to be said about finding a definitive solution to the imputation problem beyond stating as a general condition that all the elements of the economic system to which the producer goods in question belong must be taken into account, except to point out that the final result must, by the very nature of things, be in agreement with the relationship between the value of products and of producer goods expressed by Wieser's equations. The shortcomings of the subjective value theory in providing an answer to the underlying question of the imputation problem may explain why a large number of theorists see no way of solving the problem without recourse to an objective concept of cost. Yet to invoke the disutility of labor as the main cost element does nothing to advance the solution of the problem, as can be easily demonstrated. When alternative uses of the "good" labor, such as possible recreational opportunities or simply leisure, are introduced instead of the disutility of labor—something that can be done without changing any data—the same problem that one was trying to circumvent again arises with respect to their use with complementary goods.

TWO

ON THE PROBLEM OF INTEREST THEORY[1]

Ever since the publication of Böhm-Bawerk's great work, his approach to the problem of interest on capital has dominated the discussion of this topic, at least in the context of value theory. Böhm-Bawerk first examines what induces a permanent difference between the value of the capital employed and its product.[2] In more general terms, he raises the question why in any time-consuming production process the value of the product invariably exceeds the value of the goods which are used in its production. He explains the existence of interest by this difference in value, "the fold . . . in which interest lies concealed,"[3] and, ever since the publication of his work, the majority of modern interest theorists have followed suit. For Böhm-Bawerk and most other proponents of the "agio" theory of interest, this permanent difference in value is irreconcilable with a basic tenet of value theory, to wit, that the means of production and the goods they produce must be of equal value. To account for this discrepancy, they make the *ad hoc* assumption that future needs are invariably valued lower compared to the same needs at the present time. This consideration alone prevents available means of production from being distributed among production processes of varying length in a way that equalizes the marginal utility of the goods produced from a given quantity of producer goods. Were it not for the undervaluation of future needs, there could be no state of equi-

[1] ["Zur Problemstellung der Zinstheorie," *Archiv für Sozialwissenschaft und Sozialpolitik*, vol. 58, no. 3, 1927, pp. 517–32; translated by Grete Heinz as "On the Problem of the Theory of Interest," in F. A. Hayek, *Money, Capital & Fluctuations: Early Essays*, ed. Roy McCloughry (Chicago: University of Chicago Press; London: Routledge and Kegan Paul, 1984), pp. 55–70; translation revised by Hansjoerg Klausinger.—Ed.]

[2] Cf. e.g. *Geschichte und Kritik der Kapitalzins*[-]*theorien* (3rd ed.), p. 137. [The first German edition appeared in 1884. The third edition appeared as volume 1 of the set *Kapital und Kapitalzins*, 3rd ed., 3 vols.; the set also included *Positive Theorie des Kapitales* (Innsbruck, Austria: Wagner'schen Univeristäts-Buchhandlung, 1909–1914). English translation, Eugen von Böhm-Bawerk, *Capital and Interest*, vol. 1, *The History and Critique of Interest Theories*, trans. George D. Huncke and Hans F. Sennholz (South Holland, IL: Libertarian Press, 1959), p. 77.—Ed.].

[3] *Positive Theorie des Kapitals* (3rd ed.), p. 294. [See note above. English translation, Eugen von Böhm-Bawerk, *Capital and Interest*, vol. 2, *The Positive Theory of Capital*, trans. George D. Huncke and Hans F. Sennholz (South Holland, IL: Libertarian Press, 1959), p. 172.—Ed.].

librium in which the value of producer goods and of goods produced by them is not equal. Interest on capital in a static system rests on this difference in value.[4]

The specific solution that Böhm-Bawerk was forced to embrace by his formulation of the problem has not received wide support; in particular, his assertion that future needs are consistently undervalued has been sharply challenged. Yet his formulation of the problem has been generally accepted as a seemingly inevitable consequence of modern value theory.[5] As a result, more obvious explanations for the interest on capital, such as productivity theory, could not gain a foothold, whereas the only possible way out, the one chosen by Böhm-Bawerk, was contradicted by the facts.[6] We shall therefore turn to the question whether Böhm-Bawerk's approach to the problem of interest on capital allowed for no other possible explanation for the above-mentioned difference in value than the premise that future needs were undervalued. Was

[4] I am fully aware in saying this that Böhm-Bawerk gave three reasons for explaining the difference in value between present and future goods. Only the first two refer to the undervaluation of future needs, while the third refers to the well-known greater productivity of roundabout production processes. Even aside from the fact that Böhm-Bawerk's system does not fully acknowledge the legitimacy of this "third reason," its validity can be easily shown to be contingent on the existence of the other two reasons, that is, the undervaluation of future needs, so that it cannot stand on its own. This point needs no further elucidation, since the premise of the undervaluation of future needs is one of the cornerstones of Böhm-Bawerk's theory. Suffice it to note the subordinate role assigned to the third reason in the first paragraph, p. 460, of Böhm-Bawerk's *Positive Theorie* (3rd ed.) [Böhm-Bawerk, *Capital and Interest*, vol. 2, pp. 275–76.—Ed.]. K. Wicksell's last paper, "Zur Zinstheorie (Böhm-Bawerks Dritter Grund)" in the third volume of the collection *Die Theorie der Gegenwart* (Vienna, 1927), which came to my attention when the present essay was already in proof, also deserves mentioning in this connection. [Knut Wicksell, "Zur Zinstheorie (Böhm-Bawerks Dritter Grund)," in *Die Wirtschaftstheorie der Gegenwart*, vol. 3, *Einkommensbildung*, ed. Hans Meyer, Frank Fetter, and Richard Reisch (Vienna: Springer, 1928), pp. 199–209; translated by Timothy Chamberlain as "On the Theory of Interest (Böhm-Bawerk's 'Third Ground')," in *Selected Essays in Economics*, by Wicksell, ed. Bo Sandelin (London: Routledge, 1997), vol. 2, pp. 41–53.—Ed.]

[5] Cf. e.g. Schumpeter, who states in his *Theorie der wirtschaftlichen Entwicklung* (Leipzig, 1912, p. 324): "We fully accept that any interest theory has to fulfil the requirements of his (Böhm-Bawerk's) theory of value. We start from the premise that any interest theory that fails to meet these requirements and that lays itself open to his objections must not be advanced today." [Joseph A. Schumpeter, *Theorie der wirtschaftlichen Entwicklung* (Munich: Duncker & Humblot, 1912); English translation from the 1926 2nd ed., *The Theory of Economic Development: An Inquiry into Profits, Capital, Credit, Interest, and the Business Cycle*, trans. Redvers Opie (London: Oxford University Press, 1934). Some translated passages from the German edition that were excluded from the English edition are presented in Markus C. Becker and Thorbjørn Knudsen, "Schumpeter 1911: Farsighted Visions on Economic Development," *American Journal of Economics and Sociology*, vol. 61, no. 2, April 2002, pp. 387–403.—Ed.]

[6] [It is not clear what are the facts that Hayek believes contradict Böhm-Bawerk's assertion that individuals who make intertemporal choices systematically discount future-dated consumption—Ed.]

it really true that without this premise the production of future goods would expand to the point where their value declined to that of the producer goods from which they were made? Might there not be other reasons that would prevent such an expansion of production and thereby eliminate the need to derive the difference in value from the undervaluation of future needs? In other words, do we have to accept the premise about the undervaluation of future needs as a necessary consequence of Böhm-Bawerk's formulation of the problem of interest on capital? Such was undoubtedly Böhm-Bawerk's own view, which inevitably followed from a consistent application of his over-simplified value theory, but I believe that his view was erroneous, as can easily be demonstrated.

To proceed with our analysis, however, we must first introduce a partial modification of Böhm-Bawerk's formulation of the problem, which was adumbrated earlier. According to the subjective theory of value, the value of producer goods and the goods produced by them will coincide only under *certain well-defined preconditions*. In the case of produced goods these preconditions, that is, *the achievement of a state of equilibrium*, require that the production of goods (as far as is technically possible) *is just expanded to the point* where the value of the products has declined exactly to the value of the producer goods. However, from this assumption follows necessarily the equality in value between products and the producer goods from which they are processed. Hence the analysis need not address the question of value relations but its main thrust must be to determine why production will not be arranged in a way that gives rise to such an equalization of value. The proper question is what prevents the expansion of the production of goods resulting from more or less time-consuming processes to the point where goods produced with the help of the same producer goods have equal value. This differs slightly from Böhm-Bawerk's approach, in which the structure of production generally did not constitute an object of analysis but was taken as given, and comes closer to Wieser's approach, which focused on the economic causes of a specific structure of production in explaining the value relation between products and producer goods.[7]

[7] Cf. the comments in my essay "Bemerkungen zum Zurechnungsproblem," *Jahrbücher für Nationalökonomie und Statistik*, vol. 124 (Series III, vol. 69), Jena, 1926, pp. 13ff. [included in this volume as "Some Observations on the Imputation Problem"—Ed.], as well as my obituary for Friedrich v. Wieser in the vol. 125 of the same journal, Jena, 1926, p. 517. [Friedrich A. von Hayek, "Friedrich Freiherr von Wieser," *Jahrbücher für Nationalökonomie und Statistik*, 3rd series, vol. 125, 1926, pp. 513–30; translated by Grete Heinz as "Friedrich von Wieser (1851–1926)," in *The Fortunes of Liberalism*, ed. Peter Klein, vol. 4 of *The Collected Works of F. A. Hayek* (Chicago: University of Chicago Press, 1992), pp. 108–25.—Ed.] Hans Mayer and Leo Schönfeld took Wieser's approach as the point of departure for their writings in a most consistent and effective manner. In this context we should cite Mayer's various recent contributions to the fourth edition of the *Handwörterbuch der Staatswissenschaften* (especially the entry under "Produktion"), and his series

The solution to the problem of how the disposal of given goods is determined by fundamental economic data is complicated by the well-known phenomenon to which Böhm-Bawerk refers as greater productiveness of roundabout production, the higher productivity to be obtained from given producer goods by more time-consuming production processes.[8] The decision whether to use the given producer goods in shorter or longer production processes must thus be based on the relative utility of greater or smaller quantities of the same[9] product at different points in time. On the assumption that the economic data are givens, only two possibilities remain: either the quantity of the product available at the two points in time under consideration (apart from the effect of using the given means of production in different production pro-

of articles "Untersuchungen zu dem Grundgesetz der wirtschaftlichen Wertrechnung," *Zeitschrift für Volkswirtschaft und Sozialpolitik*, New Series, vol. I et sequitur, and Schönfeld's *Grenznutzen und Wirtschaftsrechnung* (Vienna, 1924). [Hans Mayer, "Produktion," in *Handwörterbuch der Staatswissenschaften*, 4th ed., vol. 6, ed. Ludwig Elster, Adolf Weber, and Friedrich Wieser (Jena, Ger.: Gustav Fischer, 1925), pp. 1108–22. Hayek later cited this work in his *Prices and Production*. The *Handwörterbuch*, published 1923–1928 in eight volumes, each volume more than 1,000 pages, contained the following additional "various contributions" by Mayer: "Konsumtion" [Consumption], vol. 5, 1923, pp. 867–74; "Bedürfnis" [Needs], vol. 2, 1924, pp. 450–56; "Preis. II. Der Monopolpreis" [Price. II. Monopoly Price], vol. 3, 1925, pp. 1026–37; "Produktionsfaktoren" [Factors of Production], vol. 6, 1925, 1122–28; "Gut" [Good], vol. 4, 1927, pp. 1272–80; "Verteilung" [Distribution] and "Zurechnung" [Imputation], vol. 8 (1928), pp. 675–78 and 1206–28. Hans Mayer, "Untersuchungen zu dem Grundgesetz der wirtschaftlichen Wertrechnung" [Investigations into the fundamental laws of economic calculation], *Zeitschrift für Volkswirtschaft und Sozialpolitik*, n.s., vol. 1, 1921, pp. 431–58, and vol. 2, 1922, pp. 1–23. Leo Schönfeld, *Grenznutzen und Wirtschaftsrechnung* [Marginal utility and economic calculation] (Vienna: Manz, 1924).—Ed.]

[8] The thesis of the greater productivity of roundabout production processes has given rise to a great deal of misunderstanding. The thesis would be far less vulnerable to criticism, however, if it were clearly stated that longer production processes are economically viable only if a given effort yields a larger result or if the same result can be achieved by a smaller effort, in short, a longer production process is economically viable only if it yields a larger product. Basically, there are any number of possibilities to yield a certain product within a period of production of given length, but for each period the various possibilities may give rise to a smaller or larger product and only the one with the highest product will be considered. The longer the time period in question, the greater the number of methods available for roundabout production, so that now production methods with a higher yield *may* become feasible, which previously have not been available. [In other words: the greater productivity of more roundabout production processes is a necessary feature of the *frontier* of non-dominated processes: any positive discount rate entails that a process taking longer to bear fruit must produce more fruit to be potentially preferred to a shorter process.—Ed.]

[9] F[ranz] X. Weiss objects with good reason ("Produktionsumwege und Kapitalzins," *Zeitschrift für Volkswirtschaft und Sozialpolitik*, new series, vol. I, [no. 4] Vienna, 1921 [pp. 493ff.]) that the greater productivity obtained from given producer goods through their use in longer production processes generally refers to the larger amount of value of a different good rather than to a larger quantity of the same good, but his objection only complicates the analysis without changing the end result and will thus not be considered any further here.

cesses) will be identical, or else that the total stock of available producer goods will be utilized. It then follows from the law of marginal utility that the utility of a smaller number of units with higher marginal utility must be compared with a larger number of units of the same product with a smaller marginal utility. Thus, according to Böhm-Bawerk's own assumptions, only when the total value of a larger product with a lower marginal utility exceeds that of a smaller product with a higher marginal utility will the use of more roundabout and more productive processes be compatible with a state of equilibrium.

Accordingly, Böhm-Bawerk's question should be rephrased as follows: what prevents the production of future goods from expanding even more than it actually does, namely, to the point where the value of the products processed from given means of production falls to the value of the products that can be made by the shortest process (in the limiting case, the value of their direct use as consumer goods)? As we have shown, as a consequence of such an expansion the marginal utility of the unit produced by the longer production process would have to decline below the marginal utility of a unit of the same product turned out by a shorter process. Only thus could the differences in utility between present and future products disappear. According to Böhm-Bawerk this would be the natural consequence, of the tendency toward a complete equalization of the marginal utilities of present and future products that can be derived from a given producer good, were it not for the general undervaluation of future needs compared to present needs.[10]

A difference in value would *necessarily* persist if production were geared to make equal provision for the present and the future, so that the marginal utility of the *product* in question must be equal at both points in time. The disappearance of this difference in value would thus presuppose that means of production would be devoted to time-consuming production processes to such an extent that consequently the overall provision with goods would increasingly improve, which means that the marginal utility of all the goods produced with the help of capital (and of all other goods as well, since means of production would thereby be released for other purposes) must steadily decline.[11] The satisfaction of current wants would thus have to be stopped at a point where the unit of consumer goods destined to satisfy present needs still yields a larger marginal utility than the unit of the same products to be attained in the future from the goods that thus have been saved in the present.

[10] [That is, according to Böhm-Bawerk, given a positive discount rate, equalization of discounted marginal utilities implies a higher *undiscounted* marginal utility of later-dated products in equilibrium.—Ed.]

[11] Cf. R[ichard] Strigl's interesting arguments on this and the following points in his illuminating and wrongly neglected study, *Die ökonomischen Kategorien und Organisation der Wirtschaft* [Economic categories and the organization of the economy], Jena, [Gustav Fischer,] 1923, especially pp, 135ff.

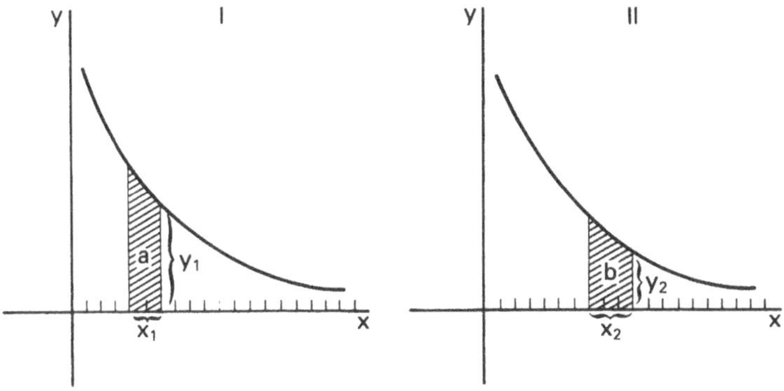

$a = b;\ x_1 : x_2 = 2:3;\ y_1 > y_2$

Conditions for achieving equilibrium between the use of a producer good in (I) a shorter, less productive and (II) in a longer, more productive process, according to the older interpretation of the isolated comparisons between individual utilities. The divisions on the abscissa represent identical units of the product, segments x_1 and x_2 represent the number of units of the product turned out by the same quantity of producer goods.

This conclusion is unavoidable. The larger amount of a product turned out by a given quantity of producer goods with the use of roundabout production processes can have the same value as the smaller quantity of the same product turned out by a shorter process under only one condition: that the same unit of the larger amount of the product available later has a lower marginal utility than the unit of the smaller amount available at an earlier date. This point is best clarified by a graphic method commonly used in mathematical economics. We must consider the alternative of obtaining from a given quantity of means of production either a larger amount of the product at a later date or a smaller amount of the same product at an earlier date. It follows from Böhm-Bawerk's concept of statics on which he bases his analysis that the utility curves for a product have the same shape for both points in time. Both curves in the graphs below will therefore express that the intensity of wants diminishes with their increasing satisfaction in terms of the quantity of the product at the dates (I) and (II) measured along the abscissa. It is further assumed that at the earlier date (I) two units of the product can be turned out with the given means of production, as shown by the segment x_1, while three units of the product that can be turned out at the later date (II) are represented by the corresponding segment x_2.

Our next task is to ascertain under what conditions an equilibrium consistent with the rules of elementary value theory will result from the disposal of producer goods between these two production processes, without having to rely on the undervaluation of future needs. Here we must keep in mind that we are comparing the utility of each quantity turned out by the shorter production process with the utility of the larger quantity of the product turned out by the longer production process, that is, a given segment of the abscissa in Figure I with a larger segment in Figure II. The total utility of the products turned out by the different production processes will be equal if the area enclosed by the different amounts of the product (represented by the segments on the abscissa) and the corresponding segments of the utility curve (value function) are of equal magnitude, these areas each representing the total utility of the product turned out by a given quantity of producer goods. This equality can only be accomplished if the ordinate of the utility curve at the point where satisfaction has to be cut off (marginal utility) is smaller for the product turned out by the more time-consuming production process than for the other product.

The question now arises whether we require Böhm-Bawerk's assumption of the undervaluation of future needs to explain why production of future goods is not expanded to the point where their marginal utility will steadily decline and why thus this marginal utility generally exceeds the direct utility of the producer goods by which they are made. Yet there are other possible explanations why production does not expand to such an extent. One is that men do not strive for achieving the maximum utility for each unit of goods but for balancing the total satisfaction of their needs over time. Thus equilibrium could be achieved without the presently available producer goods and future products having equal utility. There is little reason to doubt, off-hand, that such an explanation is plausible. In this case, the greater productivity of roundabout production suffices to demonstrate the necessity of interest on capital, though it fails to explain the actual magnitude of the interest rate, which obviously depends on concrete data about the wants and supply of goods of individual economic subjects. What is certain—and sufficient for theoretical purposes—is that any such individual valuation will result in a definite rate of interest on capital and that interest on capital cannot vanish *as long as* unutilized roundabout processes are capable of increasing the product.

Surprisingly enough, considering the voluminous literature dealing with the problem of interest on capital, no attempt has been made so far to envisage the issue from this perspective. It must be kept in mind, however, that the theoretical foundation on which our solution rests is of very recent vintage. As mentioned earlier, Böhm-Bawerk took it for granted that a good would be used in a certain way; as far as he was concerned, this use followed as a matter of course from taking the hierarchy of needs (need impulses) as a starting point or it was rather inconsistently accepted as "given data."[12] The problem

[12] It is obviously self-contradictory on the one hand to explain value formation by saying that the specific uses of goods are determined by the striving for an optimal satisfaction of wants

how to arrive at a coherent economic plan was not of special concern to him, but in any case he had no doubt that an adequate and unambiguous decision could be derived in every case from the isolated comparison of the utilities of the various possible ways in which a good could be put to use. However, it has become apparent from new studies, most notably those undertaken by Hans Mayer[13] and L. Schönfeld,[14] that such is not the case and that difficult problems may arise in this respect. Schönfeld in particular has demonstrated that it is not simple comparisons of isolated individual utilities that determine the economic plan but that such a decision invariably hinges on the comparison between the total economic utility to be realized from alternative courses of action. Isolated comparisons can at best offer an "abbreviated procedure" for this kind of analysis, insofar as they yield the same result (which he does believe to be invariably the case).

There is no need to carry this distinction to greater length. All that matters in this context is to show that comparisons of individual utilities are an inadequate basis for determining economic decisions. The inadequacies of Böhm-Bawerk's approach to value theory are obvious enough with respect to the narrow domain of interest theory. They are even more acutely evident in his direct disciples' attempts to formalize and remove psychological considerations from the foundations of economic theory. However, there are two further major problems in economic theory where the flaws of this approach have serious repercussions. Difficulties are especially pronounced in the theory of interest on capital because of two interrelated problems, for which no satisfactory solution has as yet been offered. They defy all solution as long as a fixed hierarchy of the *single* ends in question is considered to be a relevant and sufficient basis for deriving an equilibrium system. One of the problems, to which we referred earlier, is the comparison of the utility of a smaller quantity of goods consisting of units with larger marginal utility with the utility of

(equalization of marginal utilities, etc.) and that for this reason for every given system of valuation there exists a corresponding economic structure, and on the other hand to assert that the uses of goods must be considered as a given, as Böhm-Bawerk occasionally points out (*Positive Theorie*, 3rd ed., Exkurs VII, p. 209). Proof that a certain use of a good is necessary implies that it must have a certain value, hence all circumstances that influence this value also influence its use and vice versa. For this reason, the admission that we must accept the way goods are used as a given requiring no further explanation amounts to declaring the bankruptcy of value theory.

[13] See the entries "Produktion" and "Bedürfnisse" [*sic*; actual title is "Bedurfnis"—Ed.] in the *Handwörterbuch der Staatswissenschaften*, 4th ed., as well as the up to now only partially published series of articles entitled "Untersuchungen zum [*sic*; actual title reads "zu dem"—Ed.] Grundgesetz der wirtschaftlichen Wertrechnung" in *Zeitschrift für Volkswirtschaft und Sozialpolitik*, new series, vol. I et sequitur. [Correct citations to these works appear above in n. 7.—Ed.]

[14] *Grenznutzen und Wirtschaftsrechnung*, Vienna, 1924. Cf. also the article "Grenznutzen" by P. N. Rosenstein-Rodan in the fourth edition of the *Handwörterbuch der Staatswissenschaften* [vol. 4, 1927, pp. 1190–1213] and references therein to the more recent literature. [An English translation of Rosenstein-Rodan's article, "Marginal Utility," translated by Wolfgang F. Stolper, appeared in *International Economic Papers*, 10, 1960, pp. 71–106.—Ed.]

a larger quantity of goods consisting of units with smaller marginal utility. It is obvious that such a comparison must result in an equilibrium state at a certain moment, but the conditions for such an equilibrium state cannot be derived in this case by merely assuming a given hierarchy of the individual uses.[15] The second problem is the problem of time, which takes precedence over the first problem; in this context, comparisons of individual utilities become meaningless, as we shall demonstrate below. Böhm-Bawerk held an exceedingly narrow view of this problem, and neither he nor the older adherents to the theory of marginal utility recognized its full scope. Hans Mayer was the first to show in his above-mentioned recent writings that the passage of time is an indispensable element in devising a meaningful economic plan. Taking into account the disposal of goods over time is vital for an understanding of value formation.

Here as elsewhere, a simple solution that worked well for a simple case was blithely transferred to a new set of circumstances, without anyone's reexamining the applicability of its assumptions to these new circumstances.[16] There was not the least doubt that decisions about the satisfaction of needs over time could be equated with decisions about needs at one point in time (actually an "economic period" assumed to be timeless). But actually there is a strong psychological difference between these two situations. In one case the loss of utility in one place is simultaneously (or within a very short time span) compensated by a higher utility in another place, so that the sense of loss is immediately counterbalanced by a simultaneous and greater utility gain. As it takes place within a short period of time, this decision evokes the sense of a unified rise in overall utility. In the other case, the long time span between the occurrence of the loss and the subsequently achieved higher utility prevents the two emotions from merging into a single entity. Experience undoubtedly justifies the assumption that for short time spans decision-making is based on the individual utilities to be attained by the goods in question. No general experience, however, tells us how decisions will be made between two recognized utilities of a given magnitude whose realization is separated by a long time span. We do not know, in particular, whether a higher future utility, which is recognized as such, will on that account necessarily be preferred to a present utility.[17]

[15] The problem of interest on capital—as well as price theory and imputation theory—are three instances in which this still unresolved question surfaces in dealing with fundamental economic problems. The author plans to deal more systematically with all three of these cases at a later date. As other work currently prevents him from giving the topic a more thorough treatment, the above outline at least sketches out the problem in its most important application.

[16] Cf. my previously mentioned paper on the problem of imputation, p. 3. [See citation information in n. 7 above.—Ed.]

[17] To dispose of a potential, though not crucial, objection, which I might inadvertently have triggered by my formulation, let me restate the facts of the matter a little more concretely. Let us assume that in two successive economic periods, in which the needs to be satisfied are exactly identical, the product of a given quantity of producer goods may be used, but that apart from this product provision has been made for the exactly identical satisfaction of needs in these two

The "abbreviated procedure" (Schönfeld) of comparing individual utilities instead of total economic utility, which, in the last analysis, is the decisive factor, is warranted only when the two alternative uses for a good can be realized without effecting a change in the external conditions of economic behavior. This "ceteris paribus" is not applicable, however, when one of the two alternatives can *only* be realized after a long waiting period. It is a condition that also certainly does not hold when the equilibrium state between two uses can be achieved only if, as shown in the diagrams above, the same need is already more fully satisfied at the more distant than at the closer point of time, no matter which of the alternative uses is chosen. In consequence of the fact that a given producer good can turn out larger quantities of a product by a longer process, Böhm-Bawerk posits that the production of future goods must expand to the point where the utility of the larger quantity of goods produced declines to the utility of the smaller quantity of goods that can be turned out in a shorter time. This approach rests on the mistaken assumption that the comparison of isolated utilities that can be achieved with the given amount of producer goods at different points in time actually determines how needs are satisfied over time. Yet, in contrast, what determines decisions of this sort is not comparison of isolated individual utilities, as used in this context, but the urge to achieve a certain arrangement of the satisfaction of one's needs over time.[18] There can be nothing said *in general* how each individual wants to arrange the satisfaction of his needs at specific points in time. The

periods. Let us then assume that the product made from the available producer goods is greater in the second economic period than in the first. It is therefore necessary to compare with each other the utility of different quantities of the product turned out from the same quantity of producer goods. Here the marginal utility of the same physical unit of the product in the second period, in which more has been turned out from the same quantity of producer goods, must be lower *in comparison to* that derived from *the provision of goods in the initial situation*, equal in both periods, and thus lower than in the first period. When we speak of the marginal utility of one amount of product being relatively larger in one period and relatively smaller in another, we are making a comparison with the marginal utility of all the remaining products, whose quantity is constant and the same in both periods. Only in this case will the marginal utility of the product be higher in one period than in the other and will the actual decisions in this connection not give preference to the higher utility. But it is just a question of terminology whether one deduces the existence of a smaller or larger utility from the decisions made and concludes that despite an unchanged provision of goods the utility of all other goods varies from period to period. Böhm-Bawerk's formulation of the undervaluation of future needs shows in any case that he used the term utility in the former sense and any immanent criticism must adhere to the same terminology. Böhm's approach to the problem is based on this interpretation of the utility concept, because otherwise a contradiction between the valuation and the actual decision would not be possible.

[18] Once one concedes that the same means of production can produce quite different results or the same result with quite different quantities of the same means of production in both time periods, it does make a considerable difference whether one wishes to achieve the same utility from the same means of production or whether one wants to satisfy the same needs to an equal extent in both time periods.

general claim that economic subjects willingly make current sacrifices in order to achieve greater future satisfaction of their needs is just as inadmissible as is the contrary assertion to the effect that the satisfaction of current needs is given preference. Here as elsewhere it is the task of theory to create the proper framework for any concrete assumption about how individuals rank different degrees of satisfaction of needs over time, just as theory has hitherto deduced the laws of value formation at a point in time, without concrete assumptions about the hierarchy of needs at that point in time. When one deals with an economy that extends over time, the greatest total economic utility is offered by whatever "combination of uses" (Schönfeld) most closely approximates the economic subject's aim to distribute the satisfaction of his needs over time, which is not necessarily equivalent to the greatest sum of individual utilities.

For now these few suggestions delineating a possible solution to the question raised here will have to suffice. It was the primary purpose of this inquiry to determine whether Böhm-Bawerk's formulation of the question was well-founded and, hence, whether he can rightly claim that his is the only one correct answer to the question. The above arguments may be deemed incomplete, but I believe that they suffice to show that the elementary rules of value determination as he used them do not cover the issue to which Böhm-Bawerk addressed himself in presenting the problem. Consequently there is no rule according to which the values of producer goods and products that are available in different periods "should" coincide and thus there is no need to justify the existence of such a value difference by an *ad hoc* explanation. Böhm-Bawerk's formulation of the question obscures a simple fact. The use of capital does not imply the sacrifice of a more intensively experienced need in exchange for satisfying a *less intensive* one; what is at stake is the attainment of a *greater future welfare* by a *more comprehensive* satisfaction of less intensive segments of a future need at the expense of satisfying *smaller* segments of a present need.

There is only one aspect of the above discussion that requires further amplification. While it is true, as pointed out above, that the facts do not justify a generalized assumption as to the way in which the relative satisfaction of needs is sought over time, such a fictitious assumption may still be needed as a useful methodological tool in our analysis. From the above discussion—and Strigl[19] has elaborated on this point—it is easy to see why the indispensable theoretical tool of the static approach can legitimately be applied only on the assumption that economic subjects seek the same supply of goods in successive economic periods. Without this assumption, one cannot conceive of an economic process to which static theory is applicable, since it is founded above all on the constancy of needs as well as on the constancy of the means of production available in successive economic periods. Some people want to limit

[19] *Op. cit.*, pp. 136ff.

the static approach to a timeless economy.[20] For those, however, who wish to apply the methods of statics to an economic process that unfolds over time, the assumption serves to create fictitious data whereby a process is kept steady over time. Hans Mayer's previously mentioned studies, which are among the first to deal seriously with the problem of economic decisions over time, clearly view the endeavor to obtain a supply of goods of equal magnitude in successive economic periods as one of the essential prerequisites for the static approach, but he has not yet touched the problem of interest.[21]

With such a static situation as the starting point, the various factors that influence the interest rate can be explained much more plausibly than by Böhm-Bawerk's analysis. The latter starts out from a "normal state" purportedly governed by the principles of general value theory, according to which products are expected to have the same value as producer goods. The analysis then seeks out special reasons for a value difference to develop, for which a specific rate of interest must compensate. Our premise is that in the normal state derived from general value theory and from the concept of statics, the difference between the value of products and producer goods reflects the greater productivity due to the passage of time. Thus interest corresponds exactly to this physical productivity of capital. Such non-static factors as an endeavor to secure a larger supply of goods in the future (saving) or an unwillingness to provide for a constant supply in the future are only necessary for explaining deviations of the interest rate from physical productivity. The difference in value between current and future goods, as reflected in the interest rate, is an intrinsic element of a static economy. Once this is recognized, we can dismiss the "dynamic interest theories," which owe their existence in part (cf. Schumpeter, op. cit., for instance) to Böhm-Bawerk's presenting interest as a sort of abnormality in a static system.

[20] Cf. Rudolf Streller, *Statik und Dynamik in der theoretischen Nationalökonomie*, Leipzig, [Forschungsinstitut für Volkswirtschaftslehre,] 1926, especially pp. 100ff. and the literature cited therein.

[21] Basically, we can imagine three different empirical types: that people strive for a better, equal, or lower provision for the future. Only in the first, most general stage of theoretical exposition is it justifiable, on purely methodological grounds, to limit oneself to the second type. It would be an interesting task to determine inductively, by examining household accounts, which type is in fact predominant. To gauge the impact on the interest rate level of these different valuations of the present and future satisfaction of needs, one would also have to know the magnitude of the increase in physical productivity achievable from an extension of roundabout production processes. The ultimate disappearance of interest in the presence of a strong desire for a steadily improving future provision is conceivable only in theory. Any desire for a relatively better present provision would raise interest beyond the physical productivity of capital. In view of the large volume of savings, the progressive type that strives for a better satisfaction of future needs is apparently the dominant one. The rate of interest must therefore normally be lower than the physical gain in productivity of capitalistic methods of production. Cf. on this subject the previously mentioned article by P. N. Rosenstein-Rodan, [*op. cit.*,] pp. 1197f.

THREE

UTILITY ANALYSIS AND INTEREST[1]

I

Among the assumptions which are traditionally regarded as necessary for the existence of a stationary state, the most difficult to define is that of constant tastes. Without attempting to solve all the puzzles to which this concept gives rise, it is interesting to trace the effects which the usual and, it is suggested, illegitimate interpretation of its meaning has had on the treatment of the interest problem. We shall find that much of the confusion which still exists about the rôle of the psychical element in the determination of the rate of interest is due to the sort of pseudo-problems which generally arose out of the idea that the utility of a commodity can be conceived as an absolute magnitude instead of merely as a relation to some other commodity.

Although the authors mainly concerned made little or no use of algebraic or geometric exposition, it will make for clearness if we begin by re-stating their assumptions in these terms. In this first section we shall deal mainly with the assumptions underlying Böhm-Bawerk's statement of the problem, and with the quite consistent conclusions which Professor Schumpeter drew from them. Professor Schumpeter did not, of course, intend these conclusions to constitute a *reductio ad absurdum* of the initial assumptions, but to-day they appear almost as such. In later sections we shall attempt to estimate the progress which has been achieved by Professor Irving Fisher's application of the modern apparatus of utility analysis, and to show that even he did not quite succeed, at least in his terminology, in cutting himself loose from the inferences drawn from the assumptions of earlier utility analysis.

With the utility of a commodity conceived as an absolute magnitude, it was natural to define constant tastes as implying that at all successive moments the marginal utility of equal quantities of a commodity available at successive moments was the same. It makes little difference for our purpose whether this assumption is stated in the simpler and even more objectionable form $u_x = f(x)$, implying that the marginal utility of *x* depends on the quantity available of that

[1] [*Economic Journal*, vol. 46, no. 101, March 1936, pp. 44–60.—Ed.]

commodity only, or whether it is stated in the slightly more meaningful form $u_x = f(x, y, z \ldots)$, implying that the marginal utility of x depends on the quantities of all commodities available at that moment. Whichever of these alternatives we actually choose, the essential point is that in either case it is assumed that the marginal utility of any commodity at a particular moment depends only on the quantities of commodities available at that moment, that it is independent of the quantities provided for other moments, and that from this statement of the absolute utilities at different moments we can make deductions about the relative utility of quantities available at different moments. Whether the assumption actually made is that the supply of all other commodities is constant, or whether this is assumed to be irrelevant, the result is in either case that the utility of different quantities of any commodity at different moments is regarded as adequately represented by independent utility curves which, if tastes are assumed to be constant, must be of identical shape.[2]

If we proceed on the assumption of constant tastes as thus defined, it is not difficult to see how, on the one hand, Böhm-Bawerk was led to the conclusion that the existence of interest could only be explained by a systematic undervaluation of future needs, and how, on the other hand, Professor Schumpeter, rejecting this explanation as unrealistic and in contradiction with the assumption of constant tastes, came to the conclusion that the existence of interest was incompatible with stationary conditions.

Böhm-Bawerk's central problem, although he did not always state it in this form, was why people did not take advantage of the possibility of increasing by investment the product obtainable from given resources to such a point that the utility of the greater future product fell to a level equal to the utility of the services which could be obtained by the alternative current use of these resources. This is what one would expect from the general rule that all resources will be distributed among their different uses in such a way that the marginal utility of all those products will be the same, and therefore also equal to the (derived) marginal utility of the factors used. The only possible explanation why this did not happen in so far as products obtainable at different moments of time were concerned, seemed to be that people did not actually attach that true utility to future products which corresponded to the assumption of constant tastes as defined above, but attached only a smaller importance to them which decreased in proportion with the time distance. This would evidently lead people to stop investing for the future before the true future utility of the greater future product had actually fallen to the level of

[2] In an attempt made a number of years ago to clear up some of the difficulties which arise in this approach, I have myself used this construction without becoming aware of the illegitimate assumptions which it involves ("Zur Problemstellung der Zinstheorie," *Archiv für Sozialwissenschaften und Sozialpolitik*, vol. lviii/3, 1927, pp. 517–532 [included in the present volume as "On the Problem of Interest Theory"—Ed.], specially 523.

that of the smaller alternative present product, and thus would account for the existence of the "gap" between the utility of the factors and the utility of the product which, according to Böhm-Bawerk, is the true source of interest.

If, however, one denied with Professor Schumpeter the existence of such a psychical discount, the same assumptions would necessarily lead to the conclusion that saving must continue so long as additional investments brought a greater product than could be obtained from the current use of the same resources, and that, in consequence, a stationary state could only be reached after interest had disappeared. At any one moment, it is true, the amount which it would be advantageous to invest would be limited by the fact that the marginal utility of given additions to the output at any future moment would fall, and that, in consequence, even a future product obtainable from further doses of investment, which was greater in quantity than the alternative present output, might have a smaller utility than the latter. But this would only limit the rate of saving, and not alter the fact that some saving would continue so long as the physical return from any factor could be increased by investing it for a longer period. Only the complete exhaustion of all opportunities to increase output from any factor in this way could put a stop to further saving, and since a stationary state implied that there is no saving, it is possible only if the productivity of capital, and therefore interest, have disappeared.

It will be seen that this proposition is only a logical development from the assumption originally made by Böhm-Bawerk, if the initial assumption about the identical shape of the utility curves at successive moments is not subsequently modified by the introduction of a psychical discount.

II

The assumption that the tastes of a person remain constant is really meant to express that he will act in the same way at successive moments if faced with the same circumstances. Is it necessary for this purpose to assume that the utility functions at the successive moments are the same in the absolute sense implied in the traditional statement of the problem?

There can be no question now that the absolute utility functions have a definite meaning only in so far as they can be translated into a statement about the quantities of the commodities concerned, which under the given conditions will have exactly the same utility, or be perfect substitutes for each other. The utility curve for any commodity would thus express the decreasing quantity of some other commodity the total supply of which was assumed to be constant, which under otherwise unchanged conditions would just equal the utility of successive marginal additions to the supply of the first commodity. The meaning of the assumption that the two utility curves for the same commodity at two different moments should be identical, although slightly more complicated, can also be expressed as a statement about the relative quantities of the commodity available at the two moments which will have the same utility. As a little reflection will show, this assumption must mean that if the total quantities of the commodity available at each of the two dates are the same, equal quantities will have the same value, and that if the total quantities available at the two moments are different, a small addition to the smaller total and larger addition to the larger total will be equally useful.

This, however, would be merely a statement about the attitude of the person concerned at the earlier of the two dates in question, since only at this date could he actually choose between two such quantities; it would not state whether his attitude at the two dates was the same or different. In order to be able to make such a statement, we would have to know how he would decide in a similar position at the second date. It is true that if the assumption of constant utility curves refers not only to the two dates considered, but to all possible dates, this also implies that at the second date his decision would be the same. But it becomes at once obvious that this might be equally true if the utility curves for the different moments were not the same in an absolute sense. In order that my choice between to-day and to-morrow may be the same as to-morrow's choice between then and the day after, it is by no means necessary that on each occasion the quantities available either to-day or to-morrow which I regard as equally useful should be identical quantities. It is only necessary that on each occasion the proportion between a certain quantity to-day and the quantity to-morrow which I regard as equally useful should be the same.

The fact is that the assumption of identical utility curves at all successive moments states not merely the general postulate that the choice between present and future will be made in the *same* way at different moments, but implies beyond that that the choice will be made in a *particular* way. Instead of being a merely formal assumption expressing that the attitude of a person will be the same at successive moments, it is a very definite assumption of the particular attitude he will take at each moment. We shall see later whether this particular assumption has any merits which would justify one in regarding it as a particularly significant, or as representing in any sense the normal case. At this point we are interested merely in showing how it could have seemed to follow directly from the assumption of constant tastes necessary for static analysis, if utility is conceived as an absolute magnitude which can be described as a function of one variable, the quantity of the commodity in question.

But while with the modern "indifference" approach to the utility problem it is easy to see that any attitude as between present and future is compatible with the assumption of constant tastes, it is also not difficult to understand why the older approach led Böhm-Bawerk and his followers to introduce the idea of a "perspective under-valuation of future wants." The special case which they regarded as *the* case of constant tastes would indeed require that people should save and invest until the value of the present factors had become equal to the future utility of their product, *i.e.* until interest had disappeared. In fact, however, by this they did no more than overcome a difficulty of their own making. Only because they had assumed that constant tastes implied that equal quantities of a commodity at two dates ought to have the same marginal utility to a person at a particular moment, did they have to introduce a special reason why this was not the case. In the particular form in which this was done their statement has, indeed, little meaning. It implies a comparison between the present (absolute) utility of a future commodity and its future (absolute) utility which is regarded as the true utility. Such a comparison does not arise in any act of choice, since it is from the nature of things impossible to contemplate anything at one and the same time as from the present and as from the future. All comparisons of relative utilities are necessarily as from one moment of time, so that all they express are relations between present utilities of present goods and present utilities of future goods. The utilities attached at different moments can only be compared by contrasting the relative utilities of one pair of commodities at the one moment with the relative utilities of a corresponding pair of physically similar commodities at another moment.

III

In the modern notation we should, then, have to represent constant tastes by declaring the indifference map of the individual (or the indifference maps of all the individuals) to be the same at every moment. By this we should mean that, although of course the commodities referred to by the maps of successive moments were not, in the strict sense, identical commodities, they were systems in which each element stood in identical relations to all the others. The place of any commodity available next year would, in the indifference map referring to next year, be taken by a similar commodity which would still only be available next year, and so on.

In this section an attempt will be made to use such an indifference map to describe the process of saving of an isolated person. To make it possible actually to draw an indifference map, it will in the first instance be necessary to abstract from the existence of a multitude of different commodities, and to speak of income as if it were one composite commodity always made up of the same proportions of different commodities. Even so, our indifference map would have to have an infinite number of dimensions—namely, as many as there are future moments of time to be considered. We shall obviate this dif-

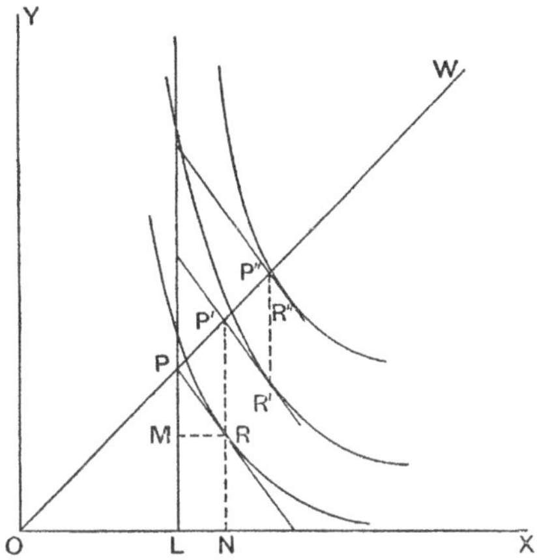

ficulty by assuming that there is only one possible investment period, say one year (as might be the case in a purely grain-growing community), and that, in consequence, there will exist at any one moment an immediate choice only between changes in this year's and in next year's product. We shall assume, however, that any investment is intended to be permanent, *i.e.* that a similar amount is to be reinvested in every successive year, and that, in consequence, only the net (and not gross) returns are considered as the addition to the income of next year (and all future years) which is due to a given investment.[3]

In the accompanying diagram next year's income is measured along the abscissa *OX* and this year's income along the ordinate *OY*. The line *OW* is drawn across the quadrant at an angle of 45 degrees to the two axes, to indicate the locus of all points representing equal incomes this year and next year (corresponding to stationary conditions).

It will be convenient to start by considering the attitude of a person who has not yet made any investments, but who, if he did not invest, would receive equal incomes this year and next year. The position of such a person is represented by the point *P* on the line *OW* in the diagram, which accordingly may serve as a starting-point. Since it is assumed that his intention will be regularly to reinvest at every successive period an amount equal to the origi-

[3] In this respect the following diagrams differ from the similar ones used by Professor Irving Fisher (*The Theory of Interest*, 1930, p. 237 *et seq.*), whose "Willingsness" [*sic*] and "Market" lines refer to gross (and not net) returns. While in consequence in his diagrams "a given rate of interest is represented by the algebraic difference between the slope of the given Market line, and the 100 percent slope of the 45° zero interest line," the rate of interest is directly represented by the slope of the curves used in the following diagrams. The advantage of this method of representation, as will be seen, is that it enables us to use the diagrams to represent the successive decisions, or the process of saving, of an individual.

nal investment, the actual choice open to him will be between—retaining a given amount of present income and a permanent net addition to his future income.[4] It may perhaps not be immediately obvious that the person will save only if such a permanent net return can be obtained, and we must be careful not to beg this question. But a little reflection will show that any other assumption is inconsistent with our previous assumptions. That the investment which is made at the first moment must be repeated at every successive moment, follows from the assumption of constant tastes and unchanged external data (including particularly unchanged technical possibilities). But if no net return were obtained (or if the gross product obtained from the investment were actually smaller than the amount invested), the sacrifice of present income would in this case not be balanced by any addition to future income (it might even lead to an actual decrease of future income). And unless we introduce here some special assumption as regards a wish to provide for uncertain contingencies, *i.e.* unforeseen changes in the data (which presumably are to be excluded from the premises of traditional static analysis), any such assumption would imply a desire to bring about a net decrease of total income, and must for this reason be excluded from consideration.

The possible attitudes which we shall have to consider will therefore range from the limiting case where every, even the very smallest, addition to the permanent income stream will induce him to give up part of his present income, to the other extreme where no addition, however large, to the permanent income stream will induce him to give up part of his present income. It is impossible to decide on *a priori* grounds what the actual attitude of the person in any given position will be. But it is a reasonable empirical assumption to make that in order to induce a person who, apart from this decision, would be certain of a constant income, to give up part of the present income in order to increase his future income, this permanent addition would have to have a definite minimum magnitude. And it is even more certain that in order to induce him to make at any one moment larger and larger sacrifices of present income, more than proportionally larger additions to future income will be required. Since the preservation of life requires a certain minimum of present income, no addition to future income, however large, will induce him to reduce present income below this figure.

If we now describe this attitude by means of indifference curves, the first limiting case—that in which every permanent addition to future income is

[4] If we start, as is convenient, from a position in which no capital yet exists, and the constant income stream which the person could command is the result of the direct use of the services of the permanent factors, an increase of present income at the expense of the future would evidently be impossible for an isolated individual. For this reason the part of the plane *YOX* in the diagram which lies to the left of the line *LP* can be neglected, as it does not contain points which represent possible combinations of present and future income.

regarded worth some sacrifice of present income—would be represented by a curve with a perpendicular slope at the point *P*. If, however, some definite addition to future income is necessary to induce the person to give up even the smallest quantity of present income, this would be expressed by a slope of the curve at this point which represents the net return which is just not sufficient to induce the person to save. In either case any point to the right of this part of the curve would represent a combination of present and future income, which would be preferred to the constant income represented by *P*.

In all cases the slope of the curve would be as indicated only at the point where it crosses the line *OW*, and, as we move along the curve farther to the right, the slope gradually diminishes. Whether at *P* the slope was perpendicular or slightly inclined, it would, for decreasing values of the ordinate, gradually turn more and more to the right, and ultimately become horizontal before present income (measured by the ordinate) had dwindled to zero. And the same would be true of all the other members of the complete family of indifference curves which could be drawn through any other point of the line *OW*.

This set of curves describing the psychical attitude of the person at any moment will enable us to derive his actual behaviour if we combine it with a corresponding representation of the technical possibilities. The simplest assumption to make in this respect, and the only assumption compatible with the case where only one commodity is produced and where there is only one possible investment period, is that up to a definite limit[5] investments bring constant returns, and that at this limit the net return falls suddenly to zero. The possibility of this constant rate of transformation of present income into permanent additions to future income could be expressed by a family of straight transformation lines of corresponding slope, as shown in the diagram.

With this representation of the technical possibilities added to the indifference curves, the action of the individual can be immediately deduced. If he starts at the position represented by *P*, he can and will move as indicated by the transformation line going through that point. Among the possible positions represented by all the points on this line the one representing a position preferred to all others will evidently be the point *R* where the line just touches an indifference curve. It means that at the first date the person will save out of

[5] Successive investments will be made, in this case, by investing successive doses of the "original" factors for the given investment period, instead of using them for current production. And all opportunities of investment will be exhausted when all the available factors are invested for that period. Up to this point we should have to expect constant physical returns unless we assume that some of the original factors are more suitable for investment than others. The point at which all factors have been invested represents our absolute limit beyond which the future income cannot be increased. In the diagram this is expressed by the fact that all transformation lines suddenly end (or become perpendicular) at the points corresponding to this maximum income.

his income *LP* the amount *MP* in order to increase next year's and all future year's income from *OL* to *ON*.

But this is only the beginning of a process that will continue for some time. As a result of the investment at the first date, the person will find himself later in command of an increased present income with an assured future income of equal magnitude, *i.e.* in the position represented by *P'*. And he will again find it to his advantage to move along the transformation line from *P'* to *R'* on to a higher indifference curve, and so on.

If, as we have assumed, the decision to save and invest takes place discontinuously at definite intervals, the person will be in successive years at the points *R*, *R'*, *R"* . . . . As the intervals at which the decisions about saving and investing are made becomes [*sic*] shorter and shorter, the lines describing the path of saving will tend to approach more and more the shape of a continuous curve.

There are two questions which must be provisionally answered before we can go on to make more realistic assumptions concerning the shape of the transformation curve. The first is, What is the relative influence of the productivity element and the psychological attitude respectively in determining the rate of interest while the process of saving continues? The second is, At what point will that process come to an end, and on what will the rate of interest depend in that final stationary state?

The answer to the first question is very simple under the assumptions made at present—(*i.e.* straight and parallel transformation lines, or constant costs). While the process of saving still continues, the rate of interest will be determined solely by the productivity of investment (the slope of the transformation curve), and the psychical attitude will merely determine how much will have to be saved at every moment in order that the marginal rate of time-preference may adapt itself to the given and constant productivity rate. The only rôle "time preference" plays in this particular case is that it determines how long it will last until a stationary position is reached.[6]

To the second question there are two different answers. It is, of course, possible that saving will go on until there is no further possibility of investment. In this case the final equilibrium position will be represented in the diagram by the point where the highest transformation line meets the line *OW*. Investment comes to a standstill simply because, although possibly the person would like to invest more, no more can be invested. Since this case is quite irrelevant to the problems which will arise later under more realistic assumptions, we can now dismiss it.

[6] The situation here is, of course, exactly the same as in the more general case where the relative costs of two commodities are constant (*i.e.* independent of the quantities produced), and where, in consequence, their relative value will be uniquely determined by their relative costs and cannot be affected (except in the very short run) by changes of their relative utility.

It is, however, also possible that the process may come to an end before the investment opportunities are exhausted. It may be that at some point on the line *OW* the transformation line coincides with the tangent of the indifference curve, and that in consequence there is no further inducement to save. In the present case this is possible only if the slope of the indifference curves at the point where they cut the line *OW* is not the same for all, but increases gradually. So far there has been no occasion to state explicitly any assumption on this point.[7] If, however, we now introduce the assumption just mentioned it is evidently possible that the time-preference in a position where present and future incomes are equal, would become as high as the technical productivity of capital. In this case the ultimate stationary equilibrium would be reached with a positive rate of interest, equal to the constant productivity of investment. The psychical attitude would merely determine at what income this point would be reached.

IV

The assumption of constant productivity, as will be remembered, had to be introduced as a consequence of two other simplifying assumptions which were made to render a diagrammatic treatment possible. These assumptions were that only one commodity (or income thought of as a complete commodity consisting of constant proportions) was produced, and that there was only one possible period of investment.[8] As soon as we drop either of these two assumptions, we come to the more realistic case in which successive investments bring decreasing returns. It will, however, be seen that the results obtained in the less realistic case are not altogether useless, since compared with time-preference, the productivity of investment will always be comparatively constant.

There is, however, the serious difficulty of exposition that as soon as we drop either of the two assumptions the diagrammatic method so far used is no longer strictly applicable. The existence of different commodities will make the returns of successive investment decrease, because the advantage of time-consuming processes will be different with different commodities, and because, if the production of some commodities is increased more than that of others, their relative value will fall. But in our diagram only decreases of physical

[7] Implicitly in the drawing of the diagram the assumption just mentioned has been made. It is for this reason only that the "path of saving" gradually approaches *OW*. Otherwise it might go parallel to, or even diverge from, *OW*. (If, as is generally assumed, "time-preference" decreases with increasing income, the latter would even be the rule.) In the two latter cases the process could, under the present assumptions, come to an end only for the first reason mentioned in the text, *i.e.* exhaustion of all investment opportunities.

[8] Probably a third condition is also required in order to obtain constant productivity—namely, that there is only one homogeneous original factor of production.

returns can be properly represented. The possibility of varying the investment periods will imply decreasing returns, because the existence of different kinds of possible methods of production will always mean that at first the most profitable ones will be selected, and the less productive uses will be resorted to only gradually, as the supply of capital increases. The difficulty of a diagrammatic representation of this case is due to the fact that if the periods of investments vary, it is no longer possible to assume that the results of investments at one date will all become available after a single and constant interval. But while it would be very difficult to take account of this in the diagram, the inaccuracy caused by neglecting it is not so serious as to make the simpler form of the diagram useless for the elucidation of this case. I shall therefore simply assume that decreasing returns occur as a result of this fact, but neglect the particular effect mentioned, in order to be able to use the same sort of diagram.

In terms of the diagram, the fact that the returns of investment decrease will be expressed by the former straight transformation lines becoming curved and concave towards the axes.[9] Since each curve represents the permanent addition to future income[10] which can be obtained by the sacrifice of successive parts of present income, the relative shape of the curves will depend on the length of the period which is called "the present," as the size of the present income which can be invested will depend on this.

But it is only the shape of the indifference curve which is affected by this. The opportunities of obtaining a return from successive investments will be practically independent of the period during which the investments have been made. They will depend (under stationary conditions) almost exclusively on the amount of investments already made, whether these have followed each other at long or at short intervals. But it is altogether different with the indifference curve which represents the psychical attitude. As the period during which a given amount is to be saved and invested becomes shorter, this amount becomes a larger share of the income of that period. For a person with an

[9] Since it must be assumed that the return on further investments depends only on the amount of investments already made, *i.e.* only on the provision made for the future, but is independent of the size of the income left for the present, it cannot be assumed that the shapes of the different members of the complete family of transformation curves are independent of each other. At any point corresponding to a given value of the abscissa the slope of all the transformation curves will have to be the same, and they will therefore all be similar in shape, but those farther up and on the right will possess additional parts which are missing with those farther down and on the left.

[10] The difficulty mentioned before concerns the date or dates when these additions to future income become first available. Contrary to the first case discussed, these periods are now no longer identical with the income period, and it is therefore, strictly speaking, no longer true that the decision to save made during every income period is directly affected by the result of the investment in the immediately preceding period. This is the complication which, as mentioned before, will be deliberately neglected.

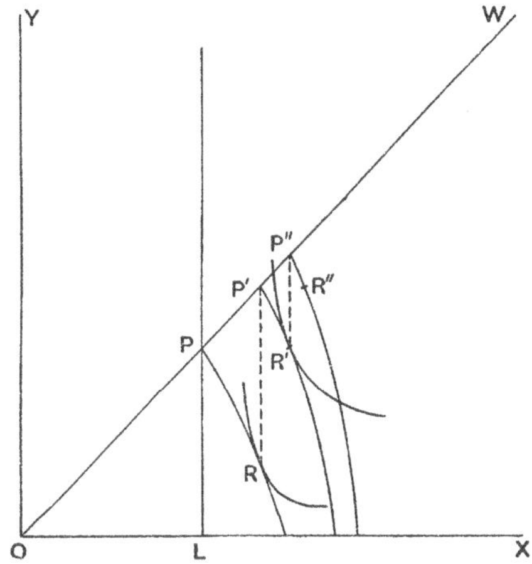

annual income of £600 it is altogether a different proposition to save £25 in the course of a year or to save the same amount in the course of a month. The sacrifice in the second case amounts to reducing one's expenditure to one-half one's income. And as we make the period shorter, the reluctance to save and invest given amounts will increase further.

In terms of the diagram, this means that as we make the income period shorter the indifference curve becomes more and more curved, while the transformation curve remains unchanged. For our purpose, however, it is evidently relatively short periods which are relevant. Compared with the totals that may be profitably invested, even the total income of a year, and still more the total income of a month, are relatively small magnitudes. But it is such relatively short periods that we have to consider if we want to understand the position of a person at different points of the path of saving.

It is, then, the ratio of the curvatures of (or the relative magnitude of elasticities of substitution expressed by) the two groups of curves which is of fundamental importance for what follows, and it is therefore necessary to dwell somewhat longer on this point. The statement just made about the ratio of the curvatures expresses the fact that, if we consider a relatively short time-interval, the sacrifice of successive parts of the income of this interval in the interests of the future will meet a rapidly increasing resistance, while, on the other hand, the investment of successive fractions of a small total income will have quite an insignificant effect on the rate of return obtainable from investment. The situation will still be similar to the case discussed before to this extent, that during any short income-period the rate of time-preference (as represented by the indifference curve) will have to adapt itself to a relatively constant rate of return. In terms of the diagram: if the process starts at P the individual will during the first time-interval move along the transformation curve until R, where the rate of time-preference on further doses of present income is equal to the rate of return which will be little affected by the comparatively small total invested. In consequence of this investment, he will some time later find himself at P', and again save until his time-preference has been raised to equal the comparatively constant rate of return, *i.e.* he will move to R'. And when, in consequence of this, he finds himself in the position represented by P'', he will again save, and so on.

The curve R, R', R'' . . . then again represents the path along which the saver moves in time. The points which are specially brought out by this representation are, firstly, that saving must necessarily be treated as a process in time the effects of which continuously change the actual position of the saver, and thereby his willingness to perform further saving, and secondly, that at any point in this process the rate of interest is determined practically by the productivity of investment alone, while time-preference is important only in determining how fast the saver will move towards a position in which the productivity of further investment, and therefore the rate of interest, will be lower.[11] It will also be seen that so long as saving continues the time-preference of the individual as represented by his marginal rate of substitution between equal present and future income streams (the slope of the indifference curve where it crosses the line OW) may be zero, or even negative, and there will yet be a positive rate of interest.

The exact direction of the path of saving will evidently depend on the shape and position of the two sets of curves. Whether and when a stationary position will be reached depends on the rate at which the productivity of investment decreases as the amount invested increases, compared with the change in the rate of time-preference consequent upon the increase of income. It is conceivable that saving will cease only when all opportunities of investment have been exhausted, because any rate of net return, however small, would lead to some saving. This would mean that at the point where they cross the constant-income-line OW, the indifference curves, at least in the region of the higher incomes, are perpendicular. In this case stationary conditions could only be reached at a zero rate of interest. But if the indifference curves have a definite slope along that line (*i.e.* if there is, in the traditional meaning, a positive time-preference), savings will cease and a stationary state will be reached with a positive rate of interest corresponding to the rate represented by that

[11] The credit of having brought out this point clearly is entirely due to Professor F. H. Knight, with whose more recent statements on this point I find myself in complete agreement. Cf. particularly his article "Professor Fisher's Interest Theory: A Case in Point," *Journal of Political Economy*, vol. xxxix/2, April 1931, [pp. 176–212,] and "Interest," reprinted from the *Encyclopædia of Social Sciences*, [ed. Edwin R. A. Seligman,] Vol. VIII, [London, Macmillan,] 1932, [pp. 131–44], in *The Ethics of Competition and other Essays*, London [George Allen & Unwin,] 1935, pp. 261 *et seq.*

slope. And in this sense it can be said that the rate of time-preference determines the rate of interest existing in the final stationary equilibrium, and there only. Since, as will be clear from what has been said before, a rate of time-preference in this sense is entirely compatible with the assumption of constant tastes, we have here the case of a stationary equilibrium with a positive rate of interest, which Professor Schumpeter regards as impossible.

Finally, there is also the possibility that as the return of investment decreases, the rate of saving becomes so small that the opportunities of investment will not be exhausted within any time in which we are at all interested. In this case saving will go on indefinitely (*i.e.* the path of saving will end at the line *OW* only after an infinitely long time), and while it continues the rate of interest will be determined, not by time-preference, but by the productivity of investment.

The important point, however, is that in real life the actual societies with which we have to deal are always progressive societies in which, for reasons into which we need not go here,[12] there is always a considerable positive rate of saving, and that in such a society it is the productivity of investment (or rather the expected rate of return on investments) which alone can be said to determine the rate of interest, while time-preference only determines the rate of saving and the point where a stationary equilibrium would ultimately be reached. The inference frequently drawn from the time-preference theories of interest[13]—that short-run changes in the rate of interest must or can be accounted for by changes in time-preference—falls to the ground.[14] Of the two branches of the Böhm-Bawerkian school, that which stressed the productivity element almost to the exclusion of time-preference represented mainly by K. Wicksell, proves to have been practically right against that represented by Professor F. A. Fetter and Professor I. Fisher, who stressed time-preference as the exclusive, or at least equally important, factor. The weakness of Wick-

[12] Growth of population, invention, and unforeseen changes which destroy part of the capital already accumulated, are probably the main reasons why the inducement to further saving never disappears.

[13] Cf., *e.g.*, A. H. Hansen and H. Tout in *Econometrica*, Vol. I/2, April 1933. [Alvin H. Hansen and Herbert Tout, "Annual Survey of Business Cycle Theory: Investment and Saving in Business Cycle Theory," *Econometrica*, vol. 1, no. 2, April 1933, pp. 119–47.—Ed.]

[14] There is, of course, another set of circumstances which accounts for the existence of short-term fluctuations of the rate of interest—namely, all the influences coming from the side of money. On the plane of abstraction on which the present argument moves, these had to be neglected.

It has been suggested to me, probably with much justice, that what was in the minds of many of the authors who spoke about time-preference as affecting short-term fluctuations in the rate of interest is really what has recently become known under the name of liquidity preference. If this is so, it clearly indicates how necessary it is sharply to distinguish between what are really fundamentally different influences which should on no account be confused.

sell's case was that he never attempted expressly to justify why he neglected the time-preference element. Professor Fisher, on the other hand, although he may claim to have furnished us with a formal apparatus which enables us to describe the interaction of all the relevant factors, even if he had attached no more than equal importance to the two factors involved—and he certainly has been *understood* to regard the psychical element as the dominant one—would have given the psychical factor much more than its due share. But, beyond that, his use of the term impatience certainly carries a misleading connotation. A person is called impatient in his terminology if, when assured of equal present and future incomes, he prefers some addition to his present income, even if only a very large one, to any permanent addition to his future income, even if only to a very small one. That means that the term impatience actually implies what it will always convey in popular language, that a person is *anxious to anticipate* his future income in order to increase his present income beyond the level at which it can be permanently kept. This is, however, by no means a necessary condition for the existence of interest in any society except a stationary one. All that is required in a progressive society is that its members should feel some reluctance to postpone income in order to increase future income beyond the present level at more than a limited rate. The importance of this reluctance is that it determines the rate of saving. Yet to say that people do not save more than they actually do because they are impatient, is not only rather a peculiar way of putting it, but it becomes definitely misleading when it suggests that there is a definite rate of impatience which determines the rate of interest.

FOUR

CAPITAL CONSUMPTION[1]

I

Today's economist finds himself in an unhappy position. Anyone else may feel justified to entertain optimism, if only for the more distant future. No matter how gloomy the economic situation at this very moment, rapid strides in our technical knowledge seem to open up vistas of a brighter future. The present state of his discipline offers no such reassurance to the economist. It is not that advances in his discipline have been slower than elsewhere. What is troubling is that his field lacks the influence on practical applications that is assured to other fields because their practitioners, as a matter of course, have some grounding in the principles relevant to the discipline. The economist, for his part, must stand by idly day after day, as statesmen and politicians base their actions on theories that in many instances nobody in the field has dared to advocate seriously for over a century. Hence he cannot avoid grave doubts as to our ever enjoying the fruits of technical progress promised by other fields of knowledge. He may well worry that all hopes of greater prosperity will shortly be blocked by interventions into the economy, whose consequences are not understood by their initiators.[2]

We seem to have almost reached a critical point, in some parts of the world at least, where technical progress can no longer outweigh the pernicious consequences of economic ignorance and where a permanent decline in the general standard of living is setting in.[3] We are now threatened by economic problems

[1] ["Kapitalaufzehrung," *Weltwirtschaftliches Archiv*, vol. 36, no. 1, July 1932, pp. 86–108; translated by Grete Heinz as "Capital Consumption" in F. A. Hayek, *Money, Capital & Fluctuations: Early Essays*, ed. Roy McCloughry (Chicago: University of Chicago Press; London: Routledge and Kegan Paul, 1984), pp. 136–58; translation revised by Hansjoerg Klausinger.—Ed.]

[2] [Hayek's concern here about the unintended and unfortunate consequences of intervention echoed the theme of Ludwig von Mises, *Kritik des Interventionismus* (Jena, Ger.: Gustav Fischer, 1929); revised English translation, *A Critique of Interventionism*, trans. Hans F. Sennholz (Irvington-on-Hudson, NY: Foundation for Economic Education, 1996).—Ed.]

[3] [Hayek was writing in 1932, at the bottom of the Great Depression. Economic growth resumed thereafter, with economic recovery occupying the next decade and technical progress returning. Conceptually, a set of bad policies imposed by economically ignorant policymakers is

for which economics has so far contributed little in the way of explanation, although it has all the necessary tools to do so.

Economics in its present state came into being during a very brief and extraordinarily propitious period in human development. It was elaborated during a time of uniquely rapid expansion of general wealth—due in no small part to the general acceptance of the doctrines of its founders. Since historical conditions invariably determine which problems are selected for scrutiny, it is hardly surprising that economics was preoccupied with problems of a progressing economy, while conditions in a hypothetical stationary economy were explored solely for the insights it provided on the former. Nor is it surprising that "the economics of decline, the dismal counterpart of the economics of expansion"[4] attracted no attention at all.

This study represents an attempt to fill this gap. It stems from the conviction—reinforced in me by many years' observation of a country that has been continuously consuming its capital—that if we ourselves do not undertake this unpleasant task, it will be left to future historians to write about the economics of decline of our time. There is considerable evidence that the problem is equally acute in a number of other countries worldwide, not just in the one whose experiences have most decisively shaped the views offered in this study. Austria's situation differs from theirs only in that it has had several years' head start along the path in which they are now engaging.[5]

Our purpose here is not to describe current developments, however. Before we can attempt to investigate any concrete situation from this perspective, we must have a clear conception of how the process of capital consumption would manifest itself and what is symptomatic of this process. We will limit ourselves here to such a theoretical analysis, in which the consequences of certain hypothetical assumptions will be developed. The few illustrations drawn from real life and referring largely to Austria—with whose conditions I am most familiar—are intended exclusively as illustrative examples, not as evidence that all the points I raise here apply to that country. Such a conclusion

a factor lowering the general *level* of living standards, but not permanently lowering the economy's *growth rate* unless the policies progressively worsen.—Ed.]

[4] Cf. W[ilhelm] Röpke, "Die Theorie der Kapitalbildung" [The theory of capital accumulation], lecture given to the Nationalökonomische Gesellschaft [Austrian Economics Society] in Vienna on February 22, 1929. (*Recht und Staat in Geschichte und Gegenwart*, 63) p.39. [Röpke's lecture appeared as no. 63 in the monograph series *Recht und Staat in Geschichte und Gegenwart* (Tübingen, Ger.: Mohr, 1929).—Ed.]

[5] [On the concerns of Hayek and other like-minded Austrian economists (especially Ludwig von Mises and Fritz Machlup) regarding capital consumption in Austria, see Hansjoerg Klausinger, "From Mises to Morgenstern: The Austrian School of Economics during the *Ständestaat*" (working paper, 2003); and Richard Ebeling, "The Economist as the Historian of Decline: Ludwig von Mises and Austria between the Two World Wars," in *Political Economy, Public Policy and Monetary Economics: Ludwig von Mises and the Austrian Tradition* (New York: Routledge, 2010), pp. 133–34 nn. 40 and 41.—Ed.]

would require far more factual material than is suitable for presentation in this kind of theoretical analysis.[6]

II

If consumption of capital resulted exclusively from a voluntary decision by the owners of capital, it is highly unlikely that over the years its scope would exceed the simultaneous formation of new capital and that the outcome would be an overall decline in the economy's available capital. However, there are two sets of measures affecting capital owners in general that could lead to capital consumption to such an extent that a decumulation of capital in the whole economy can become a serious problem. The first set of measures of this kind are direct state interventions aiming at the conversion of capital into income, among them capital levies and inheritance taxes. The second consists of actions resulting in incomes being spent for consumption purposes in an amount greater than the economy's net product, and thus in persistent capital consumption. The factors involved in the first group of measures are by no means insignificant. Nevertheless, I will focus here on the impact of the latter, because these tendencies are of much great import today, yet are much more poorly understood. I will come back briefly to the analogous effects of state intervention at the end of this essay. The following sections will therefore deal exclusively with the consequence of an increase in the economy's current production costs over and above the value of its current net income. It is symptomatic of how little our current "capitalistic"[7] process of production is generally understood that many economists will consider the very possibility of such a state of affairs paradoxical.[8]

Let us first examine what happens in a closed economy that was previously

[6] This theoretical analysis of the process of capital consumption has a secondary purpose as well. At the end of my study, *Preise und Produktion* (*Beiträge zur Konjunkturforschung*, 3) Vienna, [Springer,] 1931, pp. 87 and 120 [this is the German-language version of *Prices and Production* (London: Routledge, 1931)—Ed.], I already alluded to the essential similarity between the process whereby the capitalist structure of production undergoes persistent shrinkage and the way a cyclical depression unfolds. In that study I presented a detailed account of what happens during the boom and the crisis, but I took little note of the processes set in motion during the later stages of a depression. It is my hope that the present work complements the picture drawn in the earlier study by offering a fuller account of the mechanism of a depression. In particular I expect to be somewhat more explicit here about the significance of the prevailing rigidity in prices and wages, which were neglected in my previous study.

[7] The term "capitalistic" as used here and in the following pages always refers in a theoretical sense to a production process involving the use of capital, rather than to a particular social order in the political sense.

[8] [Hayek may have had particularly in mind Frank Knight, whose model assumes a stationary or progressing economy in which capital always yields a positive rate of return.—Ed.]

in a state of equilibrium, when this equilibrium between costs and prices is disturbed either because external influences increase the money costs of production or because productivity declines with unchanged money costs. The former may come about in many ways. Trade unions may succeed in raising wages above the equilibrium level or additional taxes or social duties may make the cost of employing workers or the use of other production factors more expensive. Or else money wages that represented equilibrium wages in the past, may have become relatively too high because of a deflationary process. A general lowering of productivity is less likely in an age of great technical progress, if we disregard the cases of an exhaustion of natural resources, or of a series of poor harvests and also the consequences of capital consumption to be discussed below. Even this case is important in principle, however, because what is true of a closed economy when productivity declines in the face of rigid money incomes applies equally to a country that is a member of an international system when its terms of trade with the rest of the world deteriorate. This may be the case because of a decline in demand for its products, mounting obstacles to its trade with other countries, or failure to keep pace with the general level of technical progress. Furthermore, a general decline in productivity, which may also occur in a closed economy, could result from the destruction of part of its capital equipment through non-economic causes such as war, a natural catastrophe, or because state intervention (subsidies to certain industries) has transformed it into less profitable forms.

III

What implications does it have if, as a consequence of one of these circumstances, money incomes rise in relation to the value of consumer goods that are currently brought to market under the existing organization of production? When dealing with this question, most economists seem to have been so utterly under the sway of two apparently self-evident notions that they hardly have considered giving them any serious thought. What they fail to keep in mind is that these notions apply only when production requires no capital. According to one notion, it is impossible to consume more than is currently produced. The other notion assumes that when money incomes increase in relation to real income, *all* prices will rise in the same proportion. However, it is at least conceivable and occurs quite regularly, as I hope to demonstrate, that part of the difference between the demand for consumer goods and the net product of the economy as a whole is taken out of capital. In that case, not only does the first notion prove to be incorrect, but doubts should also arise as to the accuracy of the second notion, which is its corollary. It is actually this second notion which most strongly supports the widespread conviction that as soon as the production of consumer goods becomes more profitable, there will be a greater incentive to invest.[9, 10]

What actually does happen in such a situation? We are assuming that wages, or rather, the total costs involved in the employment of labor, now exceed their equilibrium level. Hourly wage costs now exceed the value of the marginal hour of labor. Economists who have dealt with this problem usually limit themselves to showing that, as a result, the number of employed workers will decline until the value of the marginal product of labor again coincides with labor costs. They are of course quite right, as long as labor cooperates with land or other factors of production whose quantity is rigidly fixed. But as opponents of this theory have always emphasized, when labor is applied jointly with capital, the effects are different. In this case, the higher labor costs may then be borne at the expense of capital. The proponents of this theory are convinced that the effects are less deleterious in this case, but in fact the consequences are far more dangerous because of their far-reaching and unpredictable impact on capital. From the very fact that wages can be paid at the expense of capital, an excessive rise in wages leads not only to unemployment but to a decumulation of capital and thereby permanently lowers the equilibrium level of wages.

Under the capitalistic production process, when wages are too high or the total sum of incomes is too high, current consumption absorbs a larger part of the current stream of the original production factors than is compatible with the maintenance of real capital (or the transformation of new savings into real capital). New investment and reinvestment (that is, maintenance and renewal of circulating and fixed capital) loses out in the competition for available resources. The maintenance of capital necessitates the steady capitalistic reinvestment of a constant fraction of all the production factors (or, more accurately, the steady investment of all production factors for the same average period). If new savings are to be converted into real capital, this fraction must increase (or the average investment period must be extended). A precondition for this process is that the relative prices of consumer goods and producer

[9] J. M. Keynes has recently enunciated this set of ideas shared by all underconsumption theories with particular clarity. In keeping with these ideas, he considers it desirable that entrepreneurs obtain an abnormal surplus in current proceeds over their current production costs—including their normal profits. In his view, this surplus is the root cause of all booms, while in mine it makes crises inevitable when it is a temporary phenomenon and leads to persistent capital consumption, if it becomes a permanent state of affairs. [Hayek presumably refers here to John Maynard Keynes, *A Treatise on Money* (London: Macmillan, 1930).—Ed.]

[10] It almost seems as though the great emphasis modern subjective value theory places on the derived nature of the demand for production goods has been misleading in this respect—although it is correct in general, of course. Because of this emphasis, the potential "limitation" imposed on production by the provision of capital, which had been recognized and emphasized in classic economic works since Adam Smith, has received too little attention.

goods will make it profitable to distribute available resources between these two types of goods in such a way that capital is maintained or that it increases by the amount of new savings. When prices of producer goods rise in relation to prices of consumer goods, there will be a relative increase in the production of producer goods, that is, an increase in capital; a relative increase in the prices of consumer goods will lead to a rise in their production and a reduction in that of capital goods, which will either mean a slow-down in the growth of capital or an actual decrease in the stock of capital.

These observations make good sense when one bears in mind that there are only two choices, either increasing the output of capital goods or increasing the output of consumer goods, and that, in the long run, with a given technology and given natural resources, the physical quantity of consumer goods per capita can only be increased by consistently devoting a larger part of productive resources to capitalistic investment rather than to immediate consumption.[11] However, certain naïve preconceptions apparently make it very difficult to take these relationships consistently into account. The point that perplexes not only economic laymen is why increased revenue for the final product, that is, consumer goods, should not generally allow the entrepreneurs to invest more. Does a single entrepreneur's investment not depend on what he gets for his product? Why would then a higher demand for consumer goods not induce a general rise in investment activity if all production in the last analysis is geared to the production of consumer goods?

If we remember our starting point—that the share received by workers from the total revenue of the firm exceeded their contribution to the product of this firm—then it is easy to see why this must lead to an effective reduction in the stock of capital goods. Only if, as a consequence of increased demand for consumer goods, *all* prices, including the prices of all intermediate products, were to rise in the same proportion, production would be unaffected. But in that case one would expect neither a favorable nor an unfavorable effect from raising wages. In reality the effects are much more complicated. The fact that the price of shoes rises as much as the increase of its production costs is not much of a consolation for the owner of an iron mine from which machines for the production of shoes are manufactured. The increase in the price of shoes does not in the least imply that the steel manufacturer, who buys iron, will have more money available for the purchase of iron. On the contrary, he will actually have less money available because he will have to spend more for coal because of the increased competition for coal with the shoe manufacturer. Not only does money spent on consumer goods today fail to have

[11] [This trade-off is clearly illustrated, in Roger Garrison, *Time and Money* (London: Routledge, 2002), by a production possibilities frontier between current consumption and current investment.—Ed.]

an immediate effect on the purchasing power of those who produce for the future. Since there always is a choice of investing productive resources for a longer or shorter period, money spent on consumer goods actually competes with the demand of those who wish to produce for the future and whose purchasing power is determined not by the current price of consumer goods but by their past price. All those who tacitly assume that the demand for capital goods changes in proportion to the demand for consumer goods overlook the fact that consuming and investing are alternatives and that one cannot simultaneously consume more and delay consumption in order to increase the stock of intermediate products.[12] There is no way that producers of capital goods can increase their demand for producer goods commensurately to the increased demand for consumer goods. Consequently, an increased demand for consumer goods must divert production in the direction of goods that can be rapidly produced. This means not only that the existing labor force is used differently but that part of the available intermediate products will be used in a more direct—yet also less productive—way for consumption than originally intended and that part of the intermediate products used up will no longer be replaced. What we are faced with here is nothing but an example of capital consumption, whose features we will subsequently examine in detail.

IV

As I have pointed out elsewhere,[13] a process of capital consumption of this kind may occasionally occur during the downswing of a business cycle, and we are therefore more familiar with most of its manifestations in that context rather than as permanent phenomena. Yet when I ascribed industrial fluctuations to upward or downward changes in the average length of the production process or of the investment period, it was objected that such changes might be of interest as long-run phenomena but had no bearing on short-term phenomena like the business cycle.[14] To my mind, however, industrial fluctuations exemplify particularly violent fluctuations of this kind. Halting or curtailing the replacement of capital goods and using production factors in processes that make consumer goods available more rapidly, as illustrated above with

[12] I believe that J. S. Mill's famous and often criticized "fourth proposition concerning capital," to wit, that "demand for commodities is not demand for labor," already addressed this erroneous interpretation, although he did little to justify his proposition. (Cf. *Principles of political economy: With some of their applications to social philosophy* [7th ed.]. Edited and with an introduction by W. Ashley, London, [Longmans, Green,] 1909, I, Ch. V, par. 9, p. 79).

[13] Cf. Hayek, *op. cit.*, esp. pp. 90ff.

[14] [For this objection, see Martin Hill, "The Period of Production and Industrial Fluctuations," *Economic Journal*, vol. 43, no. 172, December 1933, 599–610.—Ed.]

respect to coal, implies a shift to less capitalistic methods of production. And when machines, whose product can be consumed only after considerable time has elapsed, are utilized to a lesser extent and capital goods decline in value compared to consumer goods, this is evidence that work invested in a more distant future is considered less valuable.

From all this we must conclude the following: the demand for consumer goods exceeds the cost value of consumer goods currently coming on the market, and therefore this rise in demand will be satisfied at least in part by resources that had originally been destined for more distant use, but whose utilization for that purpose has become unprofitable. In other words: old, frozen labor has become relatively cheaper than currently available labor and for this reason it is more advantageous to satisfy the current demand from the stock of frozen labor than to use new labor. (Conversely, a reduction in the current demand for consumer goods because of increased saving will make frozen labor more valuable than new labor, and it is therefore worthwhile to store current labor in the form of capital goods. This perspective makes it easier to understand the dissimilar impacts of a shift to more capitalistic and less capitalistic methods of production. The former is likely to proceed without serious disturbances, while capital consumption is always accompanied by unemployment.)

It is not hard to understand why this process must lead to unemployment when wages are rigid. If wages were not rigid, incipient unemployment would very soon lead to an adaptation of wage rates to the value of the productive contribution of the marginal worker. The lower wages, in conjunction with the decline in consumption that they induce would permit the establishment of a new equilibrium. But when the number of persons employed declines without wages being lowered and when, as a result, current costs per unit of the product still exceed the workers' contribution to the product, the disequilibrium persists and capital continues to be consumed. Only when consumption is reduced sufficiently, capital consumption will come to a halt.[15]

The whole economy must of necessity decline as long as consumption exceeds production, and a part of consumption is thus at the expense of the existing stock of capital. As long as this occurs, the current spending on consumer goods will exceed the current expenditures on the production of these goods. At the same time, current contributions by the original factors of production will not suffice to replace the total value of the product that has been

[15] If *money* wages are fixed and the effective quantity of money remains unchanged, higher consumer goods prices will eventually force consumption to be reduced in the face of a declining production of consumer goods. With fixed *real* wages (indexed wages), capital consumption will not only continue unabated but will progressively accelerate, because it is associated with a decline in the productivity of labor and hence with a fall in equilibrium wages.

consumed—that is, they will not replace all those expenditures that were made in the past and that should be currently reinvested for future purposes.

V

What gives rise to a general consumption of capital would not need much further elucidation, were we not all inclined—even if we have approved of the general observations above—to end up saying: "That is all well and good, but even so, to all appearances, capital does not shrink very much during a crisis." The reason that it is so difficult to recognize capital consumption in this situation is that people view existing capital equipment predominantly or exclusively from a technical point of view without taking its economic meaning, that is, its value, into account. In almost all cases, however, a reduction in capital means above all a reduction in the value of available production equipment, which continues to exist for some time in unaltered form and which only gradually diminishes physically as a consequence of its loss in value. It is quite conceivable that, as a result of changed price constellations, the best-equipped factory, the most wonderful machine that only recently could have been used to greatest advantage in production and therefore represented a large capital value, quite suddenly loses its value and consequently ceases to be capital. The fact that this factory or machine continues to maintain the same high technical quality makes it difficult for anyone who envisages things from a technical rather than an economical point of view to understand that capital has been destroyed and that we have become that much poorer because of it. It is an undeniable fact that most people and even most business people grasp technical matters more easily than abstract economic relationships. As a consequence, the meaning and all the more the causes of such a destruction of capital are quite generally misunderstood. Hardly any other economic phenomenon seems more incomprehensible to the ordinary observer than the fact that the loss in value of facilities whose technical capacity remains unchanged is anything more than a superficial phenomenon caused by the quirks of the capitalist system, and that it reflects a genuine reduction in our wealth.

It is basically not difficult to understand, however, that the reduction in value of production facilities that occurs as a consequence of any one of the causes we have discussed earlier—even if none other than that the facilities no longer generate returns in excess of production costs—soon leads to a physical reduction of their capacity, that is, a physical destruction of capital, as well as to additional capital losses. This will be so even if we assume that proceeds still cover running costs and the requisite amortization quotas but no longer cover interest costs. This remains true even if we neglect the many cases where the permanent nature of the loss in the value of equipment is not recognized and insufficient depreciation allowances are made, hence leading of course directly to capital consumption. Let us just assume that the directly affected capital owners restrict their expenses to compensate for the loss of interest, so that their gross proceeds still cover the amortization of capital. They will then lose only part of their income but not their capital. Even so, the fact that for most of the capitalists in a given industry it becomes unprofitable to reinvest their capital in the same place will lead to capital losses of other owners of capital.

Let us assume wages increase to such an extent that workers can claim the capitalist's entire interest income from invested capital and that interest income from invested capital has thus vanished. Even that does *not* mean, as Böhm-Bawerk seems to posit in his classic investigation of this problem,[16] that there are no possibilities for investing available capital[17] in interest-earning

[16] E. von Böhm-Bawerk, *Macht oder ökonomisches Gesetz* (1914). Reprinted in *Gesammelte Schriften von Eugen von Böhm-Bawerk*, edited by F. X. Weiss, Vienna and Leipzig, 1924, esp. pp. 278ff. [Eugen von Böhm-Bawerk, "Macht oder ökonomisches Gesetz?," *Zeitschrift für Volkswirtschaft, Sozialpolitik und Verwaltung*, vol. 23, 1914, pp. 205–71; reprinted in Franz X. Weiss, ed., *Gesammelte Schriften von Eugen von Böhm-Bawerk*, 2 vols. (Vienna and Leipzig: Hölder-Pichler-Tempsky, 1924), vol. 1, pp. 230–300. An English translation by John Richard Mez of the University of Oregon, "Control or Economic Law?," appeared in mimeographed form in 1931. It was later included in *Shorter Classics of Eugen von Böhm-Bawerk*, vol. 1 (South Holland, IL: Libertarian Press, 1962), pp. 139–99, and republished as a stand-alone monograph (Auburn, AL: Ludwig von Mises Institute, 2010).—Ed.] It hardly needs saying that despite my criticism of this particular point, Böhm-Bawerk's work—and the subsequent extension of his ideas in L. Mises' [*Die*] *Gemeinwirschaft: Untersuchungen über den Sozialismus*, 2nd revised ed., Jena, [Gustav Fischer,] 1932, p. 424ff. [English translation, *Socialism: An Economic and Sociological Analysis*, trans. J. Kahane (Indianapolis, IN: Liberty Fund, 1981)—Ed.]—are the most important foundation for the observations presented in this essay.

[17] J. S. Mill's "capital disposable for investment" (*On some unsettled questions of political economy*, London, 1844, p. 133). [John Stuart Mill, *Essays on Some Unsettled Questions of Political Economy* (London: John W. Parker, 1844). The phrase "capital disposable for investment" does not actually appear on p. 133 (or elsewhere in that book of Mill's), but "p. 133" is presumably a typo for p. 113, where Mill writes of "disposable capital." Mill does use the phrase "capital disposable for investment" in *Principles of Political Economy*, 7th ed., ed. William J. Ashley (London: Longmans, Green, 1909), book 3, ch. 8, sec. 1.—Ed.] This is more commonly designated as "free" capital, which consists of earned amortization quotas (or proceeds from the turnover of circulating capital), new savings, and possibly additional credits (cf. F. A. Hayek, *Geldtheorie und Konjunkturtheorie* [*Beiträge zur Konjunkturforschung*, 1], Vienna and Leipzig, [Hölder-Pichler-Tempsky,] 1929, p. 123ff.). [English translation, *Monetary Theory and the Trade Cycle*, trans. N. Kaldor and H. M. Croome (London: Jonathan Cape, 1933); reprinted in *Business Cycles: Part I*, ed. Hansjoerg Klausinger, vol. 7 of *The Collected Works of F. A. Hayek* (Chicago: University of Chicago Press, 2012), pp. 47–166.—Ed.] This is the only proper use of the unfortunate term "capital disposal," which recently has found such energetic defenders (cf. F[ritz] Machlup, *Börsenkredit, Industriekredit und Kapitalbildung* [*Beiträge zur Konjunkturforschung*, 2], Vienna, [Springer,] 1931, p. 9ff. [English translation, from a revised German edition, *The Stock Market, Credit, and Capital Formation*, trans. Vera C. Smith (London: William Hodge, 1940)—Ed.], and G[eorge] Halm, "'Warten' und 'Kapital-

new investments. It is possible, strictly speaking, to invest available capital in new investments in a profitable way—whether the capital stems from new savings or from earned amortization quotas—at any given wage level. If wages are high, relatively less roundabout methods of production will have to be adopted and interest rates for such new investments may actually be higher than previously.

But what are those new profitable uses of capital that becomes available for reinvestment because it is no longer profitable in its previous use? They are obviously in industries that stand to gain directly from the consumers' increased income, in which it is still profitable to employ labor even at higher wages, with a quick turnover of capital, that is, in industries directly producing consumer goods. Capital will thus shifts toward industries that directly serve consumer needs. Not only the industries producing consumer *goods*, but also those offering personal services, such as the hotel industry, theaters and movies, etc. will attract capital. What is critical, however, is that *only a small part of the capital used in industries that have become unprofitable can be withdrawn in this manner and shifted elsewhere.* If reinvestment becomes unprofitable in one stage of production that up to now allowed amortization quotas to be earned, it will become impossible to amortize capital invested in the higher stage because the product of this stage of production, which previously was purchased from the amortization quota earned by the next stage, now cannot be sold anymore. This is one of those cases in which it becomes apparent that what is viewed as working capital from the point of view of individual firms, often—as Dr. Machlup has demonstrated[18]—does not represent working capital for the economy as a whole. If use is made in one stage of production of the fact that it is working capital and thus can be withdrawn, the consequence is that the working capital of the preceding stages of production can no longer be withdrawn, because it is not turned over and can therefore no longer be made available. In these preceding stages of production in particular, higher wages in the next stages of production may even result in a complete standstill of production and a complete destruction of capital. What makes it so especially difficult to see the connection between the two phenomena is the fact that capital losses may be highest in firms that have not been directly affected by wage increases.

disposition,'" *Jahrbücher für Nationalökonomie und Statistik*, Jena, vol. 135, [1931,] pp. 831ff.). But no new word is needed for this concept in any case and furthermore, as Machlup himself points out, G[ustav] Cassel used the term in a broader sense, as a result of which Machlup felt obliged to distinguish between free and invested capital disposal. Free capital disposal corresponds precisely to free capital or "capital disposable for investments," while invested capital disposal is just an ugly and misleading term for the constantly fluctuating value of all capital goods in existence at a given time. So what is the purpose of a new term?

[18] Machlup, *op. cit.*, pp. 132ff.

This is one of those numerous instances in which a production process that is integrated from an economic point of view, in that it leads to the production of a given consumer good, is fragmented into a whole series of different firms or industries. Under these circumstances it becomes extremely difficult to see things that would be perfectly clear if the whole process took place within the walls of a single factory. Let us suppose that all tools, machines, and raw materials required in a production process were produced in the same firm that makes the final product. In that case one could hardly fail to notice that a wage increase that absorbs the interest income of the capitalists and therefore makes it unprofitable to continue to reinvest capital in the same way, must lead to an immediate loss of that part of the capital required for producing those capital goods that will henceforth not be replaced. In this segment of the process, production stops immediately and causes capital destruction, although the physical condition of the capital goods remains unaltered. In the next segment, the production process will continue as long as the available equipment functions without replacement, and meanwhile capital will wear out physically. It makes little difference whether capital equipment remains physically unchanged or not, as long as there is no prospect of a change that will turn a process that has become unprofitable back into a profitable one—as is indeed the case where a cyclical depression rather than a "structural" process of capital consumption is involved. The capital embodied in the equipment is lost, whether or not the technical efficiency of the capital goods has remained intact.

VI

From what we have just indicated, it also becomes apparent that one of the invariable effects of capital consumption is the creation of underutilized productive capacity, a fact that must be bewildering and misleading in the eyes of laymen. The idling of existing capital equipment is not what makes the production of additional capital goods unprofitable; on the contrary, it is a consequence of this unprofitableness.

We have already noted that unemployment triggered by excessively high wages will take on very different dimensions in the various industries (and will in general be particularly pronounced in industries producing capital goods); at the same time, the level of unemployment will by no means be commensurate with the extent of the increases in wages in the different industries. Unemployment, moreover, is slow to reach its peak, as existing production facilities, whose replacement ceases to be profitable, gradually wear out. This is an important consideration because, to the extent that the cost of maintaining unemployed workers (unemployment benefits) is paid by industry in the form of a payroll tax or something of the sort, it will only become apparent in which industries production continues to be profitable after unemployment has reached its peak. (This is equally true where the higher payments of unemployment benefits are drawn from accumulated reserves, since this implies a reduction of capital available to industry). This additional burden on industry or this reduction in the supply of capital will not only create further unemployment, but will also provoke the loss of part of the investments made in the meantime and will trigger a new wave of unemployment. In this way, excessively high wages can unleash a cumulative process of capital consumption and rising unemployment, and it is difficult to see how it can ever be brought to a standstill.

VII

Here we must mention a second effect of excessively high wages on the supply of capital available to industry. Although this is not a genuine case of capital consumption but, rather, an example of capital conversion, it does hamper a return to equilibrium and the reabsorption of the unemployed. For that reason it may in the long run indirectly lead to a reduction in productivity, even in situations where a return to a more flexible wage system is not excluded. I am referring here to the tendency of high wages to enhance rationalization, an effect that most people, erroneously in my opinion, view as beneficial. Rationalization in this connection obviously means the introduction of labor-saving machines and the implementation of other investments that become profitable as a consequence of higher wages, or to put it differently, that these wages force industry to introduce. To the best of my knowledge, it has not been claimed by anyone so far that the total amount of capital available for investments has been increased thereby. Keeping this circumstance in mind, one can easily see that the presumed benefits of such a forced rationalization are entirely fictitious. The truth of the matter is that in the face of excessively high wages, certain industries will invest more, at the expense of other industries, than would otherwise have been the case. In the long run, however, this is not an advantage but can only lead to a drop in productivity. For, obviously, as a result of excessive wage increases, those industries in which additional capital investments replace a relatively larger amount of labor than in other industries will be at a relative advantage in attracting capital. In any particular situation, a given quantity of additional capital will replace different amounts of labor in the various industries,[19] and the profitability of apply-

[19] In a state of equilibrium, the ratio between infinitesimally small additional quantities of capital and labor must of course be the same in all industries. For all realistically conceivable quantities, however, this substitution ratio depends on the relative steepness of the demand curve for additional amounts of capital or labor respectively in the industries concerned.

ing more labor or more capital will always depend on the relative price of these quantities of capital or labor that can yield the same increase in production. Whenever the price of labor rises relatively to the price of the quantity of capital which yields the same product, capital will go to those industries where relatively more labor can be replaced by the same amount of capital. Hence capital will be used wherever it is combined with relatively little labor. The upshot of all this is that the same sum spent on capital investment will be less effective in raising the marginal productivity of labor and will make a smaller contribution to employment than if its use had been determined by lower wages. The same increase in capital that might otherwise have sufficed to drive equilibrium wages up to the level at which they had been set prematurely by artificial means will now be insufficient to absorb all unemployed workers at that wage level. It is therefore completely groundless to expect, as many people do, that enforced rationalization will succeed in justifying wages that were initially set at too high a level.

To express it differently, the upshot of excessively high wages will be that industry will shape its capital equipment as if no more workers were available than can be employed after this rise in wages. The employment level may even be lower after this conversion than if industry had been compelled to maintain capital in its previous form rather than readjusting it to the higher wages. This conversion, which in effect helps to secure capitalists a larger share of the reduced social product, would not lead in itself to a loss of capital, except for the fact that under existing conditions any increase in unemployment puts a greater burden on industry, which in turn produces an increase in costs. With rigid wages, the consequences of this additional burden will be the same as an increase in wages. Ultimately, given the existence of unemployment benefits, this conversion of capital leads to capital consumption via its effect on unemployment.

VIII

Before concluding this theoretical analysis of the process of capital consumption, let me still mention that essentially the same processes that occur with an absolute diminution in the economy's stock of capital must also take place when the provision of capital per capita declines because the growth of capital fails to keep pace with population growth. Any reduction of capital per capita triggers exactly the same transition to less capitalistic methods of production and thus leads to the loss of the fixed capital invested in the higher stages of production just as it does when there is an absolute reduction in capital. Whatever small differences there are between the two processes are beyond the scope of this essay. For purposes of further discussion of the most significant secondary symptoms of capital consumption, it should be kept in mind that these apply just as much to a reduction in per capita provision of capital as they do to an absolute diminution of capital.

IX

We have shown the peculiar situation that arises when an apparent excess of fixed capital gives rise to a lower valuation of existing production facilities and an underutilization of the available production capacity, while at the same time there is a shortage of capital for investment, which manifests itself in high interest rates and a generally low liquidity. This situation is inevitably reflected in the status of the financial institutions responsible for raising the capital available for investment and investing it at their own risk. Even when, as in England, banks in the narrower sense of the word normally do not provide capital for investment, they are bound to be in difficulty, since it is in the very nature of their business to make longer-term investments with short-term funds. "Frozen credits" which in this situation generally means lost money, will inevitably increase in volume, and the permanent temptation to throw good money after bad will contribute to a further increase in losses. The banks' situation obviously becomes especially grave when they supply industry not only with working capital but with fixed capital, as is largely the rule in Central Europe. Under the Central European system, the danger of ever-present capital losses is exacerbated by the fact that savers have not learned to invest in any other way than through banks. As a result a major share of the sums available for new investments goes to investors whose decisions may be unduly influenced by concerns about the maintenance of prior irrevocably fixed investments.

X

I will dwell even more briefly on a few other symptoms that are likely to manifest themselves in a country whose capital is being consumed. Most of them are an immediate consequence of the processes already discussed. The existence of large underutilized production facilities whose value has been partially written off gives existing enterprises in the industry involved some protection against new competition, thus facilitating the formation of monopolistic organizations such as cartels and making them particularly advantageous. Another common facet of capital consumption, notably in Austria, is a continual reinvestment in firms whose value has been nearly written off, with the result that these reinvestments too must shortly be written off again and replaced by new ones, to keep step with the competition. This is merely another aspect of the rationalization process that takes place with steadily rising costs, to which I referred earlier.

How the process of capital consumption affects a country's foreign trade is too complicated to discuss here in any detail. It need only be mentioned that several forces are at work in such a situation that are likely to foster a passive trade balance. This is partly because consumption of capital results in substantial transfers of capital ownership abroad in the form of securities and partly because some of the imports of the country consuming its capital are not paid for but covered by losses foreigners incur in their investments in that country.

Another interesting phenomenon characterizing nearly all countries that may be consuming their capital is the widespread complaint about the large gap between retail and wholesale prices or production costs. It is to be expected that branches of business serving consumption directly are relatively more profitable and that food processing industries like breweries, the tobacco industry, entertainment industries etc. prosper during the process of capital consumption, though the prosperity of these industries is of course no sure proof of ongoing capital consumption. It could just as well be symptomatic of a sharp decline in a country's savings, without any actual capital consumption. But when it occurs at a time when population growth is slowing, as is commonly happening today, and, all the more, when unemployment keeps rising, it is likely to signal that capital consumption is under way.

XI

Although an absolutely certain diagnosis is hardly ever possible except in extreme cases, there is one symptom that is a useful indicator for the evolution of capital in the economy as a whole: how industrial capital fares on the stock exchange. We have seen that a reduction in the value of existing facilities amounts to an equivalent destruction of capital. At the same time, a substantial part of light industry and consumer goods industries are now organized as joint-stock companies. It should therefore be possible for their value on the stock exchange to compensate for the decline in the value of capital good industries. For this reason, the best indicator for the actual evolution of the economy's capital stock is how the value of the joint-stock capital of all of a country's industries (and the relative development of specific industries) evolves over a long period of years.

Rarely do we find comprehensive statistics also including companies that went bankrupt and all smaller enterprises. Dr. O. Morgenstern carried out such a statistical investigation at the Austrian Institute for Business Cycle

Research, and the findings were truly catastrophic.[20] According to his data, the market value of publicly traded companies on the Austrian stock exchange fell to 18.5% of their 1913 value by October 31, 1931, and this included the gold value of newly created companies as well as increases in capitalization since 1913. This change is only partially due to the effect of inflation, but mainly proceeded since the end of inflation, as can be gauged from the fact that the total value as of October 31, 1931, was actually lower than the sum of all the new companies founded and the increases in capitalization since the end of inflation. The entire capital stock of publicly traded Austrian companies on October 31, 1931, was valued at 785,255,607 Austrian Schilling. How small this amount actually is becomes more apparent when we realize that it corresponds to hardly more than a third of the sum provided by the 1931 federal budget for the Republic of Austria, and this excludes expenditures by the Länder and local communities. Here it must be kept in mind that these expenditures are predominantly earmarked for consumption and are particularly rigid because they are financed by the government. If we assumed that all Austrian companies were still under Austrian ownership and that Austria were to sell off all these companies abroad at the market value prevailing in autumn 1931, the proceeds would not even have covered half the annual expenditures of the Republic!

XII

As we pointed out at the beginning of this study, we focused our attention on the situation where the consumption of capital was the consequence of too high production costs, particularly excessively high wages. We concentrated on this constellation because in recent years it constituted the most important and certainly the least understood cause of capital consumption. This emphasis should not obscure the fact that the effect will be the same any time capital is used directly for consumption purposes. There can be no doubt that this holds true for taxes paid out of capital, such as capital levies, inheritance taxes, or taxes on amortization reserves accumulated by firms, to the extent that revenue from these taxes is used for current expenditures and not profitably invested. Oddly enough, even economists, when they talk about paying something out of capital, are all too ready to think of capital solely as a source of income for the wealthy. They fail to keep in mind that capital also represents part of the economy's productive equipment, which is thereby destroyed.

[20] Cf. O[skar] Morgenstern, "Kapital- und Kurswertänderungen der an der Wiener Börse notierten österreichischen Aktiengesellschaften 1913 bis 1930," *Zeitschrift für Nationalökonomie*, (Vienna), vol. III (1931/32), pp. 251ff.

Even if the production facilities corresponding to the amount of capital in question do not instantly vanish from earth, diverting these amounts for consumption purposes will eventually reduce capital equipment correspondingly. And the same holds true for any redirection of capital to less profitable uses, whether by subsidizing individual industries, by public works or by other such deployment. There can be little doubt that in the last years agricultural and housing policies have had this kind of impact in Central Europe. The numerical significance of these factors is exemplified by the fact that the amount invested in public housing in recent years out of taxes by the city of Vienna is considerably larger than the market value of the entire joint-stock capital of publicly traded Austrian companies.

The public's ubiquitous and ready support for measures resulting in the destruction of capital can certainly be explained to a large extent by its obliviousness of the consumption of the economy's capital. It was taken for granted that once capitalists had done their duty by providing capital, they deserved no further consideration: the previously created real capital was securely in place, was the general belief. The error implicit in this view hardly needs any further elucidation. Many of those, however, who are perfectly well aware of a possible consumption of capital in the economy, still advocate measures that have this effect. In their way of thinking, just as individuals can draw on their capital for a while in an emergency, a whole country can temporarily subsist on its capital in times of need and thereby avoid a reduction in its standard of living. Yet even individuals can avoid restricting their consumption only if they can legitimately hope that in the future they will earn as much on their reduced capital as they did in the past from their old capital and from all other sources. There is little hope that a whole country can do likewise. For a while, the effects of capital consumption may possibly be staved off by technical progress, but a more likely course is that even the first step along the path of capital consumption leads to a vicious circle from which it becomes extremely difficult to escape.

XIII

The longer a process of capital consumption has been under way, the more difficult it becomes to bring it to a halt. Every day that the process continues, the greater the requisite decline in the standard of living to bring it to a standstill. A point may finally be reached where starvation of the existing population cannot be staved off without further consumption of capital. In addition there exist strong psychological influences that act to intensify this process of capital consumption once it has gotten under way. One of these influences is the effect of discovering that the general standard of living of the population can continue to rise despite rising unemployment and the vehement protests of the business community. Another is that the growing danger of losing invested savings frightens off an increasing number of savers, so that a process of capital consumption that could at first still be counteracted by simultaneous formation of new capital finally leads to an actual diminution of the capital stock. All attempts to encourage capital formation will remain fruitless as long as loss of savings seems very likely. Reduced saving should not be overrated, however, as a cause of capital scarcity. It is likely that by the far greater part of the supply of "free capital" does not stem from new savings but from earned amortization quotas of previously invested capital and that the scarcity of capital, notably in Central Europe during the last decade, has probably been due far more to an insufficient amortization of old capital than to a reduced supply of new savings.

The special psychological reaction of the entrepreneurial class represents a third and by no means the least dangerous effect of a long-lasting process of capital consumption. There can be little doubt that the tendency in the last ten years to guarantee large fixed incomes independent of earnings to top company officials in Central Europe has been one of the consequences of companies making no profits for many years in a row. The entrepreneurial class itself thus becomes an accomplice in the process of capital consumption and loses any significant motive to counter it. Even those persons whose main function it should be to protect the capital of their enterprises are thereby forced into an antagonistic position toward the owners of capital paralleling that of the large masses. Nothing is more symptomatic of the anti-capitalist attitude prevalent even in large circles of the entrepreneurial class than the famous utterance by the president of a large Austrian stock company. When discussion arose as to the amount to be paid out in dividends, he declared that he could see no reason why the good money of his company should be thrown away on these utter strangers, the shareholders.

This brings me to the last and most general question: can capital consumption in the long run be averted in a democratic society whose majority is anticapitalist in its outlook and will it not almost inevitably be set in motion at least in a situation where the alternative would be a reduction in the standard of living? While socialist politicians and politically-oriented economists continue to deride the danger of a shortage of capital as a figment of the imagination, the true gravity of the problem is clearly enough grasped by serious socialist thinkers. In opposition to classical socialist doctrine, they are beginning to view it as one of the essential shortcomings of the capitalist system that it does not assure an adequate provision of capital for the economy and they consider it one of the advantages of socialism that it would allow an adequate amount of capital formation.[21]

[21] Cf. C[arl] Landauer, *Planwirtschaft und Verkehrswirtschaft*, Munich and Leipzig, [Duncker und Humblot,] 1931, especially pp. 79ff. [Hayek reviewed this book in the *Zeitschrift für Nationalökono-*

What makes the problem so intractable is the fact that the groups that initially benefit from capital consumption—the large mass of wage earners and persons on a fixed salary, light industries that cater directly to consumer needs, the retail trade, and craftsmen—are a numerical majority in every society, while the groups that are immediately affected by capital consumption and therefore are willing to offer political resistance against it—heavy industry and high finance—are the very people whose intentions are traditionally deemed suspect by progressively oriented people. And since today the bulk of the population has been indoctrinated to see "capital" in personified form and not as the objective productive equipment of the economy, it is of course difficult to make it clear to them why it should be in the public interest to maintain capital intact.

XIV

We have had to be exceedingly sketchy in filling in the theoretical scaffolding presented in the first part of this essay with specific examples. Any reasonably thorough examination of the concrete sequence of events and especially of the actual significance in the last decade of the economic tendencies that we have described here would require nothing less than an economic history of this period, or at the very least, a history of its economic policy. Such an attempt would be feasible only on the basis of highly detailed specialized investigations conducted from the standpoint of the general interrelationships adumbrated here, but such investigations are still almost totally lacking. It is true that very recent publications, such as the highly interesting research of the Institut für Konjunkturforschung on German capital formation[22] and E. Welter's book on capital shortage in Germany[23] have offered us much more detailed and reliable material than ever before on the actual evolution of the supply of capital in Germany. As laudable as these investigations are and as valuable as are their results, it is my impression that what is still most urgently needed is a theoretical grasp of the essential relationships. And my only purpose here has been to make a contribution to this theoretical problem.

---

mie, 4, 1933, pp. 294–98. An English translation by Grete Heinz of Hayek's review appears in *Socialism and War: Essays, Documents, and Reviews*, ed. Stephen Kresge, vol. 10 of *The Collected Works of F. A. Hayek* (Chicago: University of Chicago Press, 1997), pp. 79–84.—Ed.]

[22] G[ünther] Keiser and B[ernhard] Benning, "Kapitalbildung und Investionen in der deutschen Volkswirtschaft 1924 bis 1928," *Vierteljahrshefte zur Konjunkturforschung, Sonderheft*, 22, Berlin, [Reimar Hobbing,] 1931.

[23] E[rich] Welter, *Die Ursachen des Kapitalsmangels in Deutschland*, Tübingen, [J. C. B. Mohr,] 1931.

FIVE

SAVING[1]

The original meaning of the term saving, keeping or preserving something for future use, has gradually been extended to cover a number of different activities more or less directly connected with the original sense of the word. As is so frequently the case with discussions of economic concepts our first task must therefore be, not just to assign one definite meaning to the term, but to isolate the different concepts attached to it and to preserve them, under this or other names, as instruments of analysis. The first complication arises from the fact that once it has been decided upon to postpone an act of consumption it will often be more profitable not to just keep the goods thus saved but to use the interval till they will be needed in order to produce such goods by more efficient but more time-consuming methods. This will involve a temporary transformation of the resources saved into new forms, an accumulation of productive capital, and once this stage is reached, there arises the first difficulty about the meaning of saving, that is, whether here any particular decision to postpone a possible act of consumption constitutes really new saving or whether it merely means that the results of old saving (the capital already accumulated) is maintained. At the same time this possibility of using the results of saving in order to increase the product of current efforts will induce people to repeat the process of investing continuously and ultimately to treat the amount saved not as a reserve for future consumption but as a permanent source of revenue.

Even at this early stage in the development, saving and investment become distinct activities; even an isolated individual may save without investing; but the distinction assumes much greater importance when we consider the process of saving in a money economy. It will still be possible here that someone may keep *in natura* a stock of commodities which he expects to need in the future. But the income which he may either currently consume or save will,

[1] This is a reprint of the original manuscript of the article on "Saving" prepared for the *Encyclopædia of the Social Sciences* in 1933. It appeared with considerable editorial emendations and abridgments in Vol. XIII of that work in 1934. [First published in Hayek, *Profits, Interest, and Investment* (London: Routledge, 1939), pp. 151–70. A few commas have been added for greater readability. Edwin R. A. Seligman, ed., *Encyclopædia of the Social Sciences*, vol. 8 (New York: Macmillan, 1934), pp. 548–52.—Ed.]

in the first instance, consist of money, and the immediate choice he will have to make will be between holding this money and investing it in order to get a return. In this situation, savings which are not invested assume a special significance which has prominently figured in all discussion on saving. The possibility that savings may be neither invested nor kept *in natura* but may take the form of money hoards creates further difficulties because it will be the cause of differences between saving (and also capital) in the individual sense and in the social sense. It would probably be better to avoid using the term with respect to society as a whole. Since, however, this practice has become so firmly established, it is important to realise that saving in the social sense is really a separate phenomenon—the increase of wealth or the formation of capital—of which individual saving is but one possible cause.

But, although saving is not synonymous with the formation of capital but merely the most important cause which normally leads to this result, it is impossible usefully to discuss saving without at the same time considering, much that properly belongs only to the wider concept. To begin with, saving cannot be defined without some reference to the normal process of reproduction of capital; it would be difficult to draw the line between that source of the supply of capital which can be described as saving proper and that which cannot; nor is there any established usage as regards terminology. And many of the problems which have generally been discussed under the heading of saving refer either to the relation between saving and investing or else to the process of capital formation in general irrespective of whether it is due to saving proper or not.

Once we have recognised the necessity of distinguishing in all cases (except in that of saving *in natura*) between the activities which provide the means of investment (one of which is saving proper) and the activity of investment, we still have to make further distinctions between the various activities of the first kind—all of which are often loosely termed saving. The most convenient classification of the sources of the supply of new capital is probably that proposed by Professor Röpke, which can be roughly translated as follows:

I. Saving *in natura.*
II. Saving by means of money:
  1—individual (voluntary) saving,
  2—corporate (voluntary) saving,
  3—collective (compulsory) saving,
  4—monetary (compulsory) saving.[2]

[2] W[ilhelm] Röpke, *Zur Theorie der Kapitalbildung*, Tübingen, [J. C. B. Mohr,] 1929. [Röpke's monograph was no. 63 in the series *Recht und Staat in Geschichte und Gegenwart.*—Ed.] In the German original Professor Röpke's classification is perhaps more satisfactory since in all cases except II, 1, he uses the equivalent of "formation of capital" instead of "saving."

Of these different types of "saving," only II, 1, is generally understood by the more familiar use of the term saving. II, 2, referring to the reinvestment of undistributed profits of corporations has recently become more familiar and is now commonly included under "savings," although the voluntary character of the decision to save on the part of those who might otherwise have consumed the profits remains somewhat doubtful. Where the means for investment are raised by taxation (II, 3) the contrast between this sort of "saving" and what is ordinarily understood by this term is even stronger; while in the case of II, 4 (now familiar under the name of forced saving), the peculiar characteristic is that the money for investment is not provided by any kind of saving but is created for the purpose. A sort of "saving" only occurs here when, in consequence of a diversion of resources from the production of consumers' goods to the production of capital goods, the current supply of consumers' goods is reduced. But the use of the term saving in this connection must be regarded as an instance of the misleading practice of treating the term as equivalent to "capital formation."

Further difficulties arise in connection with the distinction between net and gross saving. Once any capital is in existence its owners will constantly have to decide whether to reinvest enough of its proceeds to maintain the stock of capital intact which involves a new decision of whether to postpone consumption or not to do so. It has become customary to consider as savings proper only savings out of net income, after allowance has been made for the maintenance of capital, a usage which has sometimes led to the dangerous confusion of the supply of new free capital with the total free capital available for investment. It is extremely difficult to draw a clear line of demarcation between the two, for this would require a satisfactory definition of what is meant by maintaining capital intact, particularly under conditions of technical progress, a task which has not yet been accomplished. The difficulties here arise already with the savings of an individual but to an even greater extent in connection with savings in the social sense. In the latter case the gross total of individual savings has to be reduced by the amount of old savings which have been delib erately used up for consumption, and there is in addition the difficult question of whether to treat involuntary capital losses as a further negative item which has to be deducted before we arrive at the figure for the net saving, which constitutes the supply of free capital available for new investment.

Any historical treatment of saving is faced not only with the difficulties arising out of the difference between saving and the creation of capital or the increase of wealth in the aggregate, but in addition with the problem of distinguishing between the causes of this and the causes of the concentration of wealth in the hands of particular persons. Much confusion has been caused in historical investigations by the lack of clear distinctions in this respect. As regards the supply of savings available for the creation of new capital equipment the first point to be stressed is that the regular investment of savings is a comparatively new phenomenon. While the storing of consumers' goods *in natura* has probably never been of very great importance (the occasional public storage of grain, etc., against famine excepted), the hoarding of precious metals must be regarded as the normal form of saving throughout most of history and is still customary among most people of non-European stock. It would certainly be untrue historically to say that the growth of this form of saving is a consequence of the introduction of money; it would probably be more true to say that the particular suitability of the precious metals as a "store of value" made them generally acceptable as a medium of exchange. Until the Industrial Revolution hoarding of money remained the normal form of saving in all cases where the saver himself was not in a position to use capital productively. In other words, throughout antiquity, the Middle Ages, and for some time thereafter, even when savings were invested this did not mean as a rule the separation of the saver and the investor; and where individual savings were not employed by their owner as productive capital, either because they were too small or for other reasons, he normally had no other alternative but to hoard them. Even entrepreneurs seeking to provide for a time when they should have ceased directly to employ capital in production or trade often accumulated hoards; and as late as the beginning of the eighteenth century we hear of London merchants on their retirement taking a chest of gold coin with them to the country with the intention of gradually drawing on that hoard for the rest of their lives.

Until the industrial revolution new capital came mainly from the reinvestment of profits by entrepreneurs. Long distance trade was the most important source of the accumulation of capital in the sense of new productive equipment. The other sources generally mentioned in this connection, particularly landed property, had probably more to do with the concentration of wealth than with the creation of capital. The most important early instrumentalities of profitable investment for the non-entrepreneurs, which offered a permanent source of income to new classes of savers and thus encouraged the development of the saving habit—government loans, annuities and mortgages—represented investments only from the point of view of the individual; their proceeds were normally used for consumption purposes and did not result in the formation of new capital. It is probable that even in the earlier stages of modern manufacture—in England of the second half of the eighteenth and the first quarter of the nineteenth century—relatively little of the capital required came from outside savings, although the growth of banking institutions had provided an agency for their collection. It was only with the development of the modern capital market during the railway booms of the 1820s and 1830s and with the simultaneous and subsequent growth of banking and other investing institutions that the modern relation between the individual small saver and the entrepreneur-investor was established. In the second quarter of the century the desire to collect and fructify not only current savings but also old accumulated hoards of money became one of the leading ideas of economic policy and the main cause of repeated waves of credit expansion. In the period preceding the World War hoarding of coin, except as a temporary phenomenon during depression, had disappeared from modern industrial societies.

But while the depositing of such savings with a bank or savings bank must still be regarded as the normal way in which savings are made available for investment, even before the Great War and still more so since, the importance of specialised institutions has steadily grown which are more adapted to the particular needs of the individual saver. Besides life insurance, as the most important, building societies and similar institutions facilitating saving for a particular purpose ought to be mentioned.

What has just been said about the disappearance of hoarding is true at least of the hoarding of hand to hand money. It was generally assumed that since people tend to bring any sum saved to a bank or similar institution, all savings would soon be invested. But in so far as people already hold their normal balances for current expenditure in the form of bank deposits, saving may simply mean that they will leave these deposits unused or at best that they will transfer them from a checking (current) to a savings (deposit) account. As both A. C. Pigou and D. H. Robertson have pointed out, saving in this case will not necessarily result in additional investments by the banks; only if the form of deposits is changed and if, as in the United States, reserves held against time (savings) deposits are smaller than those against demand deposits, will at least a part of the new savings be used for new investments. Unless the banks create additional credits for investment purposes to the same extent that the holders of deposits have ceased to use them for current expenditure, the effect of such saving is essentially the same as that of hoarding and has all the undesirable deflationary consequences attaching to the latter.

The effects usually imputed to saving are, however, imputed not to savings which are hoarded but to those which are invested. Such investment means, if the capital created by it is to remain intact, that a quantity of intermediate products, corresponding to the amount of factors invested, will be permanently withheld from consumption and that with the help of this additional capital the output of consumers' goods will be augmented but their cost per unit decreased. In a situation where all factors are already employed when the new investment is being made, this will mean that the average investment period is being lengthened, fewer consumers' goods must be produced during the transition period and less can therefore be consumed. Because of the decreased expenditure on consumers' goods, the prices of consumers' goods will tend to fall; thereby the necessary curtailment of the output of consumers' goods is brought about and the factors of production required for an increased output of capital goods are set free. Even where saving leads not to an increase in the average period of investment (*i.e.*, an increase of the amount of capital per head) but only to the provision of equipment for factors previously not employed, those factors which were already employed and which provided the savings out of their income must reduce their consumption in order to remunerate the new factors until the product of the latter is ready. While in this case only consumption per head—and not total consumption—must be reduced, in a case where saving leads only to the investment for longer periods of factors already employed, the absolute rate of consumption will have to be reduced temporarily in order to spread the existing output over a longer period, after which the product of the factors now being invested will become available.

The second effect of new investment, the reduction of cost per unit, is important because it shows that the increase in output at a later stage is due not to the fact that the product of a greater quantity of factors then comes on the market but to the fact that, with the help of the additional capital, the original factors produce more than before. The income of all these factors is therefore still equal to the cost of production of the current output and sufficient to take it off the market at remunerative prices. Serious disturbances, however, may follow large and unforeseen fluctuations in the rate of saving and, in consequence of the relative increase in the demand for consumers' goods, an increase of investment in excess of saving proper by means of additional credits.

Because of a misunderstanding of the process through which the temporary reduction of consumption brings about a permanent increase in current output (or a reduction of cost per unit), saving has since early times been persistently blamed for causing trade depressions. "Under-consumption" or "over-saving" explanations of trade slumps were at the basis of many of the earlier discussions of unproductive expenditure and of luxury consumption. Since Malthus and Lauderdale these theories have always had some following, particularly among socialist thinkers, and have gained wide popularity during depressions. In recent years they have been reflected mainly in the notion of "maintaining purchasing power" of consumers and in this form have been strongly supported by groups advocating stabilisation of the price level of consumers' goods. It is becoming increasingly clear, however, that these theories are false and that there are only the three special cases—hoarding, violent fluctuations in the rate of saving and forced saving through credit expansion—in which excessive saving may be said to cause depression. Apart from these cases it is doubtful whether there is any sense in which the rate of saving may be absolutely too high or too low. A "general glut" in consequence of too ample a supply of means for investment cannot occur so long as there are still unused opportunities for investment which offer a positive rate of interest. And even if the demand for capital in the form of new productive equipment were not very elastic, the demand for durable consumer goods is practically inexhaustible. What is commonly meant by over-investment is not an excess of investment relative to the demand for the ultimate product, but an excessive launching of new undertakings which need for their completion or utilisation more capital than is available; in other words, "over-investment" implies not too much saving but too little. Nor can it be said that over-saving may reduce the value of the product of the investment below the point where it justifies the sacrifice involved in the act of saving. This thesis, frequently advanced, offers a curious contrast to the equally current proposition that "under-estimation of future wants" prevents an increase of saving to the point where the rate of interest would fall to zero. Both views imply the existence of a normal scale of preference between present and future goods, by which the actual preferences of the individuals can be gauged. There is, however, no other basis for the determination of the relative utilities to an individual at different moments of time but his actual preference, shown at the moment when he decides either to consume or to postpone consumption.

To say that a person underestimates his future wants, even if he saves considerable amounts in order to increase his future income (as is suggested by many forms of the time-preference theories of interest) is just as unjustifiable as to say that he saves too much. Both statements are based on the observer's opinion of what he considers the appropriate distribution of resources over time.

While there is no "just balance between saving and consumption" in the usual sense and while saving at any stable rate can be absorbed without real difficulty, it is very likely that in a dynamic economy—a society with a growing population, advancing technology and a modern banking system—saving at a continuously high rate is an important safeguard of stability. This will not only facilitate the absorption of additional population, and minimise the friction connected with technical progress and shifts of demand, but will probably also tend to mitigate disturbances arising from fluctuations in credit. In the absence of a sufficient supply of new capital any unusually profitable opening for investment will tend to attract capital from other uses and so to enforce extensive readjustments; the introduction of labour-saving inventions may lead also to a lowering of wages. With a rapid increase in the capital supply, such readjustments can be effected much more smoothly or obviated altogether. Similarly, the greater the investment based on voluntary saving, the smaller will be the relative variation in the total rate of investment caused by a given rate of credit expansion. Even the inherent instability of capital created by forced saving might be counteracted if sufficient voluntary savings became available to provide a real basis for this capital.

What the actual volume of saving is depends upon willingness and capacity to save. The factors which affect an individual's willingness to save are the regularity and certainty of his income, the security of the investment opportunities available to him, and the possibility of investing in his own business. It is worth mentioning here that the systems of social insurance which, while securing incomes in old age and providing for sickness, accidents and unemployment, provide for payments out of accumulated revenues rather than accumulated reserves, are, no doubt, a very important factor decreasing the aggregate supply of savings.

It seems that in the short run the willingness to save varies very little and that it is particularly not much affected in the aggregate by changes in the rate of interest. This is mainly due to the fact that while to some people a rise in the rate of interest provides an increased incentive to save, other people who want to accumulate a definite amount for a given purpose (life insurance, house purchase, etc.) need to save less if the rate of interest is higher. While for these reasons it is very difficult to form a clear opinion as to the elasticity of the aggregate supply of savings, it is probably safe to say that, in so far as changes in the willingness to save are concerned, this elasticity is very low. This does not mean, however, that changes in the rate of interest may not affect the aggregate supply of savings very considerably in a different way, namely *via* the capacity to save of the various individuals. There can be little doubt that in general people with a given attitude towards saving will save a higher percentage of a larger than of a smaller income. A transfer of income from classes with a smaller to classes with a greater income (as might be brought about by a change in the rate of interest) is therefore likely to increase the supply of savings. And a rise in aggregate incomes which might be brought about by the same cause, will, of course, have the same effect.

SIX

ON THE RELATIONSHIP BETWEEN INVESTMENT AND OUTPUT[1]

I

The value of the stock of capital conceived as the discounted value of the expected future products, or conceived as the result of investing factors of production for definite periods, are, of course, essentially different ways of representing the same thing.[2] Both methods of approach, if they are to prove useful for purposes of closer analysis, make inevitable a more detailed investigation of what I like to call the time structure of production, *i.e.* of the different periods for which either individual services have to be discounted or for which individual units of factors are being invested. I hope to show in the course of this article that neither of the two aspects without the other is sufficient to give a satisfactory explanation of the actual relationship. But the way in which the two aspects can be combined has never been made quite clear. Even the exact nature of the concepts which underlie the two different methods of approach has hardly ever been explicitly defined. I propose here to

[1] [*Economic Journal*, vol. 44, no. 174, June 1934, pp. 207–31.—Ed.]

[2] [The thing in question is the value, at a particular date, of the stock of non-labor inputs (or goods-in-process) involved in production plans. To use an example of Alfred Marshall's, cited by Hayek at n. 4 below, consider a man who plans to build a house by combining his labor with free materials and free land, making himself any implements that he will use. Suppose that the entire process of producing the house, from gathering materials through to final assembly, takes several months. At each moment, after the first date at which he gathers materials (*i.e.*, after "investing factors of production"), until the date at which the house is ready to occupy, he will have a stock of goods-in-process—namely, gathered materials, implements, and the semi-finished house. The discounted-value perspective evaluates this stock of goods on a given date by reference to the expected value of occupying the house at future dates (minus the value of the labor needed to complete it) discounted back to the present at the appropriate interest rates. The result-of-investing-factors perspective evaluates the stock by adding up the planned labor inputs at earlier dates, plus compound interest on the labor expenditures. The evaluations are the same assuming that production and occupancy go as planned (the process is in equilibrium). Hayek is here laying the groundwork to challenge Frank Knight's theory of capital, which claimed that time taken in production is irrelevant, that the important rôles of capital can be captured in a model in which production is instantaneous and simultaneous with consumption.—Ed.]

devote myself to an attempt to elucidate the relationship between the two concepts, and to develop some consequences which seem relevant to current controversies in this field.

The next three sections of this paper are accordingly devoted to the somewhat laborious task of explaining and co-ordinating the different aspects in which the time intervals arising in the process of production present themselves. Beginning in Section II with the representation of the time-shape of the labour stream applied in any one process, in the following section the relationship of this stream to the time-shape of the output stream derived from the labour invested at a moment of time is studied, and in Section IV the corresponding magnitudes are discussed for the case of durable goods. Only in Section V then an attempt is made to show what real phenomena correspond to changes in the different magnitudes discussed, to what extent they represent real independent variables or are only derived constructions, and how the state of equilibrium described with the help of these constructions is brought about in the actual world. Finally, in Section VI, the relevance of these equilibrium-considerations for the explanation of a dynamic process is investigated and an attempt is made to show that, although it cannot be assumed that the existing capital goods are the result of a past process exactly similar to that in which current labour is invested, or that at any moment any capital goods are produced without the help of already existing capital, yet the existing stock of capital goods will always make the investment of labour for a definite range of periods necessary if the capital is to be maintained intact. It will appear that, contrary to a widely held opinion, the concept of a definite time-structure of investment is even more important for the understanding of the dynamic processes of the accumulation and consumption of capital than for the mere description of the conditions of a stationary equilibrium.

Any discussion of these problems within an article makes it inevitable to leave out a number of considerations which are highly relevant to a really satisfactory treatment of the main point. This applies in particular to the determination of a definite rate of interest, which is here taken for granted, its relation to saving, and the concept of free capital. I hope to discuss these systematically side by side with the problem selected here in a more comprehensive study.[3] Yet in spite of these inevitable shortcomings of an anticipatory treatment of the special problem selected, it seems to me to be justified in view of the light it sheds on the relationship between what has come to be known

[3] [Hayek delivered the hoped-for discussion in his book *The Pure Theory of Capital* (London: Routledge, 1941); most recent edition edited by Lawrence H. White as vol. 12 of *The Collected Works of F. A. Hayek* (Chicago: University of Chicago Press, 2007). The analysis in the present article, exposited somewhat differently, appears in chapters 15 and 16 of that book. Fig. 3 below corresponds to Fig. 18 in the book.—Ed.]

as the "Marshallian" and the "Austrian" (*i.e.* Jevons–Böhm-Bawerk–Wicksell) approach to the theory of capital.[4, 5]

It is necessary to begin by drawing a clear distinction between the two different ways in which time may be a condition to the production of the ultimate services to the consumer. This distinction between the actual time a process of production lasts and the time through which a product will give its services, to which corresponds the distinction between goods in process and durable goods, is of special importance in this connection. For in each of these two cases only one of the two fundamental magnitudes to be discussed here can be considered as a directly given independent variable, while each can be derived from the other only if the rate of interest is given, and is therefore in a sense a mere construction. Under these circumstances it is not surprising that of the two schools mentioned above, that which thought of capital almost exclusively as of durable goods concentrated almost exclusively on the one of these magnitudes, the *output function* (although this concept has not been clearly formulated by it[6]), while the other school, which thought of capital primarily

[4] Marshall himself was, of course, aware of the double aspect presented by capital, which he described as that of accumulation and discounting (cf. *Principles*, V, iv, 2, also mathematical notes v, xiii, xiv, and xxiv). [Alfred Marshall, *Principles of Economics*, 8th ed. (London: Macmillan, 1920); available online at Library of Economics and Liberty, http://www.econlib.org/library/Marshall/marP.html. The cited paragraph from Marshall's text provides the house-building example of n. 1 above and proposes that the rational house-builder will compare the value of occupancy with the *compounded* input cost. The cited mathematical notes express compound and discounted values as integrals over continuous time.—Ed.] But it is probably true to say that he impressed the latter aspect so much more strongly on his disciples that it has become dominant among English economists. And the same applies, *mutatis mutandis*, to Böhm-Bawerk and his followers.

[5] Although little attempt is made to deal directly with objections raised recently against the "Austrian" approach to the theory of capital, much of what follows is an implicit reply to some of the most important recent contributions to the subject, such as F[ritz] Burchardt, "Die Schemata des stationären Kreislaufs bei Böhm-Bawerk and Marx," *Weltwirtschaftliches Archiv*, vols. 34 and 35, 1932–33 [actual publication dates and information: vol. 34, October 1931, pp. 525–64, and vol. 35, January 1932, pp. 116–76—Ed.]; Frank H. Knight, "Capitalistic Production, Time and the Rate of Return," in *Economic Essays in Honour of Gustav Cassel*, London, [George Allen and Unwin,] 1933, and M[artin] Hill, "The Period of Production and Industrial Fluctuations," *Economic Journal*, [vol. 43, no. 172,] December 1933 [pp. 599–610].

[6] The only clear formulation of this concept known to me is to be found in a yet unpublished thesis of Mr. V. Edelberg. [In *The Pure Theory of Capital*, *op. cit.*, p. 6, Hayek acknowledges the "still mostly unpublished" dissertations of Dr. Victor Edelberg and two others. Susan Howson, *Lionel Robbins* (Cambridge: Cambridge University Press, 2011), p. 254, reports that Edelberg "won the Hutchinson Silver Medal [at the London School of Economics] in 1935 for his dissertation 'Wages and capitalist production,' . . . and began to teach [at the London School of Economics] as an assistant lecturer in 1936. But in 1939 he suffered a severe mental breakdown from which he never really recovered." Edelberg's dissertation appears to have never been published. In the area of capital theory he did publish the once well known article "The

in terms of goods in process, made the other magnitude, the *investment function* (which is the more exact formulation of what they called the period of production), the starting-point of their attack.[7] It seems to me, however, that in neither case will one alone of the two concepts provide a sufficient instrument of explanation, and that, in particular, the effects of changes in the data can be understood only if the relation between these two concepts is cleared up.

II

It is convenient to begin with the discussion of goods in process, and this and the following section of the present paper will be devoted entirely to this aspect of time in production. In order to distinguish its effects sharply from any effects due to the durability of goods and to avoid for the present all complications arising out of the fact that the phenomena are regularly combined, it is necessary to assume that in the process in question no durable goods are used, and to define as one process that series of activities which results in a product that is finished and consumed at one moment of time.[8]

Such a process of production can then be represented by Jevons Investment Figures[9] shown in Fig. 1*a*. The time during which the process proceeds is here measured along the abscissa, while the quantities of "labour" applied in the course of the process up to any one moment are shown cumulatively as the ordinates of the curve OL_1' for the corresponding points of the T-axis. "Labour" stands here and throughout this article for an assumed uniform

Ricardian Theory of Profits," *Economica*, no. 39, February 1933, pp. 51–74, which rationally reconstructed Ricardo's capital theory in Jevonian–Böhm-Bawerkian–Wicksellian terms, and the highly mathematical "Elements of Capital Theory: A Note," *Economica*, n.s., vol. 3, no. 11, August 1936, pp. 314–22.—Ed.]

[7] [In *The Pure Theory of Capital*, *op. cit.*, p. 126 n. 1, Hayek remarked, presumably in reference to the present passage: "Although I have, on an earlier occasion, myself used the terms 'investment function' and 'investment curve' in this context, the terms 'input function' and 'input curve' now seem to me to be preferable by reason both of their brevity and of the analogy to the term 'output function.'"—Ed.]

[8] This is essentially the assumption made in *Prices and Production*, where considerations of space made it impossible to show how durable goods could be included in the scheme. It is hoped that the present paper will to a certain extent make up for this deficiency. [To picture a process in which no durable goods are involved, adapt an example Hayek would use in *The Pure Theory of Capital* and imagine the just-in-time assembly of firecrackers entirely by hand, using minerals and paper produced entirely by hand from free natural resources. Inputs from durable goods, or machine services, complicate the analysis when the machines antedate or outlive the process.—Ed.]

[9] This very appropriate designation has been suggested by Dr. J. Marschak (*Archiv für Sozialwissenschaft*, Vol. 68 p. 395). [Jacob Marschak, "Volksvermögen und Kassenbedarf," *Archiv für Sozialwissenschaft und Sozialpolitik*, vol. 68, no. 4, 1933, pp. 385–419.—Ed.]

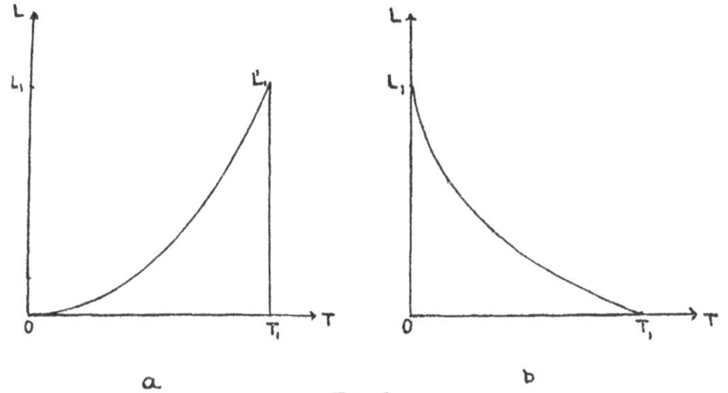

FIG. 1.

original factor of production.[10] Intermediate and final products are represented in such units as are the product of a unit of such "labour," so that each ordinate of the curve OL_1' measures the quantity of intermediate product at the respective stage of production, while the final output, obtained at the end of the period OT_1, is equal to T_1L_1', or the total quantity of labour applied in the course of the process. The slope of the curve OL_1' at any one point represents the rate at which labour is applied at the corresponding moment. The diagram, in short, shows the distribution in time of the total quantity of labour that contributes to the output of a moment of time.[11]

If we assume a completely stationary structure of production (*i.e.* if we assume that at every successive moment processes of exactly the same kind are started), we obtain a representation of the different periods for which at any one moment the different units of the total "labour" supply employed in that industry are invested, by simply inverting the first figure, as in Fig. 1*b*. The

[10] [For Böhm Bawerk, the "original" factors are labor and land, which are both unproduced and permanent (requiring no maintenance by the one who uses them). In response to Knight's criticism, Hayek in "The Mythology of Capital" (1936), included in this volume, acknowledged that the history of factors of production was irrelevant, because the theory must be entirely forward-looking. Given this acknowledgment, and following Marshall's example cited above, Hayek here by "original factor of production" presumably means an input bundle consisting of some combination of labor, land, and free materials. Near the end of this article he suggests that the input is, like labor and land, "permanent," (*i.e.*, not requiring maintenance). Otherwise the services of inherited capital goods might be considered "original" to a particular process of production in the sense of not being produced as part of the process.—Ed.]

[11] [Quotation marks appear around most instances of "labour" in the 1934 publication of the present article (to indicate that so-called "labour" refers to a bundle of inputs not limited to literal labor alone), but where the marks were missing (for example, from the last three instances), they have been left missing. The omission does not correspond in any obvious way to a distinction intended by Hayek.—Ed.]

difference between the two figures is that in the first case the product T_1L_1' maturing at the moment T_1 is connected with the preceding investment during a period of time of the quantities of "labour" which have contributed to that product, while in the second case the total quantity of "labour" invested in the industry at one moment of time is connected with the stream of output over a period of time which is due to that investment.[12]

In either of these two forms this curve, which describes the quantities of "labour" invested at successive moments of one process, or the periods for which individual quantities of the total of "labour" employed in the process are invested, represents what I call the investment function ($f(t)$).[13] As will appear later, this two-dimensional method of representing the range of different periods for which the individual units of "labour" are invested is the only adequate representation of what is usually called the period of production or of investment, and cannot usefully be replaced—except by way of a provisional simplification in an early stage of the analysis—by any one-dimensional magnitude such as the "average period of production."

In the preceding diagram the height of the curvilinear triangle measures the quantity of output at a moment of time, and its area (on the assumption of a completely "synchronised," stationary process) the quantity of intermediate products, both *in terms of "labour."* The changes in the quantity of consumers' goods produced which will be the consequence of changes in the investment structure (*i.e.* changes in the shape of the investment function[14]) cannot possibly be represented in the diagram, since from the assumption the total output will (under stationary conditions) always be equal to the total quantity of original factors invested. It should, perhaps, be specially emphasised at this point that the investment function under discussion here as well as the output function to be discussed later are entirely different from the familiar production functions which describe the dependence of the quantity of output on changes in the method of production. The types of functions used here serve merely to *describe* one single process of this sort and cannot by themselves be used to show the effects of changes in the method of production. If this were intended, the quantity of consumers' goods produced by investing

[12] In both cases, however, the periods in question are *future* periods of time. In the first case the period OT_1 refers to those future moments of time at which the corresponding quantities of "labour" have to be invested in order to obtain the product at the end of this period, while in the second case it refers to the period during which the product of the labour invested at its beginning, say the present, will mature.

[13] Strictly interpreted, $f(t)$ is to be taken to correspond to the "inverted" representation of the process (Fig. 1*b*), while the actual rate at which "labour" is supplied throughout any one process ought to be represented by $f(T_1 - t)$.

[14] In what follows I shall use the terms investment function, investment curve, investment figure and investment structure interchangeably. Occasionally I shall even speak of lengthening or shortening the investment structure as a short way of describing such changes in the shape of the function as involve positive or negative saving.

a given quantity of "labour" for different ranges of periods would have to be regarded as a functional of the investment function (*i.e.* as $\varphi(f(t))$ where the form of the function $f(t)$ is an independent variable). But changes of this magnitude are in a different dimension from those shown in the first diagram and cannot be represented in it except by introducing a third dimension.

But before we proceed to do this, the limitations of the method of representation so far employed must be pointed out in somewhat greater detail. The diagrams in Fig. 1 show how long we have to wait for the product of the different units of "labour" invested, and, consequently, how long we have to wait for such parts of the product as are to be attributed to individual units of "labour." But it would only be possible to deduce from this how long we have to wait for the different units of consumers' goods if we could assume that equal shares of the total "labour" invested in the course of the process will produce the same quantities of consumers' goods. But there is no reason why we should assume this to be so. Indeed, on the contrary, we know that it cannot be so, since equal quantities of "labour," invested for different periods, must at any given rate of interest necessarily grow into different quantities of products.[15]

But if this is so, if the product of equal quantities of "labour," invested for different periods in the course of any one process, does not consist of equal but of different quantities of consumers' goods, then the investment function which describes how long we have to wait for the product of the different units of "labour" does not directly show us how long we have to wait for the different units of the output.[16] The curve in Fig. 1*b* in particular, although it shows what part of the quantity of labour invested at the moment O matures during any part of the period OT_1, does not show immediately what quantities of consumers' goods correspond to the former. It is for this reason that it is described as an investment function which is to be clearly distinguished from the output function, which describes the latter phenomenon.

What applies to the final product also applies to the quantity of intermediate products. Without going into this problem at any length, it may be pointed

[15] [From the equilibrium condition that prospective annualized risk-adjusted rates of return to all investments are equal, it follows that a unit of input invested for a longer period must, in equilibrium, produce output of a greater undiscounted value. Otherwise, given a positive discount rate, the longer investment would not be made.—Ed.]

[16] Misunderstandings on this point, that the traditional concept of the period of production refers to units of factors and not to units of the products, are responsible for many of the objections to the proposition that an increase of capital always means an increase of the period of production. [For example, the introduction of sewing machines into the production of straw handbags, previously made entirely by hand, may reduce the expected time between the date labor gathers straw and the date a finished handbag is sold, shortening the prospective period of production with respect to *that* unit of labor input. With respect to the finished handbags, however, the range of prospective periods of production (including the production and using up of durable sewing machines) has lengthened.—Ed.]

out here that although the area of the investment figure represents the quantity of intermediate products in physical terms (*i.e.* in terms of the quantities of original factors that have gone to produce it), it does not unequivocally determine its quantity in terms of value, either relatively to the value of the factors or relatively to the value of the output.[17]

This magnitude again becomes only determinate when with the introduction of interest we are put in a position to use value as the common denominator to which to reduce the otherwise not comparable physical magnitudes.

III

All these apparently rather complicated relationships can be represented in a fairly simple way if we add to the former diagram, which showed only physical quantities, a third dimension, representing the relative value of these quantities. For this purpose we place the figure so far discussed in the horizontal plane of a three-dimensional system of co-ordinates and measure the values attaching to these quantities along the third (perpendicular) V-axis. It is assumed that the available quantity of "labour," the rate of interest and the value of either a unit of "labour" or a unit of consumers' goods (or, alternatively, the value of both, but not the rate of interest) is given. For the present it is further assumed that one of the many alternatively possible investment functions has been decided upon and that in consequence the quantity of consumers' goods produced is also determined.[18] The problem, then, is what quantity of consumers' goods is to be attributed to individual units of "labour."[19] The answer is contained in the diagrammatic description of equilibrium given by Fig. 2.

[17] [This is because the relative values will in general vary with the interest or discount rate.—Ed.] Without reference to a given rate of interest, the relative area of two investment figures will not even determine in some cases which corresponds to the greater quantity of capital in value terms. *E.g.* of two investment figures which have a similar area but of which one is longer with a more, and the other shorter with a less, convex investment curve, at one rate of interest the one and at another the other may correspond to the greater quantity of capital. [Hayek here, following Wicksell, states an important point that emerged from the "two Cambridges" capital controversy of the 1960s, that the quantity of capital in value terms cannot in general be used as a datum in determining the interest rate, because its magnitude depends on the interest rate.—Ed.]

[18] The way in which the choice of the investment function will in turn be influenced by the rate of interest and the "productivity function" of the particular line of production (*i.e.* by the function $\varphi(f(t))$) will be discussed in Section V of this paper.

[19] [This is the standard microeconomic problem of figuring the marginal physical productivity of an input, here in the context of time-consuming production with continuous input and continuous output.—Ed.]

In order to simplify the resulting figure at first as much as possible it has been assumed that the investment function is linear. This is expressed by the fact that the hypotenuse OL_1 of the rectangular triangle OL_1T_1 which corresponds to the curve OL_1 in Fig. 1*a* is a straight line; it means that during the interval of time OT_1 "labour" is invested in that process at a constant rate. Since equal quantities of "labour" must necessarily have the same value,[20] the magnitude of V along any point of OT_1 is necessarily the same, namely equal to OT_0. The value of the total quantity of "labour" invested during the course of the process would be shown by a rectangle with T_1L_1 representing the number of units of "labour," as a base, and OT_0, representing the value of a unit of "labour," as its height. But as it is assumed that this quantity of "labour" is not all invested at the moment O, but continuously throughout the period OT_1, this rectangle is, as it were, projected into the time dimension and becomes the rectangle $T_0OL_1L_1'$.

The value of any unit of "labour" invested will have to grow, while it remains invested, at the same compound rate of interest. This rate is shown by the curve T_0T_1' and the family of identical curves beginning along T_0L_1', forming together the interest surface $T_0T_1'L_1'$. Since at every point further to the right along OL these curves begin at later moments of time, they will at T_1 have risen for correspondingly shorter periods and have reached a correspondingly smaller height. A perpendicular cross-section at T_1 parallel to VOL will, therefore, cut the interest surface along the curve T_1L_1'. The height of every point on this curve represents the value (and therefore the quantity) of the final products which have to be attributed to the quantity of labour invested at the corresponding point along OL. In the same way at every preceding moment of the interval OT_1 the value of that part of the intermediate products which are the result of an earlier investment of "labour" and are accordingly shown nearer to the left will have grown more in value than the part of the intermediate products existing at the same moment which is the result of later investment and is accordingly shown further to the right. The interest surface will therefore slope upwards not only in the direction of the T-axis but also from the right, to the left along the L-axis.

As will be evident from the diagram, the shares of the total product that are to be attributed to the individual units of "labour" invested for different periods of time depend on the rate of interest. A rise of that rate, *e.g.* to the figure indicated by the dotted curves, would have the consequence that relatively larger shares have to be imputed to the units of "labour" invested for longer periods, while smaller shares would have to be attributed to the units

[20] [For "must necessarily" read "are assumed to." Hayek in the previous paragraph stated the assumption: "the value of either a unit of 'labour' or a unit of consumers' goods (or, alternatively, the value of both, but not the rate of interest) is given."—Ed.]

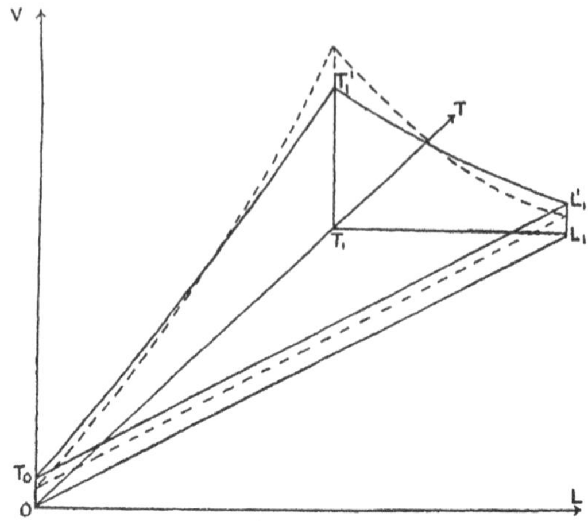

FIG. 2.

of "labour" invested for shorter periods. At the same time the relative value of "labour" and of the product would have to change. If, as has been assumed in the diagram, the value of the product remains constant, the value of "labour" would have to be reduced;[21] while the case where the value of "labour" remained constant would imply a corresponding rise in the value of the product. This situation would be represented in the diagram if the surface indicated by the dotted lines would be lifted by such an amount that the dotted line parallel to T_0L_1' would coincide with that line.

This diagram can easily be adapted to correspond to Fig. 1*b* instead of Fig. 1*a*, *i.e.* so as to represent the relationship between the total quantity of "labour" invested at one moment of time in different stages of similar processes, and the output stream derived from it. This form of representation, shown in Fig. 3, has the special advantage of enabling us to derive in a simple way the output function, which will be the starting-point for the discussion in the next section.

In this diagram OL_1 represents the number of units of "labour" invested at the moment O in different stages of the processes going on simultaneously in the industry, and OT_0 the value of a unit of "labour." The unit of "labour" shown at the beginning of the L-axis (*i.e.* nearest to the origin) is being invested in a process which is just being started and its product will accordingly mature only after the lapse of the maximum investment period, *i.e.* at T_1. Units of "labour" shown further on the right of the L-axis are invested in

[21] [The future undiscounted marginal value product of a unit of "labor" input remains the same, but the present value imputed to the input falls because the value is discounted more heavily.—Ed.]

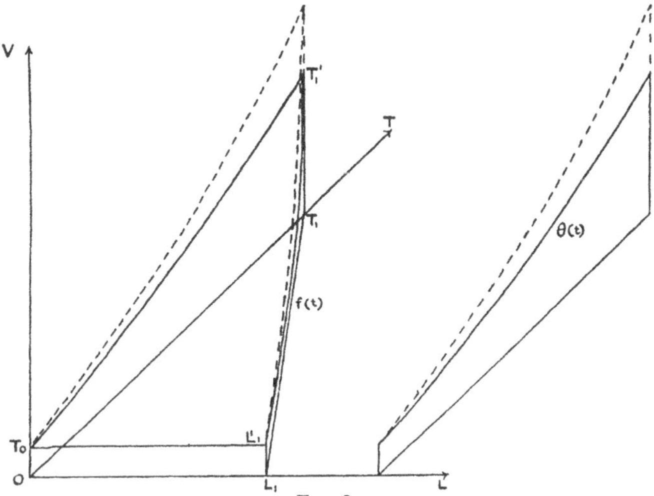

FIG. 3.

more advanced stages of similar processes and their product will mature at less distant moments, represented by the position of the corresponding points of the line L_1T_1 along the T-axis. This line again corresponds to the curve L_1T_1 in Fig. 1*b* and represents, therefore, the investment function *f*(*t*). But as the value of the product of the different units of "labour" which is shown to mature along this line will have grown at the same compound rate of interest for periods of increasing length, it will be greater as we get nearer to T_1. This increase of the V-co-ordinates corresponding to the products of the different units of "labour" maturing along L_1T_1 is shown by the upward slope of the curve $L_1'T_1'$ above it. It must be remembered here that since all the different units of labour are supposed to be employed in the same kind of process, and therefore to yield the same kind of product, the different value of the product due to the different quantities of "labour" must be due to proportional differences in the quantity of these products. But these different quantities of the product which will result at different moments of time from the "labour" invested at one moment of time represent the magnitude which we have described as the output function.

This magnitude is implicitly given by the shape of the vertical plane $L_1L_1'T_1T_1'$, and depends, therefore, in the same way as this surface on the rate of interest. The area of this plane corresponding to any interval along the T-axis is proportional to the magnitude of the output stream during the respective interval of time. As can easily be seen from the diagram, this area would vary not only in consequence of a change in the height of the curve $L_1'T_1'$, but also in consequence of any change in the direction of the investment curve L_1T_1 which forms its base. The rate of the flow of output at any moment of time will therefore correspond to the first derivative of the investment function $f(t)$ with respect to time, multiplied by the corresponding value of the interest function, *i.e.* the height of the interest surface $T_0T_1'L_1'$. The resulting function, which describes the rate of flow of the output stream at any moment between O and T_1, is the output function, represented in the diagram by the separate strip marked $\theta(t)$.[22] For the present the essential point is, that this output function can be derived from the investment function only on the assumption of a given rate of interest, and that, as is shown by the part of the diagram drawn in dotted lines, it will change its shape with every change in the rate of interest.

This section may be concluded with a short reference to the meaning of the volume of the three-dimensional body which appears in the last two diagrams. It represents the quantity of capital in value terms under stationary conditions. It shows clearly the reason why only it and not the simple investment figure which forms its base gives an unambiguous expression of this magnitude: because the reinvestment of interest accrued up to any moment of time has to be counted as part of the total investment. It is for this reason, too, that it is impossible to substitute any one-dimensional magnitude like the "average period of production" for the concept of the investment function. For there is no one single average period for which a quantity of factors could be invested with the result that the quantity of capital so created would be the same as if the same quantity of factors had been invested for the range of periods described by a given investment function, whatever the rate of interest. The mean value of these different investment periods which would satisfy this condition would have to be different for every rate of interest.[23]

[22] This strip is to be compared with the other parts of the figure only as regards its shape, but not as regards its absolute height, since it has necessarily to be drawn on a different scale. Its height should become equal to that of the body only where the investment curve becomes parallel to the T-axis. The similarity of the shape of the output function to that of the interest curve in the diagram is due to the fact that the investment function has been assumed to be linear. If this were not so, the output function might assume any other form. The relationship between the shape of the two curves (or the corresponding functions) will be discussed in somewhat greater detail in the next section of this article.

These relationships lend themselves easily to mathematical treatment, but it is not intended to burden the present article with it. Only a short re-statement of the main relationship discussed in the text may be added here. If $f(t)$ be the investment function, $\theta(t)$ the output function, $v = OT_0$ the value dimension of "labour" and ρ the rate of interest per annum computed continuously (Wicksell's *Verzinsungsenergie*), and therefore $ve^{\rho t}$ what in the text has been called the interest function, then $\theta(t) = f'(t)ve^{\rho t}$. [See also Hayek, *The Pure Theory of Capital*, *op. cit.*, ch. 13, "Compound Interest and the Instantaneous Rate of Interest."—Ed.]

[23] It should be noted that the volume of the body, and therefore the quantity of capital in value terms, will be a finite magnitude even if the investment curve approaches the T-axis only asymptotically. But this is not so important a case as has sometimes been believed, since only expected

IV

We turn now to the case of durable goods.[24] Here the situation is in many respects the exact reverse of that discussed in the previous section. In the ideal case, where a durable good is created by investing a given quantity of "labour" at a moment of time, and where that good then produces without any further aid from labour a continuous stream of services over a period of time,[25] the primary datum is apparently not of the nature of an investment function but a kind of output function. The given variable is the shape of a flow of services over a period of time. We know how long we have to wait for any unit of these services, but we do not know directly how long we have to wait for the product of the different units of "labour" invested. In order to decide this we should have to know what quantities of the final services have to be attributed to the individual units of "labour." And this can be done only on the basis of a given rate of interest. The relationship can again be described by means of a diagrammatic apparatus similar to that employed in the preceding section.

In Fig. 4 the meaning of the three co-ordinates is the same as in Figs. 2 and 3. The initial data, however, from which we have to start are, (1) the quantity of "labour" invested at zero hour and possessing a definite value, so that the total value of this "labour" can be represented by the rectangle $OT_0L_1'L_1$; (2) the shape of the expected stream of services, represented by the strip marked $\theta(t)$; and (3) a definite rate of interest at which the value of the "labour" invested at O will increase in time, represented in the diagram by the upward sloping interest surface $T_0T_1'T_1''L_1'$.

Any vertical cross-section connecting the interest surface with the base plane TOL along any line connecting T_1L_1 will represent an output stream which satisfies the condition that the discounted value of the product of each unit of labour invested will be the same. It has, however, to satisfy the further condition that it corresponds to the given time-shape of the output stream, or, if we apply the results of the preceding section, its area within any interval of the T-axis has to correspond to the magnitude of the given output stream within the same interval. The problem, therefore, is to find such a curve in the base

returns count—or since only economic and not physical duration is relevant. Even a good which is expected to last for ever, like a railway tunnel, will hardly ever be expected to remain permanently useful.

[24] [Böhm-Bawerk had omitted durable capital goods (or "fixed capital") from his model of time-consuming production. Knut Wicksell, elaborating on the work of his student Gustaf Åkerman, added durable capital goods to create a more general model. Hayek cites Wicksell's contribution below in n. 29. For an algebraic restatement of the Böhm-Bawerk and Åkerman-Wicksell models, neglecting Hayek's treatment of the issues, see Hans Brems, "Time and Interest: Böhm-Bawerk and Åkerman-Wicksell," *History of Political Economy*, 20, Winter 1988, pp. 565–81.—Ed.]

[25] [In *The Pure Theory of Capital*, *op. cit.*, p. 86, Hayek offers the example of taking "a straight branch from a tree and us[ing] it for years as a walking-stick."—Ed.]

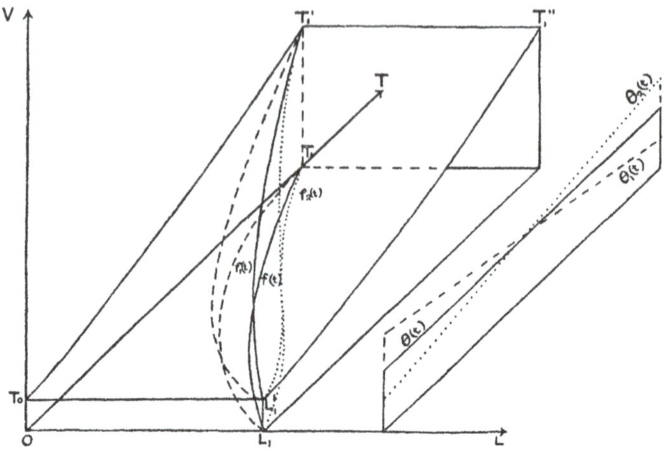

FIG. 4.

plane that the area below the interest surface of a vertical surface erected upon it, differentiated with respect to time, will be equal to that of the output function. This, clearly, is a problem of integration which in the particular case can be solved on the basis of the inverse operation carried out in the preceding section.[26]

It will, however, be sufficient for the present purpose to illustrate by a few examples the relationship between the output function and the investment function in the case of durable goods without going further into the mathematics of the problem. We shall do this by first assuming that the rate of interest is fixed but the shape of the output stream changes, and then by assuming that the rate of interest changes while the output function remains constant.

So far we have only seen (Fig. 3) that if the investment function is to be linear the output function would have to be of a peculiar and rather improbable shape. We shall now start from the more probable assumption that the durable good in question produces during its existence a constant stream of services. What will, on the assumption of a given rate of interest as that represented by the interest surface in Fig. 4, be the shape of the investment function corresponding to such a constant output stream (shown by the line $\theta(t)$ in the diagram)? In geometrical terms this question is equivalent to asking what perpendicular surface, enclosed between the base plane and the interest surface, will have within any interval of the T-axis an area proportional to that of the corresponding part of the given output stream.

As the height of this surface will increase with the progress of time, the

[26] $$f(t) = \int_0^{T_1} \frac{\theta(t)}{ve^{\rho t}}\, dt = \frac{1}{v}\int_0^{T_1} \theta(t)e^{-\rho t}\, dt$$

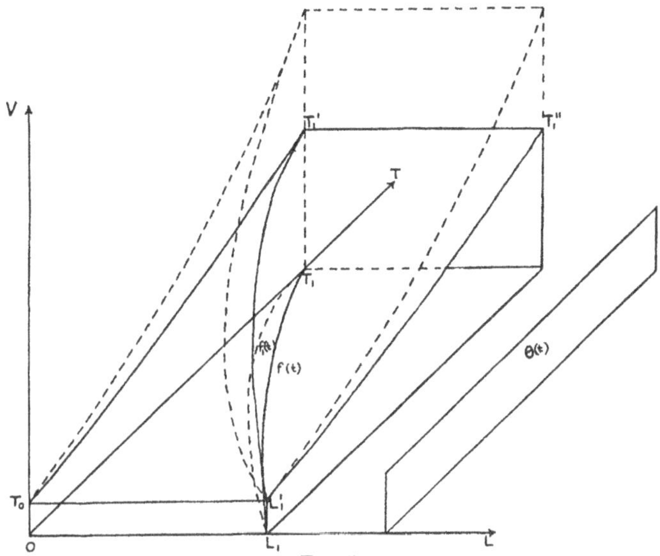

FIG. 5.

effect of this increase in height on its area will have to be compensated by a change in another dimension. And the only other change which can have this effect is a change in the inclination of this surface towards the T-axis. The area of such a surface within any given interval will evidently be greater the greater its inclination towards the T-axis, reaching a maximum where it is inclined towards it at 90 degrees, and a minimum where it is parallel to it. It will, therefore, be possible to compensate for an increase in height by decreasing the inclination towards the T-axis, with the effect that the area of the surface remains the same for any interval of the T-axis. Or, in other words, the answer to our question is that the investment curve (the line along which the surface cuts the base plane) will have to be convex towards the T and L axes and will have to increase its curvature as it approaches T_1.

This investment curve, corresponding to the constant output stream $\theta(t)$, is shown in Fig. 4 by the fully-drawn curve marked $f(t)$. It will now probably be evident without further demonstration that if the output stream were not constant but would decrease in time as that marked $\theta_1(t)$ in the diagram, the corresponding investment curve would have to be even more convex towards the origin ($f_1(t)$); while an output function which increased at an arithmetical rate as that marked $\theta_2(t)$ would have the effect of making the investment function less convex or even, in such parts where it increased faster than the interest curve, concave towards the origin ($f_2(t)$).

It remains now to show the effect of a change of the rate of interest on the shape of the investment function derived from a given output function. This effect is shown, for the case of a constant output stream, in Fig. 5. The fully drawn investment curve marked $f(t)$ corresponds here to the lower rate of interest represented by the surface $T_0T_1'T_1''L_1'$, while the investment curve marked $f_1(t)$ corresponds to the higher rate of interest shown by the second interest surface drawn in dotted lines. In words it means simply that the investment curve will become more convex as the rate of interest rises, and vice versa.

V

What is the economic meaning of the fact that in the first of the two cases discussed the investment function and in the second the output function is the independent variable, while in each case the other one of the two magnitudes is only a derived magnitude, a construction? We can only attempt a very partial answer to this question here, since its complete discussion would raise all the problems connected with the question of how the direction of current investment is determined.

It has occasionally been objected that the investment period, or period of production, is a magnitude which cannot possibly be known to, or play any rôle in the calculations of, the entrepreneur. If this were true this contention would, of course, equally militate against a concept of capital as the discounted value of expected future services as against a definition of capital in terms of (ranges of) investment periods. But surely it cannot be seriously argued that investments are made without some definite anticipation not only of the value of the services expected from them, but also of the time when they will mature. That these expectations will in most cases not be based on certainty but only on a certain chance introduces an element of uncertainty. But it does not alter the fundamental fact that the time when the product is expected to mature is as much a datum for the decision of the entrepreneur as its expected value.

A more serious problem, however, and a problem that cannot be answered generally, is whether this is not only true as regards the total investment in any one process or any one durable good, but also of any single unit of factors invested in such goods or process. Here the answer in every concrete case depends, in a way familiar from the marginal productivity analysis, on whether it is possible to isolate the physical marginal product of every unit of factors or whether we can only speak of a marginal product in terms of value. This depends, as is well known, upon whether the proportions in which the different factors can be used in any single line of production are variable, or whether only the quantities produced in the different industries, where different but fixed proportions prevail, can be changed.

The case of variable proportions in any one line of production is exemplified in this instance by the possibility of investing parts of the total quantity of "labour" used in any one process for a longer or shorter period. If again we take first the case of goods in process, it will clearly in most cases be possible to change within limits the quantities of "labour" employed in the different "stages" of the process and to compare the additions to the product obtained by employing a given quantity of "labour" in an earlier or later stage of the process. And the condition of equilibrium will evidently be, not that this "marginal product"[27] will be the same for all the units of "labour" employed in different stages, but that its value, discounted over the period for which the respective units of "labour" are invested, will be the same.

Any change in the rate of interest will in consequence change the relative value to be attributed to units of "labour" in the different stages, and, wherever this is possible, give rise to shifts of factors of production between stages. A fall in the rate of interest, *e.g.* will have the effect of increasing the value of the factors in the earlier stages relatively to that in the later stages and create a tendency towards a movement of factors to the earlier stages, until the value of the physical "marginal product" of every unit of "labour" is again equal to the value of that unit *plus* interest for the period for which it has been invested.[28]

But such a physical "marginal product" can be isolated only where the position of individual units of "labour" in the process can be changed while everything else is left the same. And although small changes of this sort will generally be possible, they are by no means possible without limits. Between the one extreme, where any form of investment curve can be changed into any other form by a continuous series of small changes of this sort, involving only the shifts of very small units of "labour," to the other extreme of a few alternative investment curves of altogether different shape, where for technical reasons no small changes are possible, and where a change from the one to the other can only be made by altering the investment period for almost every single unit of "labour," there is an infinite series of intermediate cases, which are more likely to occur in real life than either of the two extremes.

[27] This is, of course, not a marginal product in the usual sense of the product of the marginal unit of "labour" employed in the process, but in the special sense in which the term has been used in this connection by Professor Taussig, *i.e.* it is the product of the marginal unit of "labour" employed at any particular stage of production and therefore invested for a definite period of time. Units of labour invested at different stages co-operate with different quantities of capital and the process of discounting is a method of finding their true marginal product by making allowance for the share of the different quantities of capital with which they co-operate, cf. F. W. Taussig, "Outlines of a Theory of Wages," *American Economic Association Quarterly*, Third Series, Vol. XI, [April] 1910 [pp. 136–56].

[28] [This effect is an important part of Hayek's account in *Prices and Production* of how an unwarranted expansion of credit, lowering the interest rate below equilibrium, induces unsustainable top-heaviness in the structure of production during the boom phase of the business cycle.—Ed.]

In these cases where only more or less considerable quantities of "labour" which have been invested for different periods can be shifted *en bloc*, it is not possible to single out the physical product of a unit of "labour." The principle on which alone it will here be possible to attribute definite quantities of the product to the different units of "labour" is that the aggregate product of the total labour is so distributed between the individual units, that by discounting the product attributed to every unit, at the rate of interest ruling everywhere else in the system, the value of every unit of "labour" becomes the same. And the further adjustment of the value of the units of "labour" to the level prevailing in the rest of the system will have to be made by increasing or decreasing the quantity of output of the line of production concerned and so influencing the value of the product that is to be discounted.

This, of course, is the familiar principle of imputation of a marginal value product, based on the consideration that if two or more factors are combined in different lines of production in different but fixed proportions, the relative quantities of the product will have to be so adjusted that, by giving the same value to any one unit of the same factor, in all lines of production, we can distribute the total value of the product between the factors. The main application of this to our particular problem is best shown in the extreme case where the investment function is rigidly fixed in all lines of industry: a fall in the rate of interest or an increase in the supply of free capital here will lead to an increase of output in the industries with a longer structure of production (with more capital per head) at the expense of those with a shorter structure of production, and in this way increase the proportion of "labour" that is invested for relatively long periods, thus changing the investment function for industry in general without changing it for any one industry.

In the case where the investment function is variable by small amounts and where, therefore, it is possible to connect definite amounts of the product with any unit of factors there will always be one and only one output function corresponding to any one investment function, and any change in the rate of interest will lead to changes in both these functions. Where, however, these two functions are not co-ordinated by physical productivity in this unambiguous way, a change in the rate of interest will affect the relationship between the two functions and bring about changes either of the one or the other in different ways.

Now, this case where the shape of the investment function is more or less fixed and every change of the rate of interest simply leads to a change of the relative importance of the parts of the total invested for longer or shorter periods (*i.e.* to a change of the output function) is not very different from the case where the output function is given and the investment function derived from it, *i.e.* the case of durable goods.

In this case it has long been recognised that it is not normally possible to trace a physical connection between every unit of factors invested and the services of the goods due to it, and that therefore the investment period, or investment function, cannot be considered as a technical datum.[29] Only for the marginal units of factors invested in goods of variable durability, *i.e.* for the units that have caused definite extensions of its life, can such a technical connection be established. But this becomes impossible where, either the physical durability of the good cannot be varied or where—a very frequent case in real life—its physical duration has for technical reasons to be made greater than its economic usefulness will last (obsolescence). It is therefore in many ways most instructive to discuss the extreme case of a durable good of absolutely fixed duration.

The principle on which for any rate of interest an apparently purely fictitious investment curve can be derived from the output curve has been shown in the preceding section. But is this investment curve purely fictitious? Already the discussion of the effects of changes in the rate of interest have [*sic*] shown that it has some real importance. A lowering of the rate of interest, *e.g.*, which will make the investment curve less curved, means that a greater part of the more distant services of the goods will be attributed to "labour" (because less will be deducted for interest) or that a smaller part of the future stream of services will be sufficient to attract a unit of "labour" to the production of such goods. More goods (or, where possible, more durable goods) of the kind will be produced simply because the more distant part of the expected services will play a greater rôle in the considerations of the entrepreneur and will lead him to invest more on account of these more distant returns. Even a description of the equilibrium between costs and prices is hardly conceivable without a use of the relationships described by the investment function.

But the main importance of the concept of the investment function becomes apparent only when we direct attention to the more dynamic aspects of the question. From what has been said so far it will probably have become sufficiently clear that every rate of interest will direct investment in a definite direction, a lower rate so as to involve a greater total quantity of capital (a "longer" investment structure) and a higher rate so as to involve a smaller quantity of capital. It is, of course, the well-known "function" of interest to limit production to the most profitable methods for which the available quantity of capital is just sufficient. But what exactly this "given quantity of capital" means, and what will be the effects of methods of production that are not in accord with it, this, it seems to me, can only be explained by means of this concept of the investment function.

[29] Cf. K. Wicksell, "Realkapital och kapitalränta," *Ekonomisk Tidskrift*, vol. 25, [nos. 5–6,] 1923 [pp. 145–80]. [English translation, "Real Capital and Interest," trans. Solomon Adler, in *Lectures on Political Economy*, by Knut Wicksell (London: 1934), vol. 1, appendix 2.—Ed.]

Under stationary conditions, *i.e.* when the investment function remains constant and all the current income is spent on current output of consumers' goods, their prices and the prices of intermediate products will just cover cost of production. Any lengthening or shortening of the investment structure, however, will necessarily have the effect of temporarily, during the transition period, reducing or increasing output relatively to the level at which it could be permanently maintained. If the investment structure is being lengthened, the output of consumers' goods will for a time be reduced to an amount which has cost less than the total income of all factors of production (including capital); while when it is shortened, an amount which has cost more than this will come on the market. If these changes are the consequence of corresponding changes of expenditure on consumers' goods below or above net income, prices will still correspond to costs. But if they are the consequence of a deflection of the rate of interest from the equilibrium position, output will be either smaller or greater than demand and the consequent disequilibrium between prices and cost will have the tendency to restore the conditions of equilibrium which the rate of interest has failed to maintain.

These effects, of course, can merely be hinted at in the course of this discussion. But it must be clear, that in this connection the attribution of definite parts of the output stream to such units of factors as are to be considered as its costs is of the greatest importance. It is for the analysis of this process in time and of the effects of changes in the direction of investment on the cost of current output relatively to current expenditure, that the concept of the investment function becomes of real importance. That this is so is not surprising if we remember that what it does is essentially to show how the effects of present activity will be distributed in time, to point to the particular future moments when the results are expected to realise which have led to present investment.

VI

The contention that the chief value of the "period of production" approach lies in the help it renders in the analysis of dynamic phenomena may be a little unexpected, since it has frequently been suggested that while it may be applicable to stationary conditions, it loses all its meaning when applied to problems of economic dynamics. This very widespread impression is due to the fact that the concept of the period of production has generally been interpreted in an historical, backward-looking sense. For this Böhm-Bawerk's manner of exposition is mainly responsible. But, as has been pointed out at the beginning of this article, the essential concept is not that of the length of the process from which current output results, but the range of periods for which the current supply of factors is being invested.

It is true, however, that certain conclusions frequently drawn from the idea of a period of production imply such an historical interpretation. This is particularly true of what might, using a term of J. B. Clark, be called the "synchronization" proposition, if this is interpreted literally. This proposition states (what is essentially a truism) that under perfectly stationary conditions the stock of intermediate products existing at any one moment of time will exactly correspond to all the different stages through which the "labour" invested at the same moment will have to pass before it matures into consumers' goods. It was on the basis of this proposition that the diagrams used in the first two sections of this paper, which in the first instance were intended to describe a process in time, were also interpreted as a representation of the stock of capital existing at any one moment. Although this must be true under perfectly stationary conditions, it is just because the concept of stationary conditions implies this that nothing in real life will ever correspond to it; not only because the external data never remain constant, but for the simple reason that the data determining the methods of production are not only "external" data, but include always also results of preceding economic activity. Stationary conditions in this sense could only exist if the productive equipment existing at the beginning of any one period were the same as that existing at the end of that period, *i.e.* if stationary conditions had already existed, or if at any one moment all capital had been available in a free form (a real "subsistence fund" consisting of consumers' goods) and had then been invested in view of conditions which have not changed since. But once unforeseen changes occur after capital has been invested in a definite form, all further investment will be influenced by the historical accident of the existence of certain capital goods, and the movement towards a state of equilibrium will at best be an asymptotic movement.[30]

It is for this reason that the backward-looking interpretation of the "period of production" will always lead to absurd conclusions. A real identity in a physical sense between the stock of intermediate products existing at any one moment and the intermediate products that are being reproduced by the current investment of original factors will never exist. Or, to express the same idea in more familiar terms, it can never be expected that the value of the existing real capital[31] will correspond to its actual cost of production. But all this does not disprove the only essential contention, namely, that the value of the existing capital goods will stand in a definite relationship to the way

[30] "In the order of history labour precedes capital: from land and labour everything proceeds. But in the actual order of things there is always some capital already produced, which is united with land and labour in the production of new values."—J. Bentham, *Works*, Vol. III, p. 34. [*Manual of Political Economy*, in vol. 3 of *The Works of Jeremy Bentham* (Edinburgh: William Tait, 1843).—Ed.]

[31] [That is, the value of the set of existing plant and equipment.—Ed.]

in which the current factors are being invested. Before dealing with this last problem, it is necessary to say a few words on the way in which unforeseen changes will affect the value of existing capital goods.

This problem would be comparatively simple if all intermediate products were completely specific, *i.e.* if they could not possibly be used for any other purposes or in any other way than was intended when they were made. It is the assumption that such is the case which underlies and justifies most of the over-simplified statements on the relationship between the existing stock of capital and current investment. If it were true,[32] the only choice for the entrepreneur in the event of any unexpected change would be between going on as originally intended or abandoning the existing intermediate products entirely. But they could in no way become part of the new processes started after the change has taken place.

Such complete specificity of the intermediate products, however, never exists; and in fact in a great many cases the range of possible uses for any individual capital good is very wide indeed. The effect of this is that any unexpected change will lead to some of the existing intermediate products being used for purposes not originally contemplated and to which they are not perfectly adapted, but for which, once they are in existence, they can now be used with greater advantage than for their original purpose. Their movements between the different stages will be governed by the same general principles as that of the original factors; a fall in the rate of interest will tend[33] to bring about shifts to earlier stages and a rise in the rate of interest to bring about shifts to later stages. In fact, in most respects their position would become similar to that of the "original" factors of production, except that they are not sources of a permanent but only of a very limited stream of productive services.

The degree of mobility of the different intermediate products is, of course, very different and accordingly their value will be affected in very different degrees by any unforeseen change. Although this is one of the most obvious facts, it has an importance for the theory of capital which has very rarely been seen. It is perhaps one of the most urgent needs in the field of the theory of capital, that economists should at last free themselves of the idea that capital is some homogeneous mass, some given quantity of value, which will preserve

[32] The proposition that an intermediate product is irrevocably committed to the stage of production for which it was intended implies, among other things, that it is perishable, because keeping it for consumption later than was originally intended would be equivalent to shifting it to an earlier stage.

[33] There will be exceptions from this tendency, since, in some cases, after some of the intermediate products in any stage of production have been shifted to earlier stages, it may be more profitable to use the intermediate products which have remained in a lower stage. The same applies, of course, to original factors where different kinds of such factors co-operate.

its magnitude independently of the value of the real commodities of which it consists.[34]

The notion that capital as such—*i.e.* the quantity of value which it represents—is completely mobile and can at will and without any loss of value be transformed in any concrete form, has already played much havoc in economic theory.[35] It would be true only if the concrete capital goods were just so many units of homogeneous "energy" which could be put to any use, *i.e.* if they were completely non-specific. But this, of course, corresponds even less to reality than the assumption of complete specificity. It seems reasonable to suppose that *all* the capital goods existing at any one moment are at least partly the result of an historical process which again and again has put existing capital goods to other uses than those for which they were originally intended, and that in consequence the actual form that capital takes will be very different from what it would be if the structure could be built up *ab ovo* with the help of an equivalent fund of free capital.

It was, of course, considerations of this sort which led Marshall to insist on the fact, that existing capital goods (as distinguished from free capital) did not yield interest but quasi-rent, and which made Wicksell describe at least the more durable capital goods as rent-goods (*Rentengüter*). For our main problem, to which we have to return now, it will be useful to think of all real capital as consisting of rent-goods in the extreme sense, *i.e.* as of non-reproducible, non-permanent instruments of production.[36] If it can be shown that even in this extreme case there exists a definite relationship between the value of the existing stock of such goods and the range of periods for which current labour is being invested, this will apply *a fortiori* to the less extreme cases.

[34] [The idea referred to is part of Frank Knight's theory of capital.—Ed.]

[35] An example of reasoning based on this assumption is Böhm-Bawerk's discussion of the effects of a rise of wages on the investment structure, to which Mr. Hill refers in his article already quoted. The apparent contradiction pointed out by Mr. Hill between Böhm-Bawerk's conclusions and those at which I have arrived in a discussion of the same problem (see the article on "Kapitalaufzehrung," *Weltwirtschaftliches Archiv*, [vol. 36, no. 1,] July 1932 [pp. 86–108; included in this volume as "Capital Consumption"—Ed.]) is simply due to the fact that Böhm-Bawerk assumes complete mobility of capital in this sense, while my analysis is based on the fact that at any moment capital will be definitely committed to particular forms of investment from which it cannot immediately be withdrawn. For a later and more satisfactory analysis of the process of "capital consumption" see J. R. Hicks, *Theory of Wages* [London, Macmillan, 1932], Chapters IX and X.

[36] For reasons which I cannot discuss here, it seems to me advisable to substitute "non-permanent means of production" for the usual "produced means of production" as the essential distinction corresponding to the traditional one between "capital" and "land." The fact that free capital is sometimes used to create means of production which are in a physical sense permanent (tunnels, etc.) creates a certain difficulty which is, however, not likely to become very serious, since even physically permanent intermediate products are rarely expected to remain permanently useful.

The stock of all kinds of such "intermediate products" existing at any one moment represents a stream of future services[37] which can be pictured by a diagram similar to that shown in Fig. 1*b*. While almost the total quantity of goods to be consumed in the intermediate future will already be in existence in nearly completed form, the share of the more distant parts of the output stream which will already be provided for by some such products of past labour will become smaller and smaller as we look further to the future. This output stream (or alternatively possible output streams) to be expected from the existing non-permanent goods is the main factor which will determine the direction of the investment of current "labour." If output is to be maintained at a constant level, it will be necessary to distribute "labour" in such a way between the different investment periods as gradually to complete the half-finished products for the future moments and to provide for the replacement of what is used up in such a way that at any future moment there will exist a stock of intermediate products equivalent in productive capacity to that existing now. The wish to maintain the output stream at a certain level will thus make it necessary to invest current labour for definite periods, and the existence of the old stock of non-permanent products will make it possible to do so without temporarily reducing the output stream below the level at which it can permanently be maintained.

It is not possible to attempt at the end of this article a more detailed description of the actual process by which the value and the time structure of the existing stock of rent-goods affect the investment of current labour. Such a discussion would have to include a close examination of the factors which determine the value of existing rent-goods, the rate at which they will be amortised, and the rate of return at which these amortisation quotas can be reinvested. It would be complicated by the fact that the process in question is an essentially dynamic process in the course of which the shape of the investment function for current labour would undergo a gradual change. Some at least of the problems here involved I hope soon to take up in a discussion of the closely related problem of the meaning of "maintaining capital intact."[38]

[37] Under stationary conditions this stream of services expected from the existing stock of "intermediate products" will be equal to the sum of the still unexhausted parts of all the output streams attributable to the labour invested at successive moments in the past. But under dynamic conditions, where intermediate products will be used for other purposes than those for which they were originally intended, this strict correspondence between the output function which describes the output stream derived from the quantity of labour invested at a moment of time, and what one might call the integral output function, ceases to exist. This integral output function, which describes the output stream to be derived, not only from the original factors but from all goods existing at any one moment, assumes then an independent significance. It will probably prove to be the most fruitful concept for the analysis of dynamic processes. I understand that it is in this form that the concept of the output function will take a central position in Mr V. Edelberg's forthcoming publication on these problems. [On Victor Edelberg, see n. 6 above.—Ed.]

[38] [See Hayek, "The Maintenance of Capital," in the present volume.—Ed.]

It is hoped, however, that what has been said will at least make it plausible that even if there should be no correspondence whatever between the technical composition of the existing stock of real capital and the kind of capital goods in which current labour is invested, yet the value of the existing real capital limits within fairly narrow ranges the time dimension of current investment. It might, in some ways, even have been more fortunate if the connection had been stated in this way, namely, that the existing stock of real capital determines the investment structure of current labour, rather than in the inverse form, although it is, of course, true that it is by changes in this investment structure that changes in the quantity of real capital are brought about.

That anything which will tend to lengthen this investment structure of current labour will lead to increases of the quantity of capital and anything which tends to shorten it will lead to a reduction of capital, remains a point of fundamental importance. But the main point to remember here is that it is not simply changes in the value of the existing capital goods in general, but changes in their relative value, which will cause such changes in the direction of current investment. A rise of the value of those parts which will give their returns in the more distant future will lead to the investment of a greater part of the current labour for longer periods and vice versa. It is the emphasis which the concept of the period of production (investment function) places on this time structure of the stock of real capital, on the fact that it is not a homogeneous mass but that it is organised in a definite way and that the only method by which we can understand this organisation is by concentrating on the place of individual capital goods in this time structure, that constitutes its true usefulness.

SEVEN

PROFESSOR HAYEK AND THE THEORY OF INVESTMENT[1]

by Frank H. Knight

In the remarks which follow, I am not concerned with the technical problems of the "structure of investment" actually discussed in Professor Hayek's recent article,[2] and shall take no notice of what may be right or wrong in that connection. I am concerned rather with the fact that the article pretends to do something far more fundamental, but which, as I think, cannot be done. The author asserts (page 208, note 2)[3] that his paper contains implicitly the answers to objections recently made to the Austrian theory of capital, and names among other references a paper of mine published in the volume of *Economic Essays in Honour of Gustav Cassel.*[4] In this connection, he asserts or assumes, on the average of at least once to a page, that he has proved, or is proving, or that it is self-evident and requires no proof, that a change in the amount of capital in society is identical with a change in the "investment structure," an increase corresponding to a lengthening, and a decrease to a shortening, of that structure (cf. p. 211, especially footnote 2; p. 231, etc.).[5] And increase of investment is further identified, if not quite so clearly and emphatically, with a lengthening of the production process or production period, the interval between the time when "labour" is performed and the time when its product is consumed (*e.g.* pp. 208, 209, 223).[6]

If, however, this theory, or either part of it, is anywhere argued, or any reason given for believing it, I have not been able to locate the passage in question. Indeed, on page 225,[7] just preceding another assertion of the point at issue, there is a statement which is very nearly a direct "give-away." It reads:

[1] [*Economic Journal*, vol. 45, no. 177, March 1935, pp. 77–94.—Ed.]

[2] "The Relationship between Investment and Output," *Economic Journal* [vol. 44, no. 174,] June, 1934 [pp. 207–231; included in the present volume as "On the Relationship between Investment and Output."—Ed.]

[3] Hayek, "On the Relationship between Investment and Output," this volume, p. 77 n. 5.

[4] [Frank H. Knight, "Capitalist Production, Time and the Rate of Return" in *Economic Essays in Honour of Gustav Cassel* (London: George Allen & Unwin, 1933), pp. 327–42.—Ed.]

[5] Hayek, "On the Relationship between Investment and Output," this volume, p. 80 n. 14 and p. 99.

[6] *Ibid.*, pp. 77, 78, 91.

[7] *Ibid.*, p. 93.

"More goods (or, where possible, more durable goods) of the kind will be produced . . . ." It should be apparent that as regards a relation between capital quantity and investment structure the essential issue lies in the difference between constructing more goods and constructing more durable goods (in response to a fall in the interest rate); also that Professor Hayek is bound to maintain (*a*) that the sole effect would be the substitution of more durable for less durable goods (not that this is a contingent possibility, as indicated by the parenthesis); and (*b*) that this change lengthens the interval between production and consumption.

If the question were considered at all, it would surely be immediately evident that in neither of the two senses discussed by Professor Hayek does the investment of more capital necessarily involve, still less is it equivalent to, a lengthening of the time structure of investment—and *still* less to a lengthening of the production process. Moreover, there is no production process of determinate length, other than zero, or "all history." New investment may or may not involve either (*a*) an increase in the average durability of the goods involved in economic activity, or (*b*) an increase in the average construction period for such goods. It is to be assumed that, other things being equal, an increase in investment would involve both an increase in the amount of goods of the same kind and the construction of new kinds (see quotation above from Hayek, p. 225) according to what happened to be most *profitable*. "Possibility" is not in question, as generally in economic matters. More goods of the same kind would mean no permanent change in either investment function or output function, as defined by Professor Hayek, and new kinds would mean changes in both directions nearly at random, as regards both period of construction and durability.

It is true that there is a partial, *temporary* exception, in connection with an expansion of production not associated with any change in the composition of the product or in technology. If such an expansion takes place in perfectly rational order, there will be, *temporarily* (while the expansion is taking place, but not after it is completed), a slight increase in the proportion of goods in the earlier stages of processing operations, in comparison with later stages. It is to be noted, too, that there is little rigour in the complementary relationships between goods representing different stages of a given process, that *inventories* play a large *and flexible* rôle at every stage.

There is also a presumption, though no necessity, that both the average construction period and the average durability of wealth items will increase somewhat, though in no determinate degree, with an increase in the proportions of wealth to (labour and to) total income in a society. The reason is that, on the one hand, increased durability is *one way* of investing more capital and securing more income (because the annual deduction from gross yield for depreciation is reduced); and, on the other hand, interest during construction is one element in cost, and would probably increase along with other costs; and especially, a reduction in the cost per unit of time, through a lower interest rate, might well lead to an increase in the time. In both cases the particular element of time is one among a practically infinite number of variables, and the relative importance of the effects in question in the total of effects will be measured by a corresponding fraction. It is presumed, too, that any increased use of capital will find its expression in part in the making of altogether new products, and the time relations in this connection are entirely unpredictable.

For the general theory of capital, and for appraising Professor Hayek's claim mentioned above that he has met the objections to his theory, to which he makes reference (notably those of the present writer), the question is whether increasing the amount of capital invested lengthens the production process, rather than what is its effect on the investment structure. This general theory of capital is, of course, that promulgated by Böhm-Bawerk and his followers and generally accepted and taught in the past generation.

On the face of it, there must be plausible reasons for holding that the use of more capital is equivalent to the use of more time in production; otherwise the doctrine would not have been so generally expounded and believed. It unquestionably requires time to construct capital goods, and since these are subsequently used in processes requiring time, to make a product, and are more or less typically used up, it is natural to consider their production and use as an indirect in place of a direct application of the productive capacity going into them, and to consider the time involved in their creation, during which no final product is forthcoming, as added to that of their use to form a total production period for the final product. Reasonableness is harder to discover in the doctrine that labour produces capital in any sense not just as valid reciprocally, but this also is generally accepted by many of the best economists.

A brief statement of the reasoning which shows this entire procedure to be false may start from the personal statement that I myself completely accepted it for years, taught it in class lectures and expounded it in text materials manifolded for student reading, and of course it was never questioned by the "innocents" who were the victims.[8] Realisation that the whole argument is funda-

[8] The theory of profit developed in my book on Risk and Uncertainty [Frank H. Knight, *Risk, Uncertainty, and Profit* (Boston: Houghton Mifflin, 1921), online at http://www.econlib.org/library/Knight/knRUP.html—Ed.] rests upon the general view of the entrepreneur or business unit buying productive services "now" and selling the products in the future, and the theory needs to be entirely reworked. Profit must be computed with respect to some definable basis, either a dated interval of time, or a particular item of product, or to a project or venture somehow defined. It is, of course, the first of these which is actually and in general necessarily

mentally wrong came through working over the meaning of the wage-fund theory, particularly as expounded by Smith, in relation to Böhm-Bawerk's defence in the last few pages of the *Positive Theory* against the self-accusation of being a wage-fund theorist.[9] Let us glance at this original form of the theory.

Here, neglecting "land," it was argued that the capital produced in one year, thought of as food and other provisions for the use of labourers, supports the same amount of labour the next year, while the original capital is being reproduced. There is here, in the first place, a real and definite "cycle." Moreover, if in such an agricultural situation some crops are biennial or require several years to produce, their value will be increased accordingly by accumulated interest. And it is evident that if plants requiring more years to mature are to be substituted for others growing in a shorter period, a greater accumulation of the final product will be necessary to initiate and to support the operations (two different matters!), and the yield of the more slowly maturing crop will have to be greater to induce men to make the change of introducing it. This is undoubtedly the logic of the Böhm-Bawerk theory, which further assumes that the construction and using up of auxiliary instruments such as tools and machinery is equivalent in principle to the alternate production and consumption of supplies for the use of labourers. But such a production period explanation of capital is reasonably sound only with reference to assumptions which are almost entirely false to the facts of modern industrial

adopted. In any case, the essentials work out in the same way. The crucial element in the profit problem in a society in which capital is employed has to do with asset values. It is a question of (expenditures and receipts and of) the relative value of assets at the beginning and the end of the accounting period. For any basis other than a time interval, the elements will be (direct charges and credits to a particular account, together with) any and all effects upon asset values which can be attributed to the project or entity with which the account in question is kept.

The main point for emphasis is that the outlays and returns compared to determine profit are not separated by any time interval, but belong to the same accounting period, however short it may be. For any outlay in business or production the corresponding return is not in the future, but contemporary. Time and uncertainty enter into profit in a different way altogether—namely, through the capital account, or specifically, through inventories and depreciation. But capital itself is always a matter of anticipation to the infinite future. [Knight seriously meant *infinite*. His model of capital narrowed intertemporal allocation to the choice between present consumption and provision for a *perpetual* stream of future consumption, and he seemed to believe that there was no other coherent way to theorize about capital.—Ed.] Of course the concrete anticipation may relate to capital value at a future date rather than to perpetual income, and the capital may at various times and to a greater or less extent assume for the individual owner the particular form of money; but neither fact affects its character of a perpetual anticipation. This comes to be limited only if business in the entire system is conducted on the anticipation of a universal disinvestment.

[9] [Eugen von Böhm-Bawerk, *Positive Theorie des Kapitales* (Innsbruck, Austria: Wagner, 1888); English translation available to Knight, *The Positive Theory of Capital*, trans. William Smart (London: Macmillan, 1891).—Ed.]

life, and cases which it reasonably fits are obviously special cases under other principles having general validity.

Even with reference to such primitive agricultural conditions the really critical student (such as hardly exists) might have had disturbing queries in connection with treating quantity of capital as a matter of length of production cycle. In fact, the quantity of the capital bears no simple or definite relation either to its durability or to any definable time interval. Taking population as given, raising *more* plants of the *same* growth period will also require more "stock," but *will not* affect the length of the cycle, while the *addition* to total production of new varieties of *shorter* growth, say yielding two harvests per year instead of one, will involve an increase in the capital, while *shortening* the average cycle. It will, moreover, require time to make the change in all these cases, but additional capital is involved in very different ways for lengthening the cycle and for increasing production without this lengthening, and the transitional relations are different from those of the new routine when established. In the third case, which is intrinsically as probable as the other two, production may be maintained with a shortened cycle, and capital released or production increased and the same amount of capital used. The fact that time is required for changing from any system to any other is confused with change in the length of the cycle itself, is one of the basic fallacies of the modern theory. It will be noted, too, that the service life of capital goods in the form of an annual crop of supplies for the support of labourers is not due to any intrinsic quality, but simply to the production period for a new crop. The amount of supplies which last one year is highly variable with the seasons, and will change (for a given population) with any change in productive efficiency and living standards (leaving the cycle unaffected).

The crux of the wage fund situation is first that the capital, while constant in amount, passes by investment and disinvestment through a real and regular physical cycle; and second, that it could be said to be produced by labour, if capital constituted support for labour at a fixed level (as the classical economists always really assumed),[10] or if, at least, variation in the level of support

[10] This involves rejection of the wage-fund doctrine as a theory of *wages*. The wage theory of the classical system was an "absolute" standard of living theory. Its basis was the assumption that the employer (miscalled capitalist) gives the labourer some fixed amount (not fraction) of the product, which is necessary to enable him to live and work, or perhaps a merely conventional payment, in any case one determined in some absolute manner, unrelated to competitive bidding among purchasers of labour, and hence unrelated to product value. Only in such a way could a residual theory of the capital share be given foundation. The "system," then, was this: First, land gets its differential or residual product. If this is stated so as to make any sense at all, it means a marginal-productivity theory for labour-plus-capital, and the residuum is easily seen to be identical with the marginal product of the land itself. Second, labour gets what it "has to have." And third, capital gets the final residuum. And this nonsense passed for an economic theory of distribution for a century, until Jevons and Menger demoralised it without seeing much

or standard of living for labour were not associated with any variation in the output of the combination. In fact, however, labour is also produced as well as "maintained" by capital (if there is any difference), and there is no real priority either way, even if we go back to the historical beginning of economic life.

It is only under the arbitrary and absurd assumption that capital is eaten up at a fixed rate (such as the fixed scale of support for labour) that there is any correspondence between a quantity of capital and the length of a productive cycle. Under competitive conditions, where alone quantity of capital is at all definite, the quantity is the capitalised perpetual net income of any capital good (after full maintenance, including replacements) and is *also* its cost[11] of production, which includes a capital charge. Thus both these magnitudes involve a rate of return, which is "determined" by their equality. In determining both construction cost and service life, time is one factor or dimension among a practically infinite number, and quantity of capital may and does vary quite independently of either of these time intervals. *Caeteris paribus*, it of course increases with either, according to the compound interest formula.

It is if possible even more fatal to a production period theory of capital that no such period can be defined under modern conditions, either before, or after, or during an increased application of capital. The sum of the construction period and service life averaged for individual capital instruments is neither determinate in itself nor significant for theory. Even in 1776, provisions for the support of labourers—reproduced by labour, or by labour and land or even labour, land and capital—annually or in any other definite period, was only a part of capital. And even for a strictly interpreted wage fund it is arbitrary to call any point in the cycle a beginning or an end; it is a hen-and-egg sequence. Under modern conditions there simply is no cycle. It cannot now escape observation that "capital" is an integrated, organic conception, and the notion that the investment in a particular instrument comes back periodically in the form of product, giving the owner freedom to choose whether he will re-invest or not, is largely a fiction and a delusion. To show this conclusively it should suffice to mention the case of a part of a machine. The part cannot be liquidated without liquidating the machine. And the machine

as to how a real distribution theory was to be built. This achievement had to wait at least two more decades, or until Wieser, Hobson, J. B. Clark, and especially Wicksteed, gropingly indicated the circularity and symmetry of the relations. If economists had known the rudiments of analysis as put in shape by Leibniz, Newton and others [that is, had they known calculus—Ed.] a generation before Adam Smith was born, the history could have been more pleasant to look back upon. But the only theory which makes sense at all is still rejected by a large fraction of the teachers of economics, as well as indignantly by labour leaders and reformers; and it is not in the least degree understood by either the men who manage business or those who make laws, most of whom still believe that labour alone is really productive.

[11] More generally, where conditions are not stationary, the estimated cost, discounted for uncertainty, of any new item yielding the same net perpetual income.

as a unit is in a similar sense a "part" of an integrated productive organisation which is not bounded by the scope of "plant" or firm, but extends outward indefinitely to indeterminate limits.[12] Moreover, the capital structure and every unit in it is typically planned to perpetuate itself, and not for liquidation.

The animus underlying Smith's theory of capital was plainly the downright fear that the owners of capital might eat it up without replacement. (And this is, if possible, even clearer in Mill.) There never were serious grounds for such a fear, though the difference and even opposition between the two interests, of maximising consumption and providing for the future, ought to be stressed. But under modern conditions the possibilities of liquidation without serious loss are very limited, and the possible scope and speed of liquidation are only remotely related to the normal durability of the physical thing (or other "condition") in which any increment of capital is invested. In a stationary or progressive society, small increments are indeed liquidated from the standpoint of the individual owner (consumed); but no real liquidation from an aggregate viewpoint is typically involved in the process, and real liquidation, into consumption, is hardly in question.[13] The individual owner desirous of consuming any increment of capital naturally sells out at full value (for future production, above maintenance including replacement) to some other owner, and the productive organisation is not affected. In connection with the business cycle, and the depression problem in particular, the liquidation which is at issue is

[12] [In asserting that the capital owner's freedom to re-invest or disinvest is "largely a fiction and a delusion," Knight seems to assert that normally a firm will never lower output using fewer or cheaper non-labor inputs. Standard neoclassical price theory (including Hayek's theory), by contrast, teaches that normally a firm *will* reduce output, and *will* reduce particular non-labor inputs, when relative price changes call for it. In Hayek's famous example of how the price system responds to a tin mine collapse that raises the price of tin, tin-using producers reduce their outputs and substitute away from tin input.

In the case of a machine part, other examples (not Hayek's) illustrate that many machine parts have cheaper substitutes, that some parts can be completely discarded without their machines becoming useless, and that whole machines are expendable. A plumbing firm that is compelled by profitability considerations to reduce its output of plumbing services can sell one of the trucks in its fleet, and replace it with a smaller truck or none at all, without reducing its output to zero.

Given that Knight goes on to recognize the possibility of capital consumption by the economy as a whole, we might wish to give him the benefit of the doubt and suppose that he instead only meant to assert here (as he goes on to say explicitly) that in a *stationary or growing* economy one entrepreneur's disinvestment is necessarily offset by investment elsewhere. The truck sold by one firm will be purchased by another firm. Any one entrepreneur's disinvestment will be offset elsewhere unless there is disinvestment throughout the entire economy. This truism, however, hardly makes irrelevant Hayek's firm-level and industry-level analysis of the choice between reinvestment and disinvestment.—Ed.]

[13] [In the retrogressing economy of interwar Austria, by contrast, the real liquidation of capital into consumption was very much in evidence. See Hayek's article "Capital Consumption" elsewhere in this volume.—Ed.]

almost entirely conversion into *money*, not into current consumption.[14] Failure of physical maintenance sometimes results from the helplessness of owners, and is connected with the unexpected loss of earning power consequent upon economic disorganisation. This confusion between real liquidation and pecuniary liquidation, or saleability—which is not liquidation at all—needs fuller consideration. By way of preparation, it is needful to pass in more systematic review some of the essential facts in the problem of capital.

1. The most important fact requiring clarification is the nature of capital *maintenance*. This topic is a detail under a general consideration which is the source of much confusion in economic analysis—namely, the necessity of a clear distinction between stationary conditions and growth (increased provision for want-satisfaction for a given population). In a society which is maintaining or increasing its capital (per capita), all production of capital goods axiomatically represents either replacement or growth. (The situation in a retrograde society would have to be considered separately, but involves little change in the reasoning.)

No rational analysis of economic process is possible without making a sharp distinction between the "production" of "plant"—meaning *new or additional* plant (and properly including both the material and the human elements) and production in the sense of using plant to produce output. Use of plant in the production of the output (of *services*) consumed in any time interval must include the maintenance of plant, and this may involve replacement of particular items of plant. Obviously, if the plant "used up" in any interval is not maintained, the consumption of that interval is to a corresponding degree not produced in the interval, but represents the eating up of resources existing at its beginning (a process of disinvestment). The least experience with, or knowledge of, accounting must certainly make this clear, but it should be self-evident without even that elementary preparation.

Obviously, too, "replacement" of any concrete item of plant is, as already suggested, an accidental, technical detail in maintenance. What we call an item of capital itself is largely arbitrary. If any item is replaced bit by bit, the operation is correctly seen to represent routine maintenance, and the distribution of replacement through time does not change its theoretical character. The only reason for ever taking notice of replacement is to effect uniform

[14] [It is true that a business owner-manager who wants to consume more leisure will want to sell off a successful business firm rather than shrink it. But Knight here neglects, as if of no importance, cases like Hayek's tin mine where supply or demand shifts bring about relative price changes that *do* call for shrinkage in a line of production. Hayek clearly did not accept Knight's view of the business cycle problem: in a Hayekian crisis caused by unsustainable over-expansion of roundabout lines of production (without corresponding under-expansion elsewhere), real liquidation into consumption (a shrinkage in the planned structure of production) *is* at issue, not merely the reshuffling of ownership.—Ed.]

distribution of cost and return from the standpoint of a particular business unit. If the construction period is comparable to the service life, the technical activity itself is necessarily distributed. Many plant items last indefinitely without any maintenance expenditure distinguishable from the costs of operation or use of the items in question; another large fraction lasts indefinitely under purely routine maintenance, such as oiling, painting, cleaning and the like; another large fraction is permanent except for replacement of particular parts, which may be an insignificant fraction of the entire item; a fourth fraction is replaced piecemeal, as already suggested, with no particular date of superannuation (and in reality this category includes all replacement of material things); finally, a very large fraction has no natural or physical limitation of life, but may or may not pass out of use through supersession, in connection with technical and other changes involved in social evolution. Analytically, not only is all reproduction of wealth items (capital goods) included in the category of maintenance, but maintenance itself is only for special reasons, if at all, to be distinguished from other forms of "operating expense" which represent the division of joint product with the other agencies, physical and human, co-operating in production with the item in question. An analytically correct designation for new investment or disinvestment, from the aggregate standpoint, would be over- and under-maintenance respectively.

The consumable output of any "plant" or other productive organisation in any time interval, however short, assuming full maintenance, *i.e.* no disinvestment, is produced in that interval. Production in the sense of utilisation of a given plant and consumption of the product are simultaneous, and the "period of production" of consumed output is zero. The time required to put any particular unit of material through any physical process has nothing to do with the case, since it is a part of the production of any portion of output to maintain the plant involved, in its original condition; and plant maintenance includes replacements. This applies alike to materials which render final services, or are said to be "consumed," to raw materials, and to "auxiliary" goods, machines, tools and the like, which contribute to any quantity of output and which the consumer never sees.[15]

[15] The basic fallacy of the Böhm-Bawerk theory of capital is a twofold one which has vitiated the entire theoretical system of classical economics. Production is viewed as production of wealth, and wealth is viewed as concrete things. In reality, what is produced, *and consumed*, is services. The production of any service includes the maintenance of things used in the process, and this includes reproduction of any which are used up. Apart from such reproduction, really a detail of maintenance, things are "produced" only when added to a total stock. (This was seen by Mill, to the confusion of his definition of production—*i.e.* of productive labour—which refused to include services. See *Principles*, Ashley edition, p. 49.) [John Stuart Mill, *Principles of Political Economy with Some of Their Applications to Social Philosophy*, new ed., ed. W. J. Ashley (London, New York, and Toronto: Longmans, Green & Co., 1909 [and reprinted on seven dates between 1909 and the publication of Knight's article in 1935]). There Mill wrote, on p. 49, "All

On the other hand—in contrast with production as the correlate of consumption—the creation of any addition to plant is, at least "theoretically" (meaning in so far as correct accounting is possible), a process having a definite beginning and end, and hence occupying a definite time interval. The time required to produce the entire plant in use in any society at any time is simply its entire past history—or all history down to some antecedent date at which growth may have stopped. Regarding the social plant, however, some explanation is necessary as to the part to be *called* "capital," and the same explanation will make it clear that there can be no sound distinction between "primary" and "secondary" factors of production.

2. At any moment, or "as of" any particular date, and with reference to economic use and value, everything in existence which bears or represents productive capacity is without exception primary, *given*; viewed historically, all have been produced, in the economic process as a whole, extending down from the beginning of economic history. It is true that different items are in various degrees produced under "economic" conditions, *i.e.* by the use—in the case of creating new wealth, the investment—of existing resources on the basis of complete foreknowledge, and quantitative estimation in purely economic terms, of the results to accrue in the future from such investment. In "free" society, the human resources are presumably to a relatively minor extent produced under these conditions; and in the production of "property," including real estate, mineral workings, etc., rational foresight and the pecuniary motive control in varying degrees. It may be true that particular items are

---

labour is, in the language of political economy, unproductive, which ends in immediate enjoyment, without any increase of the accumulated stock of permanent means of enjoyment. And all labour, according to our present definition, must be classed as unproductive, which terminates in a permanent benefit, however important, provided that an increase of material products forms no part of that benefit."—Ed.] Moreover, the creation of an addition to wealth is production only in an accounting sense; for there is no corresponding consumption, either in the same interval or at any future time, as long as the wealth (in any physical form) is used to *produce* consumed services.

Secondly, wealth, which is identical with capital, can be treated quantitatively only by viewing it as capacity to render service. A service is measured by its economic value (equal to relative marginal utility) and wealth by *capitalised* service value. [Here Knight adopts Irving Fisher's view that the key analytical distinction is between stock (capital = wealth) and flow (income = consumption of subjectively valued services).—Ed.] Capitalisation is most naturally and realistically conceived as involving the transformation of all service-income from wealth which is not intrinsically permanent to a perpetuity basis by "depreciation." The quantity of wealth, or capital, in any item is the value of its net perpetual income, whether the life of the concrete item is zero or infinite or anything between. (Regarding the rate of capitalisation, see above, p. 82 [this volume, p. 105]; also, the article "Interest" in the *Encyclopedia of the Social Sciences* [Frank H. Knight, "Interest," in *Encyclopædia of Social Sciences*, ed. Edwin R. A. Seligman (New York: Macmillan, 1932), vol. 8, pp. 131–44], and an article in *Economica* for August 1934, referred to at the end of the present paper [Frank H. Knight, "Capital, Time, and the Interest Rate," *Economica*, n.s., vol. 1, no. 3, August 1934, pp. 257–86].)

simply "found," without any planned economic expenditure; but such finding must be accidental, unanticipated, or the competitive struggle for the opportunity of finding will itself tend to involve an investment equal to value realised. (The moral significance or social productivity of the investment is a separate issue.) The relation in production between various types of agencies is one of strictly mutual complementarity.

3. In "free" society, the creation of productive capacity in the form of human beings or human qualities is not *called* "investment," and the result is not *called* "capital." This usage is scientifically correct, because in free society human beings—the "things" bearing or embodying productive capacity in the form of "labour"—cannot be actually bought and sold, or their services mortgaged, or made the subject of an enforceable contract for a long period, and hence no definite money value can be placed upon them. They are not quantified and are not "wealth." The human being has no economic value to anyone but himself, and he has no reason for keeping a capital account with himself, even if it were possible to do so with any degree of accuracy. In connection with human beings, it is therefore impossible to distinguish among the three forms of consumption (*a*) for enjoyment and (*b*) for the purpose of maintaining productive capacity or (*c*) that of adding to the latter. All consumption directly by human beings, since it does not affect capital values in the marketable sense, has to be treated as ultimate consumption, even though we are well aware of the mixture of ends actually involved.[16]

4. Every new increment of investment, whatever physical or other form it may take, is added to an organised productive system. In fact, this is true in a doubly complex sense. In the first place, practically without exception, it will be added to some kind of more or less distinct primary technical production unit, a "plant" in the narrow sense (if not to a particular individual "machine"). But this individual plant will be technically interrelated with other plants, in both a "horizontal" and a "vertical" series. In the second place, any new increment of capital is the property of some owner, individual or corporate, and its rôle in production, and more especially in changes in production, will be profoundly affected by these ownership relations. In consequence, as noted above, the replacement of any physical item of equipment has in greater or less degree the character of replacing a part of a machine. The cost, yield, and value—*i.e.* the quantity—of an investment item or increment, reside largely in organic relationships, rather than in particular physical things or conditions.

5. Enough has been said to make it clear that neither of the processes dis-

[16] It is to be noted, however, that there is a form of capital, called "good will," which is created by investment, and owned and bought and sold, the real substance back of which is a state or attitude of human beings.

cussed by Professor Hayek in connection with the structure of investment (*i.e.* neither changes in the durability of goods nor changes in their construction period) exerts an identifiable effect on a definable "period of production" in society as a whole. Moreover, they are similarly unconnected with quantity of investment, and quantity of investment is likewise unconnected with any production period. Correspondences in this field are limited and accidental, without theoretical significance for the nature and rôle of capital. It is extremely difficult to give any intelligible meaning to a "period of production," and it certainly has no meaning of the sort assumed in the Böhm-Bawerk–Hayek theory of capital. The production period for consumed services, if the expression is to be used at all, is zero, while the production period for the capital equipment of society is all past economic history.

It is true that in production particular materials go through technical processes and exist in the form of particular named things for intervals which can be *more or less* definitely dated as to beginning and end. If a particular method of identifying and naming the things and dating the life termini of each could be agreed upon, and if the list itself remained unchanged, it would be possible to speak of a change in the average length of all such processes.[17] Both these assumptions are widely contrary to fact, and the period in question would have no meaning for economic analysis if determined. A practically indefinite number of "things," in every relation of simultaneity and succession, are involved in the production of any increment either of satisfaction or of wealth. There is also more or less used in business management discussions a notion of an average "turnover" of investment. This might be defined in several different ways and is not scientifically usable even for accounting purposes.[18] But none of these concepts is a genuine average, and none of them either corresponds to the Böhm-Bawerk conception of a production period, or has any significance for the theory of capital; none of them will at all necessarily increase in length with an increase in total investment.

If an account with a particular "thing" is set up and kept from the moment it begins to affect economic plans to the moment it ceases to do so, and even if the end of the interval really represents approximately complete liquidation into products already consumed—it is evident: First, that no assignment of a time interval can be made either (1) to the production and consump-

[17] The mode of averaging would be restricted by the fact that items approach zero and infinity as limits.

[18] In the *Economic Journal* for March 1934, Marschak very neatly shows that the conception of the production period, developed by Mr. Gifford (*Economic Journal*, Dec. 1933) reduces to one of these possible turnover formulas, namely capital divided by total income—incidentally one of the least meaningful. [J. Marschak, "A Note on the Period of Production," *Economic Journal*, vol. 44, no. 173, March 1934, pp. 146–51; C. H. P. Gifford, "The Concept of the Length of the Period of Production," *Economic Journal*, vol. 43, no. 172, December 1933, pp. 611–18.—Ed.]

tion of the increment of output consumed in any small increment of time, or (2) to the period of investment of the increment of resource services expended in any small increment of time. (Professor Hayek in effect admits this in his paper.) Second, it is also evident that if the capital-creation-and-use in question is profitable at all, the time required to produce the total amount of output yielded before final liquidation is probably *decreased* by the project. (If the product is unique this is true of its value.)

6. Exceptionally, if ever, strictly speaking, is real liquidation of a concrete item into consumed product in question, and only within fairly narrow limits is it possible. Where an enterprise as a whole is initially planned for liquidation (closing of its books) at a foreknown date, a part of the equipment used will be planned for the life of the enterprise, and another part not amenable to this treatment will be planned primarily for the largest possible recovery or "salvage" value. Even then, capital is typically invested in some other form as it is written off out of its gross yield. In general, capital investment is planned for perpetual maintenance, as capital, including any necessary replacement by items of some kind. Possibility of liquidation, and occasionally the fact, is important to an individual, but normally this means sale to a new owner. Mobility of investment is important both technically and economically; but the relation of construction period and service life to mobility constitutes two distinct problems (see below, section 8).

7. With reference to a new venture of any kind, which represents a net addition to capital—whether it is a new enterprise or plant, or a nominally distinct concrete device, an "improvement" in any existing item, the creation of good will, or whatever form it may take—the interval between the decision which is the starting point of the venture, marked by setting up an account with it, and the date when the result as a productive unit begins to operate at something like normal capacity, is more or less determinate. This is the construction period in the proper, accounting sense, for the item. It is a fallacy to treat this interval as a part of the production period for the output subsequently made by the aid of the capital produced. This might be reasonably done only if either (*a*) the entire future output of the investment increment through all time is considered as a unit, or[19] the investment is really liquidated and consumed, which implies a general net liquidation of the economic system. In any case, the entire social equipment in existence when the venture is started—accumulated through all past time—is included in the "primary factors" used indirectly through producing the new capital increment, which means that technically the production period is all past time. The fact that making an investment requires time no more adds to the production period for any subsequent product of any "unit" to which any incre-

[19] [Presumably "(*b*)" belongs here.—Ed.]

ment of investment is added than does the fact that disinvestment (see next section) requires time mean that that time, if it could be determined, would be added to the production period for the subsequent output of society, or of any definable unit of capital from which the particular decrement is subtracted.

In any society which as a whole maintains its total capital quantitatively intact, all liquidation is in effect transfer of investment from one holder or one form to another holder or form, or both.[20] No particular item of investment once made and incorporated into the productive system of a social economy can ever be said to be liquidated at any particular time, and this would remain true if the end of the world could be foreseen by any interval in advance, and if the entire system went through the most rational and complete possible process of liquidation. Thus the duration of an investment is to be completely separated in thinking from the durability of any particular thing or group of things in which the investment is "embodied." In general, the duration of all investments, in a society which is at least fully maintaining its total capital, is infinite, even though the investment "in" a particular thing, or the investment "owned by" a particular individual or corporate person, is liquidated, either through sale or through consumption of the replacement fund.

It is also to be emphasised that the amount of capital which can be withdrawn from any investment by under-maintenance has no definite relation to its cost of production. It is largely relative to the speed of withdrawal; but neither the amount "disinvestable" nor the possible speed of disinvestment has any definite relation, either to the construction period or to the "normal" annual maintenance charge. Amount and speed of withdrawal are both further relative to distance and accuracy of foresight, especially to plans at the time an investment is physically committed. The amount of the present wealth of any nation which could be liquidated into consumption in any interval before an announced annihilation catastrophe would be limited, however remote the date. But, as already noted, any investment item which is the subject of a capital account can be "written off" in any interval, if, and only if, it has a sufficient yield above pure interest; and no investment in things of limited productive life will ever knowingly be made unless the imputed income is adequate to write it off (with allowance for salvage value) and replace the source with one of equal yield, in that period.

8. The connection in which time is really significant is that of the *mobility*

[20] The notion of maintaining any capital quantitatively intact cannot be given exact definition; but this limitation applies to all quantitative analysis in economics, and the notion itself is clear and indispensable, and measurement, even, is fairly accurate. For most problems, moreover, the total in an absolute sense is not important; an addition to or subtraction from one account not involving a directly offsetting subtraction from or addition to some other is all that need be identified.

of capital, freedom to transfer it to some other use. But in this connection we must avoid a common and fatal confusion between real, technical and economic mobility, and something utterly different. What people really want to do, in the main, by way of liquidating investments, especially in connection with a depression, is to convert them into "money," not into consumable product, and this is, of course, a problem in the theory of money, and not one in the theory of capital or production.

Real movement of capital from one field to another may involve either of two processes, either the use of the same concrete things in a different connection, or their replacement by other things differently specialised. Physical transfer may, of course, in addition, be accompanied with more or less alteration or reconstruction. In the transfer of capital from one field to another, durability (*i.e.*, its opposite) is an element, but one the importance of which it is natural to exaggerate enormously. Mobility, whether through physical transfer or replacement, must be considered in connection with the structural integration of a particular item in the entire industrial system in which it is used, and this includes the "labour" of every kind and grade as well as the "property" element. Obviously, mobility has no meaning in connection, say, with a part of a machine, apart from the machine as a whole. But this is true, with a difference in degree at most, of the production unit of which the machine is an element. Even the business enterprise cannot be considered independently. (Any unit separately owned will, if mobile, be in an independent position in that it can always force the larger, relatively immobile unit of which it is a part to give it an income share on the basis of the best opportunity which may be open to it.) In general, the mobility of any item tends to be less than that of the most immobile item with which it is complementary in use—rather that of any organisation as a whole of which it is a part, and this immobility is likely to be much greater than that of any single item in it.

The discussion of mobility is confused by the further fact that the real problem is almost entirely one of uncertainty. As already shown, there is no problem of mobility if the time and conditions of transfer are anticipated when an investment is made. When either a particular transfer, or general fluidity at a known date in the future, is planned for when the investment is made, the effect on the durability or permanence of particular concrete items will run partly in each of the two possible opposite directions; in a complex unit as a whole, some items will be built more cheaply and of shorter life, in order to minimise loss on abandonment, while others will be made more expensive and more durable, but of more standardised design, so as to have the maximum value for other uses when the given project is liquidated. The latter case is common enough in connection with buildings, for example, where extra expense in construction is often incurred to facilitate re-adaptation to some other use in the event of a decline in the demand for the service for which they are initially designed.

9. Particularly in connection with cycle theory, actual mobility of investment is approached in importance by the possibility of temporary, partial postponement of maintenance, without loss of use value. Here it is of some consequence that the part of maintenance which figures as replacement superficially appears to be postponable by an interval bearing some relation to the service life of the items involved. But this is the standpoint of the individual enterprise and an accident of its scope. Actual technical possibility of postponing production of replacements without interrupting operations depends on a complex of conditions.

10. Of comparable importance, again, is the freedom to leave an item out of use without deterioration or other upkeep cost. There are, of course, types of property which deteriorate as fast when kept idle as when used at normal capacity, or even faster. Under this last item, again, the ramifying complementary technical relationships and connections of ownership must be considered in determining what is the effective investment unit for which freedom of use or non-use is in question.

So important that it must be repeated in conclusion, is the fact mentioned in connection with mobility (section above), that the entire notion of fluidity in investment in connection with crises and depressions is largely an individualistic delusion—a "fallacy of composition." In a time of depression, when people are clamouring most madly to convert assets into money, there is little or no question of an actual physical liquidation of plant into consumption. The phenomenon is partly one of maladjustment, mainly one of money, prices, and debts. The fluidity chiefly in question is marketability for cash, and the practical difficulty and the theoretical problem lie in the field of "cash" rather than in the technical properties of investment goods.[21]

[21] In this connection it is, of course, fundamental that in the modern world "cash" itself arises largely out of debts whose power to perform this function depends on their own liquidity in terms of "money" in a narrower sense. But the confusion of this liquidity of loans with the "disinvestability" of capital which is implied in the Hayek theory of crises is a fallacy even more egregious than those considered in detail above. Loan liquidity means, and can mean, nothing but marketability for money, either of the evidence of indebtedness as such or of disposable assets of the debtor. Maturity dates are largely illusory, superfluous and evil, but only their meaning is in question here. They make some or all of the assets of the borrower a guarantee of the money value of the debt at a stated date. To interpret a maturity as meaning an obligation of the debtor to "liquidate" in a real sense, *i.e.* convert his capital goods into products and turn these over to the creditor, is surely an absurdity difficult to surpass. There is small likelihood that the lender would want the products, and little more presumption that they would be more convertible into any particular amount of "money" than any other assets.

In connection with the "jam" which occurs at a time of depression, the way in which the situation would be altered if the "investment structure" in the dual sense discussed by Professor Hayek were lengthened or shortened, is a problem of almost infinite complexity. Only two or three considerations can be briefly mentioned here. First, it is undoubtedly true that the time required to carry out any industrial expansion involves a lag in yield which is an important factor affecting the amount of "over-investment," whether relative or absolute—or whatever that apparent over-development of capital goods industries which is of undoubted importance in cycle theory may finally be found to mean. And the time required to construct capital goods is a factor, but only one among other factors, in the lag of increase in output behind expansion activities. Second, immobility of the productive agencies tied up in any over-developed line is undoubtedly an important fact in the depression phenomenon. But (third) whatever rôle is assigned to technical maladjustments of any and every kind in cycle theory, it is perfectly certain that the durability of capital goods is only one factor in the economic immobility of capital itself, and also (fourth) that the immobility of labour (including, of course, specially trained people) is of fully comparable importance with the immobility of property; and furthermore (fifth), that economic inflexibility in the large is in large part a matter or price "stickiness," along with physical considerations.

In short: A depression, in its critical aspect of serious unemployment (of persons and of property) no doubt generally involves more or less previous mistaken commitment of resources, human and non-human, sustained by immobility. But it is essentially a matter of price maladjustment, sustained by price stickiness. If labour were mobile and wages flexible, no fixity in the capital structure would give rise to unemployment, of labour or capital, though efficiency might be greatly reduced. The importance of the first is in any case relative to the second. The rôle of capital durability and production period is limited to contributing toward the wrong commitment and immobility of a relatively small fraction of the productive resources of a system. It is at most a not very large fraction of another similar fraction of the cause or means of cure of the basic evils.

There is no theoretical reason why there should not be fully developed and completely typical cycles in a society in which no capital goods whatever were used. Such a situation may be visualised by considering what might happen if all economic production had the form of personal services, say, of vocal music, especially if largely organised in the form of the chorus. The phenomena of training periods and resistance to retraining, in relation to changes in demand, and to money, credit, and price changes and resistance to change, would be present and adequate to give rise to all the characteristic manifestations now met with. The example is especially in point since the "production period" would clearly be of zero length. Under these conditions no one would think of trying to compute an average period of immobility for a fraction of the productive resources of society and treat it as a "period of production."[22]

[22] Since the publication of the *Economic Essays in Honour of Gustav Cassel* and of Professor Hayek's article ["The Relationship between Investment and Output"], there has appeared in *Economica* an article of my own entitled "Capital, Time, and the Interest Rate" covering some of the same ground as the foregoing. If there is for some readers some repetition, no one is under compulsion to read both articles; and I am also reminded of the apology for repetition with which Herbert Spencer concluded the Preface to his *Data of Ethics*: "Only by varied iteration can alien conceptions be forced on reluctant minds." [Herbert Spencer, *The Data of Ethics* (London: Williams and Norgate, 1879), p. iv.—Ed.]

EIGHT

THE MYTHOLOGY OF CAPITAL[1]

> With every respect for the intellectual qualities of my opponent, I must oppose his doctrine with all possible emphasis, in order to defend a solid and natural theory of capital against a mythology of capital.
>
> —E. v. Böhm-Bawerk, *Quarterly Journal of Economics*, vol. xxi/2, February 1907, p. 282.

Summary

I. Professor Knight's argument, 119. — II. On some current misconceptions: 1. The investment periods and technological progress, 123; 2. They refer to factors, not products, 123; 3. The aggregate of such periods cannot be reduced to an average, nor is measurability essential, 124; 4. The periods refer always to the future, never to the past, 125; 5. The concept does not depend on a distinction between original and produced means of production, 126; 6. Nor is it only the original means of production whose investment periods can be changed, 127. — III. Professor Knight's criticism based on a misunderstanding, 127. — IV. His own position prevents him from giving any explanation of how the limitation of capital restricts the increase of output, 130. — V. An erroneous assertion following from his fundamental position: the value of capital goods when interest disappears, 136. — VI. Problems of capital and "perfect foresight," 138.

[1] [*Quarterly Journal of Economics*, vol. 50, no. 2, February 1936, pp. 199–228. The page references provided in the summary section have been silently updated to reflect the present volume.—Ed.]

I

Professor Knight's crusade against the concept of the period of investment[2] revives a controversy which attracted much attention thirty and forty years ago but was not satisfactorily settled at that time. In his attack he uses very similar arguments to those which Professor J. B. Clark employed then against Böhm-Bawerk.[3] However, I am not concerned here with a defense of the details of the views of the latter. In my opinion the oversimplified form in which he (and Jevons before him) tried to incorporate the time element into the theory of capital prevented him from cutting himself finally loose from the misleading concept of capital as a definite "fund," and is largely responsible for much of the confusion which exists on the subject; and I have full sympathy with those who see in the concept of a single or average period of production a meaningless abstraction which has little if any relationship to anything

[2] The following are the main articles in which Professor Knight has recently discussed the problem in question, and to which I shall refer in the course of this article by the numbers given in square brackets [ ]:

[1] ["]Capitalist Production, Time and the Rate of Return.["] *Economic Essays in Honour of Gustav Cassel*, London [George Allen & Unwin,] 1933, pp. 327–342.

[2] ["]Capital, Time, and the Interest Rate.["] *Economica* (new series), vol. 1, No. 3, August 1934, pp. 257–286.

[3] ["]Professor Hayek and the Theory of Investment.["] *Economic Journal*, vol. xlv, No. 177, March 1935, pp. 77–94.[Reprinted in this volume, pp. 100–117.—Ed.]

In addition, certain other articles by Professor Knight which bear closely on the subject and to some of which I may occasionally refer may also be mentioned.

[4] ["]Professor Fisher's Interest Theory: A Case in Point.["] *Journal of Political Economy*, vol. xxxix, No. 2, April 1931, pp. 176–212.

[5] Article on Interest, *Encyclopædia of Social Sciences*, [ed. Edwin R. A. Seligman,] vol. viii, [New York, Macmillan,] 1932, pp. 131–144.

[6] ["]The Ricardian Theory of Production and Distribution.["] *The Canadian Journal of Economics and Political Science*, vol. i, No. 1, February 1935, pp. 3–25.

The classical "Austrian" position has recently been ably and lucidly restated and defended against Professor Knight's criticism by Professor Fritz Machlup in an article, "Professor Knight and the 'Period of Production,'" which appeared, together with a Comment by Professor Knight, in the *Journal of Political Economy* [vol. 43, no. 5] for October 1935. [Machlup's article occupies pp. 577–624; Knight's "Professor Knight and the 'Period of Production': Comment," pp. 625–27.—Ed.] But this as well as Professor Knight's answer to Mr. Boulding (["]The Theory of Investment Once More: Mr. Boulding and the Austrians,["] in the last issue of this Journal [*Quarterly Journal of Economics*, vol. 50, no. 1, November 1935, pp. 36–37]) reached me too late to refer to them in the body of the article. But one or two references to these latest publications have been added in footnotes where I refer to the Comment and the Reply to Mr. Boulding with the numbers [7] and [8] respectively.

[3] [John Bates Clark (1847–1938) was an important American developer of marginal productivity theory. On his debate with Böhm-Bawerk, see Avi J. Cohen, "The Mythology of Capital or of Static Equilibrium? The Böhm-Bawerk/Clark Controversy," *Journal of the History of Economic Thought*, 30, June 2008, pp. 151–71.—Ed.]

in the real world. But Professor Knight, instead of directing his attack against what is undoubtedly wrong or misleading in the traditional statement of this theory, and trying to put a more appropriate treatment of the time element in its place, seems to me to fall back on the much more serious and dangerous error of its opponents of forty years ago. In the place of at least an attempt of analysis of the real phenomena, he evades the problems by the introduction of a pseudo-concept devoid of content and meaning, which threatens to shroud the whole problem in a mist of words.

It is with profound regret that I feel myself compelled to dissent from Professor Knight on this point, and to return his criticism. Quite apart from the great indebtedness which all economists must feel towards Professor Knight for his contributions to economic theory in general, there is no other author with whom I feel myself so much in agreement, even on some of the central questions of the theory of interest, as with Professor Knight. His masterly expositions of the relationship between the productivity and the "time-preference" element in the determination of the rate of interest[4] should have removed, for all time I hope, one of the worst misunderstandings which in the past have divided the different camps of theorists. Under these conditions anything which comes from him carries great weight, particularly when he attaches such importance to it that he tries "to force his views on reluctant minds by varied iteration." It is not surprising that he has already gained some adherents to his views.[5] But this only makes it doubly necessary to refute what seems to me to be a series of erroneous conclusions, founded on one basic mistake, which already in the past has constituted a serious bar to theoretical progress, and which would threaten to balk every further advance in this field, if its pronouncement by an authority like Professor Knight were left uncontradicted.

This basic mistake—if the substitution of a meaningless statement for the solution of a problem can be called a mistake—is the idea of capital as a fund which maintains itself automatically, and that, in consequence, once an amount of capital has been brought into existence the necessity of reproducing it presents no economic problem. According to Professor Knight "all capital is normally conceptually, perpetual,"[6] "its replacement has to be taken for

[4] Cf. particularly articles [4] and [5] quoted above.

[5] Cf. H[oward] S. Ellis, ["]Die Bedeutung der Productionsperiode für die Krisentheorie,["] and P. Joseph and K. Bode, ["]Bemerkungen zur Kapital- und Zinstheorie,["] both articles in *Zeitschrift für Nationalökonomie*, vol. vi, [no. 2,] 1935. [Ellis' article occupies pp. 145–69; Joseph and Bode's, pp. 170–195.—Ed.] R[agnar] Nurkse, ["]The Schematic Representation of the Structure of Production,["] *Review of Economic Studies*, vol. ii, [no. 3, June] 1935 [pp. 232–44]. S[une] Carlson, ["]On the Notion of Equilibrium in Interest Theory,["] *Economic Studies*, No. 1, Krakow, [published by the Economics Institute, Polish Academy of Science,] 1935 [pp. 1–25].

[6] [2], p. 259; a few pages later (p. 266) the treatment of capital once invested as "perpetual" is even described as the "realistic" way of looking at the matter.

granted as a technological detail,"[7] and in consequence "there is no production process of determinate length, other than zero or 'all history,'"[8] but "in the only sense of timing in terms of which economic analysis is possible, *production and consumption are simultaneous*."[9] Into the reasons why the capital maintains itself thus automatically we are not to inquire, because under the stationary or progressive conditions, which alone are considered, this is "axiomatic."[10] On the other hand it is asserted that "making an item of wealth more durable" or "using a longer period of construction,"[11] i.e. lengthening the time dimension of investment in either of the two possible ways, is only one among an "accurately speaking, infinite number" of possible ways of investing more capital, which are later even described as "really an infinite number of infinities."[12] According to Professor Knight, "what the Böhm-Bawerk school's position amounts to is simply selecting these two details which are of the same significance as any of an infinity of other details"[13] while in fact "additional capital is involved in very different ways for lengthening the cycle and for increasing production without this lengthening."[14] "Time is one factor or dimension among a practically infinite number, and quantity of capital may and does vary quite independently of either of these time intervals."[15]

[7] [2], p. 264. At one point Professor Knight does indeed say that "the most important fact requiring clarification is the nature of capital maintenance" ([3], p. 84 [this volume, p. 107]). But instead of the patient analysis of how and why capital is maintained, which after this we feel entitled to expect, we get nothing but a concept of capital as a mystical entity, an "integrated organic conception" which maintains itself automatically. Professor Knight does not actually use the word "automatic" in this connection, but his insistence on the supposed fact that the replacement of capital "has to be taken for granted as a technological detail" can hardly have any other meaning but that it needs no explanation in economic terms and is, therefore, from the point of view of the economist "automatic."

[8] [3], p. 78, cf. also [8], p.64. [Hayek omits a comma that followed "zero" in the quoted passage from Knight.—Ed.]

[9] [2], p. 275.

[10] [3], p. 84.

[11] [2], p. 268.

[12] [2], p. 270.

[13] [2], p. 268.

[14] [3], p. 81.

[15] [6], p. 82. An attempt to clear up by correspondence at least some of the differences between us has only had the effect of making the gulf which divides our opinion appear wider than ever. In a letter written after reading an earlier draft of the present paper, Professor Knight emphasizes that he "categorically denies that there is any determinate time interval" "which elapses between the time when some product might have been obtained from the available factors and the time the product actually accrues." This can hardly mean anything more than either that no postponement whatever of consumption is possible, or at least that, once such a postponement has taken place, it is impossible to use for current consumption any of the factors which would be needed to maintain or replace the capital goods created by the first investment. I find it difficult to believe that Professor Knight should want to assert either. Quite apart from the

Against this I do indeed hold that, firstly, all the problems which are commonly discussed under the general heading of "capital" do arise out of the fact that part of the productive equipment is non-permanent and has to be deliberately replaced on economic grounds, and that there is no meaning in speaking of capital as something permanent which exists apart from the essentially impermanent capital goods of which it consists. Secondly, that an increase of capital will *always* mean an extension of the time dimension of investment, that capital will be required to bring about an increase of output only in so far as the time dimension of investment is increased.[16] This is relevant, not only for the understanding of the transition to more capitalistic methods, but equally if one wants to understand how the limitation of the supply of capital limits the possibilities of increasing output under stationary conditions.

This is not a dispute about words. I shall endeavor to show that, on the one hand, Professor Knight's approach prevents him from seeing at all how the choice of particular methods of production is dependent on the supply of capital, and from explaining the process by which capital is being maintained or transformed, and that, on the other hand, it leads him to undoubtedly wrong conclusions. Nor does this discussion seem necessary solely because of the objections raised by Professor Knight. In many respects his conclusions are simply a consistent development of ideas which were inherent in much of the

---

fact that such statements would, as it seems to me, stand in flagrant contrast to all empirical evidence, the contrary has been asserted by Professor Knight himself as the first of "the three empirical facts that form the basis of a sound theory of capital." This, in his words ([2], p. 258), is "the simple 'technological' fact that it is possible to increase the volume (time rate) of production after any interval by the use during that interval of a part of existing productive resources—in large part the *same* resources previously and subsequently used for producing 'current consumption income'—to produce, *instead* of current consumption income, instruments of agencies of various sorts, tangible or intangible, which when produced become 'productive' of *additional* current income. This activity or process we call *investment.*" (In giving permission to quote the above sentence from his letter Professor Knight adds: "It would induce to clearness to add that it is my view that the interval in question approaches determinateness as we impose stationary or given conditions in a sense so rigid that such an expression as 'might have been obtained' loses all meaning." I am afraid this explanation leaves me more perplexed than ever. As I have tried to show in the last section of this paper, all Professor Knight's former argument *against* the concept of a determinate investment period depends exactly on the most rigid static assumptions of this kind.)

[16] [This statement surprisingly seems to deny the possibility of a "horizontal" expansion of capital and output. The argument behind it can be found in n. 19 below and in section 3. Hayek there assumes that the work-age population is constant. An increase in employment awaits an increase in the marginal productivity of those unemployed or out of the labor market, so as to enable firms to pay higher wages that meet or exceed the value that these potential employees put on leisure, and thereby awaits the construction of more capital goods per head, which means capital "deepening" for the economy as a whole. The argument does not rule out horizontal expansion of a regional economy's production by adding immigrants who bring capital with them, or by annexation of territory.—Ed.]

traditional treatment of the subject,[17] and which lead to all kinds of pseudo-problems and meaningless distinctions that have played a considerable rôle in recent discussions on the business cycle.

II

Before I can enter upon attempting to refute Professor Knight's assertion, it is necessary to dispose of certain preliminary matters. There are certain ideas which Professor Knight and others seem to associate with the view I hold but which in fact are not relevant to it. I do not want to defend these views but rather to make it quite clear that I regard them as erroneous. Practically all the points to which I now call attention were either implicitly or explicitly contained in that article of mine which Professor Knight attacks.[18] As he has chosen to disregard them, it is necessary to set them out in order.

(1) It should be quite clear that the technical changes involved, when changes in the time structure of production are contemplated, are *not* changes due to changes in technical knowledge. The concept of increasing productivity due to increasing roundaboutness arises only when we have to deal with increases of output which are dependent on a sufficient amount of capital being available, and which were impossible before only because of the insufficient supply of capital. This assumes in particular that the increase of output is not due to changes of technical knowledge. It *excludes* any changes in the technique of production which are made possible by new inventions.

(2) It is not true that the periods which it is contended are necessarily lengthened when investment is increased are periods involved in the production of a particular type of product. They are rather *periods for which particular factors are invested*, and it would be better for this reason if the term "period of production" had never been invented and if only the term "period of investment" were used. To give here only one example: it is not only conceivable, but it is probably a very frequent occurrence that an increase in the supply of capital may lead not to a change in the technique of production in any particular line of industry, but merely to a transfer of factors from industries where they have been invested for shorter periods to industries where they are invested for

[17] For an effective criticism of related earlier views cf. particularly F. W. Taussig, ["]Capital, Interest and Diminishing Returns,["] in this Journal [*Quarterly Journal of Economics*], vol. xxii, [no. 3,] May 1908, pp. 339–344.

[18] ["]On the Relationship between Investment and Output,["] *Economic Journal*, [vol. 44, no. 174,] June, 1934, [pp. 207–31; included in the present volume—Ed.] cp. particularly p. 212, note 1, and p. 226 for point (2), p. 217 for (3), p. 210, note 1, and p. 227 for (4), p. 230, note for (5), and p. 228 for (6). [Knight specifically criticizes this article by Hayek in Knight's above-listed article [3], also included in the present volume.—Ed.]

longer periods. In this case the periods for which one has to wait for any particular type of product have all remained unaltered, but the periods of investment of the factors that have been transferred from one industry to another have been lengthened.[19]

(3) *It is not proposed, and is in fact inadmissible, to reduce the description of the range of periods for which the different factors are invested to an expression of the type of a single time dimension such as the average period of production.* Professor Knight seems to hold that to expose the ambiguities and inconsistencies involved in the notion of an average investment period serves to expel the idea of time from capital theory altogether. But it is not so. In general it is sufficient to say that the investment period of some factors has been lengthened, while those of all others have remained unchanged; or that the investment periods of a greater quantity of factors have been lengthened than the quantity of factors whose investment periods have been shortened by an equal amount; or that the investment period of a given quantity of factors has been lengthened by more than the investment period of another equal amount has been shortened. It is true that in some cases (e.g. when the investment period of one factor is shortened, and at the same time the period for which a greater quantity of another factor is invested is lengthened by a smaller interval) the determination of the net effect of the changes of the investment periods of different factors in different directions raises problems which cannot be so easily answered. But the concept of the average period, which was introduced mainly to solve this difficulty, does not really provide a solution. The obstacle here is that the reinvestment of accrued interest has to be counted equally as the investment of an amount of factors of corresponding value for the same period. In consequence the only way in which an aggregate of waiting can be described, and the amount of waiting involved in different investment structures can be com-

[19] A similar case is that where an addition to the supply of capital makes it possible to employ factors (say labor) which before were unemployed. The first question to ask here is how exactly is it that an increase of capital makes their employment possible. We shall have to assume that without this capital the marginal product of this labor would have been lower than the wage at which they would have been willing to work. In what sense can it now be said that an increase of their marginal product is conditional upon more capital becoming available, i.e. why was it impossible, without this increase of capital, to employ them in the more productive processes? I cannot see that the necessity of previous accumulation can mean anything but an increase of the periods for which either the factors immediately concerned, or some other factors employed in providing the former with equipment, are invested.

In the traditional exposition of the theory of roundabout production this case, where only total capital, but not necessarily capital per head of those employed, has been increased, has been taken account of by saying that the average period of production (i.e. the average period for which the labor actually employed is invested) will only increase when capital per head increases, but will remain constant when capital is increased by an extension of its "labor dimension" instead of its "time dimension." Altho this mode of expression is sometimes useful, I think it has to be abandoned together with the concept of the average period of production.

pared, is by means of a process of summation, in the form of a double integral over the function describing the rates, at which the factors that contribute to the product of any moment are applied, and at which interest accrues.

It should, however, be especially noted that the assertion that it is conceptually possible to conceive of the aggregate capital of a society in terms of possible waiting periods does not mean that *the total period of production* (or the aggregate of all periods of production) of an economic system is necessarily *a phenomenon capable of measurement.* Whether this is the case (and in my opinion it is very unlikely) is altogether irrelevant for the problem at issue. What is essential is solely that whenever a change occurs in any part of the economic system which involves that more (or less) capital is used in the industry or industries concerned, this always means that some of the factors used there will now bring a return only after a longer (or shorter) time interval than was the case in their former use. As Professor Knight himself rightly says, "the rate of interest which determines the value of all existing capital goods is determined exclusively at the *margin of growth*, where men are comparing large, short segments of income flow with thinner streams reaching out to the indefinite future."[20] It is at this margin of growth (of every individual firm and industry) where the extensions of investment occur and where the decisive question arises whether the productivity of investment is a function of time and whether the limitation of investment is a limitation of the time we are willing or able to wait for a return.[21]

(4) It is quite erroneous to regard propositions concerning the greater productivity of roundabout methods as depending upon the possibility of identifying the contribution of the "original" factors of the remote past. In order to be able to give an intelligible description of a continuous stationary process

[20] [2], p. 278. Cp. also [8], p. 45. The disagreement here concerns the question whether it is true that men directly and irrevocably exchange "short segments of income flow" against "thinner streams reaching into the *indefinite* future" or whether it is not essential to take into account that the immediate result of the sacrifice of present income is an equally limited income flow of a different time-shape which must be clearly defined as regards size and shape in order to make it possible to decide in the particular case whether the sacrifice is justified. And this limited income stream which is the result of the first investment becomes a permanent income stream only by an infinite series of further decisions when the opportunity of consuming more now and less in the future has to be considered every time. By jumping directly to the desired result, the permanent income stream, Professor Knight slurs over so much that is essential for an understanding of the process that any use of his concept of capital for an analysis of the rôle of this capital in the course of further changes becomes quite impossible.

[21] As Professor Knight now admits "that in so far as any single investment, negligible in size in comparison with the economic system of which it is a part, represents things consumed and reproduced in a regular cycle, the quantity of capital in that investment does bear a mathematical relation to the length of the cycle" and that in this connection some of his "previously published statements have been too sweeping," there is perhaps some hope that ultimately some sort of agreement can be reached along these lines. (Cf. [7], p. 627.)

in which factors are invested at any one moment, some of whose products will mature at almost any later moment, one of two methods is possible. Either we can concentrate on all factors invested in any one interval, and relate them to the stream of product derived from it. Or we can concentrate on the product maturing during a short interval, and relate it to the factors which have contributed to it. But whichever of the two methods we select, in all cases *only the future time intervals* between the moments when the factors are, or will be invested, and the moment when the product will mature are relevant, and *never the past periods* which have elapsed since the investment of some "original factors." The theory looks forward, not back.[22]

(5) It is equally erroneous to regard the theory as depending on any distinction between "original" or "primary" and produced means of production. It makes no fundamental difference whether we describe the range of investment periods for *all* factors existing at the beginning of the period,[23] or whether we just describe the range of periods for which those services of the permanent factors are invested that only become available for investment at successive moments as they accrue. I think it is more convenient to use the second method, and to describe the investment structure by what I have called the investment function of the services of these permanent factors. But whether this distinction—which is based on the fact that some of the productive resources have to be deliberately replaced, while others are regarded as not requiring replacement on economic grounds—is accepted or not, in no case is a distinction between "primary" or "original" and "produced" means

[22] In so far as Professor Knight's aim is merely to drive out the remnants of a cost-of-production theory of value which still disfigure many expositions of the theory of capital (cf. [8], p. 45) I am all with him. But while I fully agree that there is no necessary connection between the present value of capital and the volume of past investment, I do maintain that there is a very close connection between the present and anticipated future values of capital on the one hand and the periods for which resources are invested at present on the other.

[23] A peculiar confusion in this respect occurs in the article of Miss Joseph and Mr. Bode quoted above (p. 174) where it is asserted that if all existing productive resources were taken into account, the period of production would "of course" become *zero*. It is true that the impossibility of drawing a fundamental distinction between the "original factors" and the "intermediate products" is one of the considerations which invalidate the construction of an "*average*" period of production. But whether we describe the investment structure by an expression representing the rate at which the product of all resources existing at any one moment will mature during the future, or by an expression representing the rate at which the marginal additions will mature which are due to the services of the permanent factors applied at that moment, is merely a difference of exposition. As will be easily seen, the former is simply the integral of the latter and can be represented by the area of the figure which is bounded by the investment curve which represents the latter. [These last two sentences sketch the concepts that Hayek would elaborate in *The Pure Theory of Capital*, ed. Lawrence H. White, vol. 12 of *The Collected Works of F. A. Hayek* (Chicago: University of Chicago Press, 2007), ch. 8, as the "output curve" and the "input curve."—Ed.]

of production necessary in order to give the concept of the investment function a definite sense.

(6) Last and closely connected with the preceding point, it is not necessarily the case that all "intermediate products" or "produced means of production" are highly specific, and that in consequence any change in the investment structure can only be brought about by investing the "original" factors for longer or shorter periods. This seems frequently to be implied in analysis which follows Böhm-Bawerkian lines. But of course there is no reason why it should be true. The periods for which non-permanent resources are being invested are as likely to be changed as the periods of investment of the services of the permanent resources.[24]

III

Most of the critical comments in Professor Knight's articles are due to misunderstandings of one or more of these fundamental points. But while each of them seems to be the source of some confusion, probably none was in this respect quite as fertile as number two. The idea that lengthening the process of production must always have the result that a particular kind of product will now be the result of a longer process, or that a person who invests more capital in his enterprise must therefore necessarily lengthen the period of production in this business, seems to be at the root of his assertion that capital can be used otherwise than to lengthen the time dimension of investment, as well as of his statement that I have practically admitted this.

As a proof of the former contention Professor Knight cites a single concrete example, taken from agriculture. "Taking population as given," he writes,[25] "raising *more* plants of the *same* growth period will also require more 'stock,' but *will not* affect the length of the cycle, while the *addition* to total production of varieties of *shorter* growth, say yielding two harvests per year instead of one, will involve an increase of capital while *shortening* the average cycle." Unfortunately Professor Knight only adds that "additional capital is involved in very different ways for lengthening the cycle and for increasing production without this lengthening," but does not tell us how exactly the additional capital

[24] It is perhaps necessary, in order to forestall further misunderstandings, to add as point (7) the main conclusion of the article of mine which Professor Knight attacked. It is that the periods of investment are not in all cases given as technical data but can in many instances only be determined by a process of value-imputation. This is particularly true in the case of durable goods, where the technical data only tell us how long we have to wait for a particular unit of its services, but not to what share of the factors invested in it this unit has to be attributed. This attribution, however, involves an imputation purely in value terms.

[25] [3], p. 81.

is used for increasing production otherwise than by lengthening the period for which some resources are invested. If he had stopped to inquire he would soon have found that even in the cases where his quite irrelevant "cycle" of the particular process remains constant, or is actually shortened, additional capital will be used in order to invest some resources for longer periods than before, and will only be needed if this is the case.

As Professor Knight has not stated why, in his example, either of the two new methods of cultivation will only be possible if new capital becomes available, it will be necessary to review the different possibilities which exist in this respect. Changes in technical knowledge must clearly be excluded and apparently Professor Knight also wants to exclude changes in the amount of labor used, altho it is not quite clear what the assumption "taking population as given" exactly means. If it is to mean that the quantity of all labor which contributes in any way to the product is assumed to be constant, and to be invested for a constant period, it is difficult to see how, with unchanged technical knowledge, they should suddenly be able to raise more plants and to use more capital. There seem to be only three possibilities, and all of them clearly imply a lengthening of the period for which some of the factors are invested.

(1) It may be assumed that the additional capital is used to buy instruments, etc., which are now made by people who were before directly employed in raising the crop;
(2) or it may be used to buy instruments to be made by people who before were employed to produce something else and have been attracted to making instruments, and thereby contributing to the output in question, by the new capital which has become available for the instruments;
(3) or that the additional capital is used to employ additional people.

Case (1) clearly contradicts the assumption that the periods for which the units of the given labor forces are invested are not lengthened, since the amount of time that will elapse between the making of the instrument and the maturing of the crop will clearly be longer than the period which elapses between the direct application of labor in raising the crop and its maturity. Cases (2) and (3) seem to be in conflict with the assumption of constant population. But in these cases, too, an increase of stock in society will only take place if the labor drawn to this particular line of production from elsewhere is now invested for a longer period than before. (I take it for granted here that additional capital means capital newly saved, and not merely transferred from elsewhere, since nobody, of course, wants to contend that a mere transfer of capital from one line of industry to another, which is accompanied by a similar transfer of the labor for whose investment the capital is required, need lead to an extension of the period for which any resources are invested.) Only if the labor which is now drawn to the process in question has before been invested for shorter periods than it will either in producing agriculture implements (case (2)), or in directly raising the crop (case (3)), will its diversion to the new use cause a temporary gap in the stream of consumable income, which will fall short of the value of the current services of the factors of production, and therefore require some saving or "new capital."

In Professor Knight's second case, that of additional production of shorter duration, he has again neglected to state why this should only become possible if additional capital becomes available. For the same reasons it seems to me to follow that this new production can be dependent on a new supply of capital coming forward only if the other factors required have before been invested for shorter periods.[26]

Evidently this example in no way proves that a case is conceivable where additional capital is used without having the effect of lengthening the investment period of some factor yet this example is the only thing in Professor Knight's article which even attempts a demonstration of his main thesis.

The same failure to see the point here involved at all leads Professor Knight also to misinterpret completely a statement of my own, and to describe it "as very nearly a 'give away,'" while in fact it simply refers to this case, where the lengthening of the investment structure is brought about not by lengthening any particular process (choosing a more time-consuming technique in the production of a particular product) but by using a greater share of the total factors of production than before in the relatively more time-consuming processes. What I actually said was, that a fall in the rate of interest would lead to the production of a greater quantity of durable goods, and that—explaining this further—"more goods (or, where possible, more durable goods) *of this kind* will be produced simply because the more distant part of the expected services will play a greater rôle in the considerations of the entrepreneur and will lead him to invest more on account of these more distant returns." Even if this statement was not very fortunately phrased[27] it should have been evident to anyone who has ever made an effort to understand the different ways in which extensions in the time dimension of investment may take place that it referred to the case where the periods for which particular factors are invested is being lengthened in consequence of their transfer from a less to a more capitalistic process of production. The production of more goods of the same

[26] I am afraid I am unable to see to what case the sentence in the same paragraph beginning with "in the third case" refers.

[27] My meaning would have been expressed better if, instead of speaking of the production of more goods of the kind, I had said "a greater quantity of the relatively more durable goods will be produced," or "goods of still greater durability made in place of those produced before." [In quoting himself, Hayek adds the emphasis and changes "the kind" to "this kind." See "On the Relationship between Investment and Output," this volume, p. 93.—Ed.]

(relatively durable) kind *does* therefore mean a change in the investment function for society as a whole in the direction of lengthening the time dimension of production.

IV

More serious than these misunderstandings about what the "period of production" analysis implies is the failure to see that without such an analysis no answer whatever can be given to the fundamental question: how the limitation of the available capital limits the choice among the known methods of production. This question is closely connected with the further problem, whether, and in what sense, the non-permanent resources existing at any one moment can be regarded as one homogeneous factor of determinate magnitude, as a "fund" of definite size which can be treated as a given datum in the sense in which the "supply of capital" or simply the "existing capital" is usually treated.

It is necessary first to say a few words about the reason why it is only in connection with the non-permanent resources that the problems which can properly be called problems of capital arise. The very concept of capital arises out of the fact that, where non-permanent resources are used in production, provision for replacement of the resources used up in production must be made, if the same income is to be enjoyed continually, and that in consequence part of the gross produce has to be devoted to their reproduction. But the fact that it may be regarded as the "normal" case that people will do so, with the aim of obtaining the same income in perpetuity, does not mean that therefore capital itself becomes in any sense perpetual. On the contrary the very problem of capital accounting arises only because, and to the extant that, the component parts of capital are not permanent, and it has no meaning, in economic analysis, to say that apart from the human decision, which we have yet to explain, the aggregate of all the non-permanent resources becomes some permanent entity. The problem is rather to say how the existence of a given stock of non-permanent resources makes possible their replacement by newly produced[28] instruments, and at the same time limits the extent to which

[28] I am afraid I feel compelled to disregard the special meaning which Professor Knight wants to attach to the term production. A concept of production which would compel us to say that a man engaged in the production of some instrument which is to replace some similar existing instrument, and which at some time in the future will contribute to the satisfaction of a desire, either produces not at all or produces not the final product in whose manufacture the instrument he makes is actually used, but a similar product which is consumed at the moment when he applies his labor to the instrument, seems to me an absurd abuse of words. But it is on this "concept" and nothing else that the assertion that production and consumption are simultaneous is based (like J. B. Clark's theorem of the "synchronization" of production and consumption).

this can be done.[29] And this raises the question in what sense these different capital goods can be said to have a common quality, a common characteristic, which entitles us to regard them as parts of one factor, one "fund," or which makes them to some extent substitutable for each other. What creates the identity which makes it possible to say that one capital good has been effectively replaced by another one, or that the existence of the one makes its replacement by another possible? What is that medium thru which the substance, commonly called capital in the abstract, can be said to be transformed from one concrete form into another? Is there such a thing, as is implied in the habitual use of terms by economists? or is it not conceivable that the thing which they all have in mind is that condition affecting the possibilities of production which cannot be expressed in terms of a substantive quantity?

Altho Professor Knight rather overstresses the case where a stock of capital goods is maintained by the preservation or replacement of the same items, his assertion that capital is permanent is of course not based on this assumption. The crucial case on which its meaning must be tested, and the only case where the question arises whether capital as something different from the individual instruments is permanent at all, is the case where capital goods that are worn out are replaced by capital goods of a different kind, which in many cases will not even help to produce the same services to the consumer but will contribute to render altogether different services. What does the assertion that the capital is permanent mean here? It must evidently mean more than that there will always be some capital in existence. If it has any sense it must mean that the quantity of capital is kept constant. But what is the criterion which determines whether the new capital goods intended to replace the old ones are exactly their equivalent, and what assures us that they will always be replaced by such equivalent quantities?

To these questions Professor Knight provides no answer, but, altho admitting that he has no exact answer, postulates that the idea must be treated as if it had a definite meaning if we are to get anywhere. "The notion of maintaining any capital quantitatively intact" he writes,[30] "cannot be given exact defi-

[29] On the general subject of the amortization of capital Professor Knight is not only rather obscure but his different pronouncements are clearly inconsistent. In [2], p. 273 he writes: "In reality most investments not only begin at a fairly early date to yield their income in consumable services . . . but in addition they begin fairly soon to yield more than interest on cost in this form, and *entirely liquidate themselves in a moderate period of time.* This additional flow of consumable services is ordinarily treated as a replacement fund, but *is available for consumption or for reinvestment* in any form and field of use at the will of the owner." [Emphasis added by Hayek.—Ed.] But in [3], p. 83, in order to support his thesis about the perpetuity of capital, this periodic liquidation is denied: "It cannot now escape observation that 'capital' is an integrated, organic conception, and the notion that the investment in a particular instrument comes back periodically in the form of product, giving the owner freedom to choose whether he will re-invest or not, is largely a fiction and a delusion."

[30] [3], p. 90. Footnote.

nition; but this limitation applies to all quantitative analysis in economics, and the notion itself is clear and indispensable, and measurement, even, is fairly accurate."

Now, as I have tried to show in considerable detail in another place,[31] the notion of maintaining capital *quantitatively* intact, far from being either clear or indispensable, presupposes a behavior of the capitalist-entrepreneurs which under dynamic conditions will sometimes be impossible and rarely reasonable for them to adopt. To assume that under changing conditions capital will be maintained constant in any quantitative sense is to assume something which will never happen and any deductions derived from this assumption will therefore have no application to anything in the real world.

In some places[32] Professor Knight does, it is true, come somewhat nearer a realistic assumption by stating that what people aim to maintain constant is not some physical or value dimension of capital, but its "capacity to render service."[33] But even accepting this assumption it proves in no way that people will also always be capable of maintaining this capacity to render service, and, what is more important, it does not in any way help us to explain in what way this "capacity to render service" is limited, why and how it is possible to transfer it from one concrete manifestation in a capital good into another one. It still leaves us with the impression that there is a sort of substance, some fluid of definite magnitude which flows from one capital good into another, and it gives us no indication of the set of conditions which actually at any given moment allows us to maintain output at a particular figure.

The fact that we possess at any one moment, in addition to those natural resources which are expected to render services permanently without any deliberate replacement, an amount of non-permanent resources which enable us to consume more than we could if only the former were available, will help us to maintain consumption *permanently* above this level only if by investing some of the services of the permanent resources for some time they will

[31] ["]The Maintenance of Capital,["] *Economica*, [n.s., vol. 2, no. 7,] August 1935 [pp. 241–76]. [Included in the present volume.—Ed.]

[32] [3], p. 86, note: "Wealth, which is identical with capital, can be treated quantitatively only by viewing it as capacity to render service." Also [2], p. 267: "As long as capital is maintained by replacing the capital goods, *if* their life is limited, by others of any form with equal earning capacity in imputed income . . ."

[33] Professor Knight, however, by no means consistently adheres to this view. The idea that the quantity of capital which is to be regarded as "perpetual" is a quantity of value occurs again and again. He says, for example, that "there is 'of course' no product yielded by an agency until after full provision has been made for maintaining it, or the investment in it, intact, *in the value sense*." ([2], p. 280.) [Emphasis added by Hayek.—Ed.] And similarly, a few pages later (p. 283): "New investments represent additions to all the investment previously made in past time. The amount of such investment cannot indeed be stated quantitatively in any other way than as the capitalized value of existing income sources under existing conditions."

bring a greater return than they would have given if they were used for consumption when they first became available. If this were not the case no existing quantity of "capacity to render service" in a non-permanent form would enable us to replace it by some new instruments with the same capacity to render service. We might spread the use of the services of these non-permanent factors over as long a period as we like, but after the end of this period no more would be available for consumption than could be obtained from the current use of the permanent services.

That actually we are able to replace the "capacity to render service" represented by the non-permanent resources, and by doing so maintain income permanently higher than what could be obtained from the permanent services only, is due to the *two* facts: first, that the existence of the non-permanent resources allows us to forego for the present some of the services of the existing resources without reducing consumption below the level at which it might have been kept with the permanent resources only, *and*, second, that by investing certain factors for some time we get a greater product than we would have otherwise got from them. Both these factors, the extent to which any given stock of non-permanent resources enables us to "wait" and the extent to which investment enables us to increase the product from the factors invested, are variable. And it is for this reason that only a very detailed analysis of the time structure of production, of the relationship between the periods for which individual factors have been invested and the product derived from them, can help us to understand the forces which direct the use of the current resources for the replacement of capital.

By stressing this relationship the period-of-production analysis (and to some extent already the older wage-fund and abstinence theories) introduced an element into the theory of capital without which no understanding of the process of maintenance and transformation of capital is possible. But the idea was not sufficiently worked out to make it quite clear how exactly the existence of a given stock of capital goods affected the possibilities of renewed investment. The Böhm-Bawerkian theory in particular went astray in assuming, with the older views that Professor Knight now wants to revive,[34] that the quantity of capital (or the "possibility to wait") was a simple magnitude, a homogeneous fund of clearly determined size. The particular assumption made by Böhm-Bawerk and his immediate followers, which may have some justification as a first approximation for didactic purposes, but which is certainly misleading if

[34] [8], p. 57: "The basic issue is the old and familiar one of choice between two conceptions of capital. In one view, it consists of 'things' of limited life which are periodically worn out or used up and reproduced; in the other, it is a 'fund' which is maintained intact tho the things in which it is invested may come and go to any extent. In the second view, which of course is the one advocated here, the capital 'fund' may be thought of as either a value or a 'capacity' to produce a perpetual flow of value."

it is maintained beyond the first stage, is that the existing stock of capital goods corresponds to a fixed quantity of consumers' goods and is therefore, on the further assumption of a given rate of consumption, uniquely associated with a definite total or average waiting period which it makes possible. The basis of this assumption was apparently the idea that every existing capital good was completely specific in the sense that it could be turned into only one particular quantity of consumers' goods by a process which could in no way be varied. On this assumption any present stock of capital could, of course, be regarded as equivalent to one, and only one, quantity of consumers' goods which would become available over a fixed period of time at a predetermined and invariable rate. This simplified picture of the existing stock of capital representing a "subsistence fund" of determined magnitude which would provide a support for a definite period and therefore enable us to undertake production processes of a corresponding average length is undoubtedly highly artificial and of little use for the analysis of more complicated processes.

Actually the situation is so much more complicated and requires a much more detailed and careful analysis of the time element because any existing stock of capital goods is not simply equivalent to a single quantity of consumers' goods due to mature at definitely fixed dates, but may be turned by different combinations with the services of the permanent factors into a great many alternative streams of consumers' goods of different size, time-shape and composition. In a sense, of course, capital serves as a "subsistence fund," but it is not a fund in the sense that it provides subsistence for a single uniquely defined period of time. The question which of the many alternative income streams which the existing stock of capital goods potentially represents shall be chosen will depend on which will best combine with the services of the permanent factors which are expected to become available during the future—best in this context meaning that it will combine into a total stream of the most desired time-shape. The rôle of the existing capital goods in this connection is that they fill the gap in the income stream which would otherwise have been caused by the investment of resources which might have been used to satisfy current needs. And it is only by making their investment for these periods possible that those resources will yield a product sufficient to take the place of the products rendered in the meantime by the already existing capital goods. *But there is no other "identity" between the now existing capital goods and those that will take their place than that the results of current investment*, which leads to the creation of the latter, *dovetail with one of the potential income streams*, which the former are capable of producing, into a total income stream of desired shape. And what limits the possibility of increasing output by investing resources which might serve current needs is again nothing but the possibility of providing in the meantime an income "equivalent" to that which will be obtained from the investment of current resources. ("Equivalent," strictly speaking, means here, not equal, but sufficiently large to make it worth while to wait for the increased return that will be obtained from the invested resources because of their investment.)

It should be clear that an analysis of this effect of the existence of capital goods on the direction of the investment of current resources is possible only in terms of the alternative time structures of production which are technically possible with a given equipment. What makes this analysis so particularly difficult, yet the more necessary (and at the same time lets the traditional approach in terms of an average investment period appear so hopelessly inadequate except as a first approach), is the fact that the existing capital goods do not represent a particular income stream of unique shape or size (as would be the case if it consisted of goods which were completely "specific") but a great number of alternative contributions to future income of different magnitude and date. Nothing short of a complete description of these alternative time-shapes can provide a sufficient basis for the explanation of the effect of the existence of the capital goods on current investment and, what means the same thing, of the form and quantity of the new capital goods that will replace the old ones.

In this article no positive attempt can be made to provide the technical apparatus required for a real solution of these problems. Apart from the particular aspect which I have discussed in the article which Professor Knight attacked, this task must be reserved for a more systematic study. I may mention that most of the serious difficulties which this analysis presents are due to the fact that it has to deal largely with joint-product and joint-demand relationships between goods existing at different moments of time. For the present discussion the task has been only to demonstrate why such an analysis of the time structure is necessary and why no description of capital in terms of mere quantity can take its place. The main fault of the traditional analysis in terms of the period of production was that it tried to argue in terms of a single time dimension in order to retain the connection to the conventional but misleading concept of capital as a definite fund. But it has at least the merit of stressing that element in terms of which the real relationship can be explained.

All the other attempts to state the assumptions as regards the supply of capital in terms of a definite fund and without any reference to the time structure, whether this is attempted by postulating given quantities of "waiting," or "capital disposal,"[35] or a "subsistence fund," or "true capital," or "carrying

[35] It is not surprising that Professor G. Cassel, to whom we owe this particular version of the mythology of capital, should now have joined forces with Professor Knight. Cf. his book *On Quantitative Thinking in Economics*, Oxford, Clarendon Press, 1935, p. 20. [Gustav Cassel, a leading Swedish economist, taught at the University of Stockholm. In his work *The Nature and Necessity of Interest* (London: Macmillan, 1903), he had characterized interest as the price of a homogenous service, "waiting," and the supply of capital as the supply of waiting. On p. 20 of the book that

powers," are just so many evasions of the real problem of explaining how the existence of a given stock of capital limits the possibility of current investment. Without such an analysis they are just so many empty words, harmful as the basis of that noxious mythology of capital which by creating the fiction of a non-existing entity leads to statements which refer to nothing in the real world. And the concept of capital conceived as a separate factor of determinate magnitude which is to be treated on the same footing with "land" and "labor" belongs to the same category.[36] It is no better to say, as Professor Knight did at an earlier stage, that "time as such" is a factor of production,[37] since no definite "quantity" of time is given in a way which would enable us to distribute this "fund" of time in alternative ways between the different lines of production so that the total of "time" used will always be the same. But it is certainly much worse to attempt, as Professor Knight does now, to eliminate time entirely from the analysis of the capitalist process of production. This inevitably prevents him from giving any answer to the question how the limitation of capital limits the possible size of the product and why and how capital is maintained, and compels him to treat this as a datum. And, as we shall see in the next section, it also leads him into positive errors about the function of interest.

V

How the neglect of the fundamental fact that capital consists of items which need to be reproduced, and that these serve as capital only in so far as and to the extent that their existence is a condition for taking advantage of more productive time-consuming methods, led to the most erroneous conclusions is well illustrated by Professor Knight's remarkable assertion that "the rate of

Hayek cites, Cassel singled out for criticism Hayek's 1934 article "On the Relationship between Investment and Output." On p. 23, Cassel argued like Knight that the overriding importance of the distinction between the stock of wealth and the flow of consumption gives us "reason for abandoning the whole concept of an 'average period of production,' and for concentrating our attention instead on the clear and measurable concept of the quotient between capital and income." On p. 25, he approvingly cited Knight's 1935 article "Professor Hayek and the Theory of Investment," *op. cit.*—Ed.]

[36] If, as seems generally to be the case, one can never be certain that one will not be carried away occasionally by the construction of a quantitatively fixed "fund" which undoubtedly attaches to the term capital, it would probably be advisable to follow Professor Schumpeter's suggestion and avoid the use of the term altogether. (Cf. [Joseph Schumpeter's] article ["]Kapital,["] in *Handwörterbuch der Staatswissenschaften*, [ed. Ludwig Elster, Adolf Weber, and Friedrich Wieser,] 4th ed., [Jena, Gustav Fischer,] 1923, vol. v, p. 582.)

[37] [4], p. 198: "It has long been my contention that the best form of statement to indicate the essential fact on the technical side is simply to say that time as such is a factor of production the only really distinct, homogeneous 'factor,' as a matter of fact."

interest could be zero only if all products known, empirically or in imagination, into the creation of which capital in any way enters, were free goods."[38] This statement seems to me to be about as plausible as if it were asserted that the price of air could fall to zero only if all commodities in the production of which the presence of air were an indispensable condition were free goods. Clearly, unless one of several factors cooperating in the production of a number of goods can be substituted for the others without limit, the fact that this one factor becomes a free good will never mean that the product itself must become a free good. In the case in question, however, not even the capital goods need become free goods in order that the rate of interest may fall to zero. All that is required is that the value of the services which depend on the existence of a certain capital good be no higher than the cost of reproduction of a good that will render the same service or, what amounts to the same thing, than the value in their alternative current uses of the services of the factors of production required for this reproduction. There is no reason why, in order that this may come about, these services should also become free goods.

I do not, of course, contend that a fall of the rate of interest to zero is an event in the least likely to occur at any future time in which we are at all interested. But, like all questions of what is *probable*, this is altogether irrelevant for theoretical analysis. What is of importance are the conditions under which this would be possible. Now if a condition were reached in which no further lengthening of the investment periods of individual resources (either by lengthening the process or by increasing the durability of goods in which they are invested) would lead to a further increase of output, new savings could not help to increase output. In the usual terminology the marginal productivity of capital would have fallen to zero because no more satisfaction would depend on a particular capital good ("stored up labor") than would depend on the quantity of labor and other products which are needed to replace it. So long as any of the factors required for this purpose remain scarce, the capital goods themselves and *a fortiori* the final consumers' goods made with their help will also remain scarce. And there can be no doubt that this point where further accumulation of capital would no longer increase the quantity of output obtainable from the factors used in its production, even if almost infinitely distant, would still be reached long before the point where no satisfaction whatever would be dependent on the existence of these factors.

It is not difficult to see how Professor Knight's habit of thinking not only of capital in the abstract but even of particular capital goods as permanent has led him to his peculiar conclusion. Permanent goods which can be produced—if there is such a thing, namely a good which is expected not only to last forever physically, but also to remain permanently useful—stand in this respect in a somewhat exceptional position. The value of such a good

[38] [2], p. 284.

expected to render permanently useful services would at a zero rate of interest necessarily be infinite so long as its services have any value at all, and goods of this kind would therefore be produced until the value of the services of one more unit would be zero. And until the services of these goods had become free, there would be a demand for capital for producing more and the rate of interest could not fall to zero. The person making a final investment of this kind, bringing the value of the services down to zero, would of course find that he had made a mistake and lost his investment; and the demand for capital for this purpose would stop when it became known that the investment of one further unit had this effect.

But even if the value of the permanent goods should have to fall to zero in order that the rate of interest may become zero also, this does, as shown above, by no means imply that the value of the non-permanent goods should also have to fall to zero. On each good may depend no more utility than can be had from the current use of the factors required for its reproduction, but the value of such goods will still be equal to that utility.

In concluding this section it may be pointed out that there is, of course, a very important reason why in a changing world the rate of interest will never fall to zero, a reason which Professor Knight's assumption of the permanence of capital would exclude, namely, that in a world of imperfect foresight capital will never be maintained intact in any sense, and every change will always open possibilities for the profitable investment of new capital.

VI

There remain a number of points of not inconsiderable importance which, however, if this article is not to grow to disproportionate size, can be touched upon but shortly. Perhaps the most interesting is the suggestion, which occurs here and there in Professor Knight's articles, that all his deductions about the nature of capital are based on the assumption of perfect foresight.[39] If this is to be taken quite seriously it would represent a main addition to the older Clarkian doctrine of the permanence of capital and to some extent also justify it. It would do so, however, at the expense of restricting its validity to a sphere in which problems of capital in the ordinary sense do not occur at all and certainly deprive it of all relevance to the problems of economic dynamics. But

[39] Cf. particularly [2], pp. 264 (n.2), 270, 273, and 277. In his latest articles ([7] and [8]) Professor Knight seems however inclined to concede that the period of production analysis has some limited application to static conditions most rigidly defined, and is inapplicable under dynamic conditions! Are we to understand that Professor Knight now wants to abandon all that part of his earlier criticism which was based on the most extreme static assumptions imaginable, i.e., on the assumption of perfect foresight?

since Professor Knight's purpose is, *inter alia*, to demonstrate that my analysis of certain types of industrial fluctuations is based on a fallacy in the field of the theory of capital it can evidently not be his intention to base all his argument on this assumption. Hence it seems worth while to explore shortly the question what problems of capital still exist under such an assumption.

If we assume that perfect foresight has existed from the beginning of all things, a question of how to use capital as a separate factor of production would not arise at all. All processes of production would have been definitely determined at the beginning and no further question would arise of how to use any of the instruments created in the course of the process which might be used for other purposes than those for which they were originally intended. If indeed there are natural non-permanent resources in existence at the beginning, a "capital problem" might arise in connection with the original plan.[40] But once this original plan is made and so long as it is adhered to, no problem of maintenance, replacement or redistribution of capital, nor indeed any other economic problem, would occur.

Economic problems of any sort, and in particular the problem how to use a given stock of capital goods most profitably, arise only when it is a question of adjusting the available means to any new situation. In real life such unforeseen changes occur, of course, at every moment and it is in the explanation of the reaction to these changes that the existing "capital" is required as a datum. But the concept of capital as a quantitatively determined self-perpetuating fund does not help us here in any way. In fact, if the justification of this concept lies in the assumption of perfect foresight it becomes clearly inapplicable, since a "factor" which remains in any sense constant only if complete foresight is assumed cannot possibly represent a "datum" on which new decisions can be based. As has been shown, it would be erroneous to assume that this given "factor" is given as a definite quantity of value, or as any other determinate quantity which can be measured in terms of some common unit. But while the only exact way of stating the supply condition of this factor would be a complete enumeration and description of the individual items, it would be hasty to conclude that they have no common quality at all which entitles us to class them into one group. This common quality of being able to substitute to some extent one item for another is the possibility of providing a temporary income while we wait for the services of other factors invested for longer periods. But, as we have seen, no single item represents a definite quantity

[40] It might be mentioned, incidentally, that this would not be a problem of the preservation of natural resources in the usual sense, i.e., of preservation of the particular resource, but only of its replacement by some produced means of production which will render services of equivalent value. This applies equally to the practical problem of the preservation of exhaustible natural resources where it is by no means necessarily most economical to extend their life as far as possible rather than to use their amortization fund for the creation of some new capital goods.

of income. How much income it will yield and when it will yield it depends on the use made of all other goods. In consequence the relevant datum which corresponds to what is commonly called the supply of capital and which determines for what period currently [*sic*] factors will be expediently invested is nothing but the alternatively available income streams which the existing capital goods can produce under the new conditions.

It would be difficult to believe that Professor Knight should for a moment have really thought that the concept of capital as a self-maintaining fund of determinate magnitude has any application outside a fictitious stationary state if he had not himself at least at an earlier date clearly recognized that the problems of capital fall largely outside the framework of static analysis.[41] In view of these utterances it would seem unlikely that he should now take pains to develop a concept which is valid only on the most rigidly "static" assumptions. The emphasis which he now places on the complete mobility of capital certainly conveys the impression that he wants to apply his concept to dynamic phenomena. It is at least difficult to see what other purpose this emphasis can serve, because certainly nobody has ever doubted that where all the future is correctly foreseen and always has been so no problem of mobility of capital will arise. And altho he qualified his statements about the mobility of capital by the assumption of complete foresight[42] this does not prevent him from disparaging the value of any reasoning based on the limitations of the mobility of capital under dynamic conditions. This attitude is not very far from the assertions sometimes found in the literature that apart from "frictions" invested capital ought to be regarded as completely mobile between different uses (presumably without any loss in value), and that "any theory that is based on partial immobility of invested capital is essentially a frictional one."[43] This clearly assumes the existence of a separate substance of capital apart from its manifestation in concrete capital goods, a "fund" of a mystical quantity which cannot be described or defined but which, if Professor Knight has it his way, is to have a central position in our analytical apparatus. It has the somewhat questionable advantage that there is no way of deciding whether any statement about this quantity is true or false.

[41] [4], p. 206: "The one important difference between price analysis in the case of interest and that of ordinary prices arises from the fact that saving and investment is a cumulative process. It is a phase of economic growth, outside the framework of the conventional 'static' system, unfortunately so called."

[42] [2], p. 270

[43] H[ans] Neisser, "Monetary Expansion and the Structure of Production," *Social Research*, vol. I/4, November, 1934 [pp. 434–57].

NINE

TECHNICAL PROGRESS AND EXCESS CAPACITY[1]

I

Many readers may think that someone fortunate enough to watch world events from a vantage point that is currently, without overstatement, the center of economic and political activity, should come up with a more important and interesting topic than a seemingly specialized one like "Technical Progress and Excess Capacity." My decision to announce this lecture under such a title shows that I do not share this view. I, for one, am convinced that *academic economists* do well to leave journalistic reportage to other, probably more experienced hands. I am even more firmly convinced that economists have a much broader field of view, which in fact almost obliges them to take a stand on those *fundamental ideas of our time* that dominate the actions of statesmen and politicians. These ideas are likely to exert a greater influence on the course of world development than even the most spectacular events of our time. And I hope to show you that prevailing ideas about the nexus of problems that is—only partially—suggested by this title in many ways have as permanent an effect on the hopes and desires of the masses as they do on the economic policies of statesmen.

It is conceivable, however, that the title of the lecture does not fully reveal the scope of its main theme. My intention was to use the term excess capacity as a striking but not as the sole example of how technical progress might seem to waste and squander economic vitality rather than lead to a betterment of our situation. My real question is this: *Does a competitive economy fully exploit the opportunities for increasing general prosperity offered by technical progress? Or is it true*, as has often been maintained, *that our social system prevents our making full use of existing opportunities and that in a rationally conducted economy our income could increase by a*

[1] [Lecture held at the Österreichisches Institut für Konjunkturforschung (Austrian Institute for Business Cycle Research), April 3, 1936. First published as "Technischer Fortschritt und Überkapazität," *Österreichische Zeitschrift für Bankwesen*, vol. 1, June 1936, pp. 9–23; translated by Grete Heinz as "Technical Progress and Excess Capacity," in F. A. Hayek, *Money, Capital & Fluctuations: Early Essays*, ed. Roy McCloughry (Chicago: University of Chicago Press; London: Routledge and Kegan Paul, 1984), pp. 163–80.—Ed.]

multiple of what it actually is? I cannot hope to treat such a broad subject exhaustively in one lecture. For this reason I will disregard claims by various prophets and sects, such as the now almost entirely forgotten Technocrats.[2] It is not, generally speaking, the extreme proponents of mistaken views that are the most dangerous. World views and economic ideologies are most likely to exert their influence through those components that slip unnoticed into the thinking of our time and quickly turn from unproven assertions to unquestioned dogma. I will therefore limit myself here to the examination of a number of typical trains of thought that turn up in hundreds of different cases and in a great variety of concrete guises. They may lead to plausible conclusions in individual instances, yet rest, as I shall try to show, on fallacies that are revealed most clearly in general and in abstract cases. I will not deny an additional motive, pardonable in an academic economist, namely, to demonstrate with concrete examples the value of abstract speculations such as the ones in which, much to the dismay or annoyance of their fellow men, theoretical economists overwhelmingly indulge.

II

The discussion of these problems often assumes the form of a question: should the exploitation of technical progress be left in the hands of *unregulated competition* between different firms or should *industrial development* be *scientifically planned*? Before proceeding any further, I would like to begin with one observation. An affirmative answer to the above question[3] is very often tac-

[2] [The Technocrats called for rule by technical experts, typically including central economic planning by industrial engineers. The Technocracy movement in the early twentieth century was associated in the United States with progressivism, and in Europe with socialism, social democracy, and fascism. A seminal technocratic writer was Thorstein Veblen, who in his 1921 book *The Engineers and the Price System* (New York: B. W. Huebsch) imagined policymaking by what he called a "Soviet of Engineers." In the United States the movement's importance peaked in the early years of the Great Depression, when it influenced Roosevelt's first New Deal programs of 1933 via the economist Rexford Tugwell and others. The fact that Hayek here, speaking in 1936, calls the Technocrats "now almost entirely forgotten" suggests that he had in mind the Technocrats of the Weimar Republic in Germany, a varied group that included the Marxian Karl Kautsky, the industrialist and WWI mobilization planner Walther Rathenau, and the engineer and WWI planner Wickard von Moellendorf, the last of whom is credited with introducing the term *Planwirtschaft*, or "planned economy," in 1917. On the German Technocrats, see Kjetil Jakobsen, Ketil G. Andersen, Tor Halvorsen, and Sissel Mykelbust, "Engineering Cultures: European Appropriations of Americanism," in *The Intellectual Appropriation of Technology: Discourses on Modernity, 1900–1939*, ed. Mikael Hård and Andrew Jamison (Cambridge, MA: MIT Press, 1998), pp. 119–22.—Ed.]

[3] [That is, to the second part of the question: should progress be "scientifically planned"?—Ed.]

itly based on the assumption that an economic dictator would be much wiser and more farsighted than entrepreneurs, in whose hands the decision now lies. In particular, when the state is invoked as the central planning authority, its omniscience is almost taken for granted, in contrast to the inadequacies of the entrepreneur. But the state too, or whoever might act as economic dictator, consists of human beings, and if there really existed such omniscient persons, there would be every reason to assume that they would be the most successful entrepreneurs as well. It is highly dubious that a selection mechanism exists for appointing the most capable persons to head an economic administrative apparatus.[4] I do not wish to deny that a central planning agency would dispose of information sources that are not available to individual entrepreneurs. But the intrinsic advantages are more than outweighed in my mind by the difficulty that, under centralized planning, decisions to questions that can be judged only by their actual success, will be placed more or less arbitrarily in the hands of a few people. It seems to me that the general assumption that a central planning agency would show greater foresight is based in the main on its power to force consumers to take what they are offered. It remains to be seen in how far this can be viewed as an advantage. But apart from this case it seems clear to me that there is no reason at all to assume that a central planning authority would have more knowledge or foresight than individual entrepreneurs.

After these preliminary remarks, I will now turn to the problems at hand. Self-evident as it may seem that the future is only imperfectly predictable in any economic system, it is a fact that has a bearing on our problems and one that is erroneously presented as a peculiarity of our competitive economy. For this reason its universal character deserves special emphasis. It will at once become obvious in discussing specific points that unpredictability more than anything else is at the root of all the apparent wastefulness and losses that technical progress entails.

III

Technical inventions, which by their very nature constitute spontaneous advances in our technical knowledge that are not predictable in detail, are the first and most striking example of technical progress. It is unquestionable, of course, that each time an invention with immediate applications emerges, many of

[4] [In chapter 10 of *The Road to Serfdom* (London: Routledge, 1944), Hayek would famously argue that in a centrally planned economy, the tendency created by political selection mechanisms is that, as the title of chapter 10 put it, "the worst get on top." Most recent edition, *The Road to Serfdom: Texts and Documents, The Definitive Edition*, ed. Bruce Caldwell, vol. 2 of *The Collected Works of F. A. Hayek* (Chicago: University of Chicago Press, 2007)—Ed.]

the previous investments and expenditures seem to be inappropriate in the light of this new knowledge. This may be viewed as wastefulness in the light of a superior wisdom and perhaps also from the standpoint of certain individuals who were acquainted with the invention before it became generally known. But as long as we know of no method to determine in advance who at any given time is knowledgeable on this point, that is, as long as we have no reason to assume that X's opinions about the prospects of a new production method are always more pertinent than Y's, all we can do is to ask what reaction is socially most desirable and advantageous in dealing with the new fact, once the new invention is known and successfully tested.

When this question is raised in popular discussion, two different and opposite objections are often elicited against the way that a competitive economy reacts to such an invention. On the one hand it is asserted that *technical progress is not exploited to the desirable extent.* It is hard to understand why an invention that reduces the cost of production would not be introduced in a truly competitive economy. I believe that anyone who raises this objection would agree, after giving some thought to the matter, that the blame should not fall on competition but rather on the existence of a *monopoly* or a monopoly-like constellation. It is undeniable that the owner of capital equipment that would lose its value with the introduction of a new invention would often have a motive for preventing this from happening. But at the same time others have an interest in making a profit by applying the cheaper method of production. Therefore it is only when access is denied to others that interested parties might succeed in blocking the invention. In truth, *patents* constitute the most important restriction on competition created by modern legislation, and they are largely responsible for imposing a far-reaching monopoly in this connection. Patents make it both possible and advantageous for individuals *to purchase an invention* not in order to put it to use but *to prevent its utilization.* However, this is obviously not the consequence of competition but the consequence of the special monopoly position created by patent law, into whose significance I cannot enter more fully here.[5]

[5]The interconnections, incidentally, are by no means as straightforward as is commonly assumed. The instances in which it is actually profitable to acquire a patent in order to prevent its utilization are quite exceptional. If we start from the assumption that the patent is profitable at all, whatever considerations make it attractive for anyone at all to exploit it will as a rule also apply as well to the entrepreneur who acquired it. From his standpoint he must weigh the destruction of the value of existing facilities against the value of the patent. For him too the value of the patent lies in its enabling him to attain total production costs that are lower than the running costs of the facilities currently in use. He will remove the patent from use only if he loses more by writing off his equipment than he does by the savings he can make on his total production costs. A possible exception is where a new process can be profitably applied only in conjunction with certain production factors that are not available everywhere. An invention might be profitable only, for example, for firms with an especially cheap labor supply, while the invention

But are there no instances where it would be desirable to *prevent an invention from being immediately introduced*, cases where its application might be *individually profitable* but *socially wasteful*? That leads me to the second and much more persuasive-sounding objection to the way in which a competitive economy responds to technical progress. Is it not obviously a waste of economic resources when competition forces an entrepreneur to discard machines that might still serve many years and replace them with new ones? Would capital used for producing goods which would have been produced even without it not be better spent bringing other additional goods to the market?

This argument, which in my view is *totally fallacious*, has had an *enormous influence on modern economic policy*, even if not in this simplistic and overly transparent guise. It is pointed out, for one, that there are capital losses that must be chalked up against profits but are not calculated if these losses affect someone other than the one who makes the profit. Or else it is asserted that as long as many needs remain unmet, it is more important to turn out new goods than to produce existing ones with new methods. In this context it seems particularly persuasive that competition tends to create unnecessary and wasteful excess capacity instead of satisfying the most urgent needs.

The most significant example of this type and one that has loomed large in discussions of economic policy in all countries is of course the *competition between automobiles and railroads*. I will not dwell here on the particular difficulties of properly calculating and allocating the costs of road construction and road maintenance to vehicle traffic. These costs—like the comparable costs that affect the railroads—must be taken into account in assessing efficiency. But quite aside from this technical problem, this controversy brought to the fore the very same arguments that emerge in any situation where technical progress makes expensive investments obsolete and worthless. Loss of national wealth, squandering of capital, conflict between individual profitability and social utility, all these issues have been raised as arguments against the apparent wastefulness of technical progress.

would not be profitable in districts with high labor costs. In this case it might be advantageous for an entrepreneur who employs expensive labor and who lacks the requisite information etc. to move to the more favorably situated district, to acquire the invention for the sole purpose of preventing its introduction in the other district. This he can do at an advantageous price, however, only if the inventor does not realize that his patent has greater value to other entrepreneurs. Otherwise competition would drive up the price of the patent to a level that is greater than the loss in value against which the entrepreneur in question was hoping to protect himself. Taking a patent out of the market thus becomes profitable only in the face of unequal production conditions and an imperfect market that allows the patent to be purchased below its true value. And even in this case it might actually be more rational for the first entrepreneur to sell the patent he has acquired to his competitors at a higher price than to remove it from use, though other psychological considerations make it unlikely that he will act in this manner.

IV

And what is the true state of affairs? When is it desirable to introduce a new invention? Would a wise economic dictator be guided by other principles than those ruling in a competitive economy? Let me ask you to go along a little way in a rather abstract investigation. I shall first endeavor to show *under which circumstances it is generally advantageous for an entrepreneur in a competitive economy to introduce a new and improved method of production*, and I shall then examine what meaning these individual considerations have from the point of view of society as a whole. This will allow us to determine whether the economic dictator would act differently on rational considerations and whether he would obtain a better utilization of productive resources.

Replacing old machines with new ones and scrapping the old ones is not necessarily profitable for every invention that lowers production costs. If the cost reduction is relatively small, as a rule, only a small quantity will at first be produced in the new way—namely, the extra amount that can be sold at the lower price corresponding to the new production costs. The owners of the old machines will have to accept a lower price in view of the new competition. As a consequence, they will probably be unable to amortize fully the capital invested in these machines. But as long as the cost reduction resulting from the new invention is not very great, neither will it be in their interest to replace the old machines immediately by new ones, nor can others who use the new machines underbid them to such an extent that they must stop producing altogether. Only when cost reductions have reached a certain point, will it become appropriate as well as unavoidable for the machines to be scrapped—even if they still offered many years of use—and replaced by new ones.

At which point does this critical change occur? Our answer to this question determines how we view the whole problem. At this juncture, technical details are of the essence, and unfortunately the terminology is so confused both in practice and in theory that I will have to start out by defining one or two concepts that I will be using. In what follows I will apply the terms "*capital costs*" and "*running costs*" of a firm in a special, technical sense, which will allow me to deal with my problem in a relatively simple way. This usage does not completely coincide with any of the many cost concepts used elsewhere. In this context, I take *capital costs* to mean the yield and amortization of the firm's capital assets, that is, of the value of its fixed investments such as buildings, machines, etc., calculated on the basis of their replacement costs. To avoid minor complications, I will assume that the existing assets have no other use than the one for which they were originally intended and that their scrap value is zero. This assumption substantially simplifies our exposition. It is easy enough to generalize the results by later making the appropriate modifications.

Running costs, on the other hand, refer to all those current expenditures that are necessary to keep a given fixed investment in operation. I fully realize that it is generally not feasible to make such a sharp distinction between running costs and capital costs and that in actuality it depends on the time period we have in mind. In the short run we may consider something as capital costs that turns into running costs when the firm's operations over a long, uninterrupted period of time are considered. Most repairs and maintenance costs belong to this ambiguous group. But for our purposes the distinction is adequate without delving into these complexities.

To return to my original question, the answer is that it will be appropriate and feasible to keep the old facilities running if and as long as *total costs* (that is, capital costs plus running costs) *of the new, improved method of production exceed the running costs of the old facilities*. As long as that is the case, it will be more advantageous for the owner of the old facility to continue production and to write off part of the old capital investment than to close down and have it turn into a total loss. Only when the total costs of production of the new invention fall below the running costs of the old process, will the old facilities have to be closed down and the entire production taken over by new facilities.

V

What can be concluded from all this with respect to *the economy as a whole*? Would it not be just as true that new capital, which could have been put to better use, was being applied to producing something that could have been created with existing facilities? No, for herein lies the *fallacy*: in reality the new capital does not serve to accomplish the same thing as the old capital. As long as the new machines offered no savings compared to the old ones, they would not have been introduced, as we have already seen. To become profitable, the new process would have had to induce lower total costs than the old running costs, in other words, it would have had to save more than the irretrievably fixed capital costs of the old facilities.[6] In other words, *the new process will be adopted only when the capital costs it induces are lower than the saving in running costs it yields compared to the old process*. Hence the purpose of new capital is not to replace the old capital that has lost its value, but, rather, to save on other production factors. It releases other productions factors, workers and machines, which can now be employed elsewhere. The choice in this case is effectively between putting *more capital or* putting *more labor and raw materials* into the pro-

[6] Entrepreneurs will obviously take into account in their calculations the possibility that this capital is not rigidly tied to a particular use and that existing facilities retain a positive value after being dismantled, and the results of the calculation will be modified accordingly.

duction process to turn out *the same amount of product*. And the decision will obviously rest on *what costs less*, that is, whether that amount of capital or the other factors will have a higher yield elsewhere. "This is, at least, how *a wise economic dictator* would decide." But this is *exactly* what *a competitive economy* will achieve, since the price individual entrepreneurs will have to pay for capital or for the other factors clearly depends on their utility in another use. By opting for whatever costs less, he will be doing exactly what an intelligent planner should do, that is, he will be producing a given quantity with the least possible resources and will free additional resources for other uses.

To restate the main point: it is not true that in these cases capital is used to achieve something that old assets could have produced just as well. This fallacy rests on the mistaken assumption that new capital replaces old capital, while everything else remains unchanged. What happens in reality is that whenever individual entrepreneurs are forced by competition to close down their old facilities and either to replace them with new facilities or else to make room for other entrepreneurs, abandoning the old facilities represents a saving *to the economy*.

Here we are finally confronted with a situation where technical progress creates excess capacity, insofar as the productive capacity embodied in the old facilities constitutes productive capacity at least in a purely technical sense. From an economic point of view, the matter looks different. Supposing, for instance, that demand for the product in question increased, the old facilities would not be used (except perhaps temporarily), as it would be more economical to build more of the new kind. In a *technical* sense the productive capacity still exists, but in *economic* terms it has disappeared. By this we mean that it has lost its value. It may occasionally be appropriate not to scrap facilities but to retain them for temporary (seasonal or such) *peak demand*, whose irregularity may not justify constructing new facilities.

VI

Does it follow from this that the loss in value of the old facilities, which is obviously a severe blow to the owner and which he has every interest to avert, is meaningless from the point of view of the economy as a whole and should not be viewed as a loss? Are all the familiar arguments about the need to protect and maintain existing capital values simply erroneous? In my view, that is undeniably the case. It is perfectly true that the maintenance of capital is in general a precondition for making efficient use of available resources. However, by turning the "*maintenance of capital*" into *an end in itself*, this principle is invoked even when it collides with the true goal of all economic activity: the most complete possible satisfaction of needs. The *utility of a capital good for the economy as a whole* is obviously contingent on its *rendering an indispensable service*—just as is its owner's claim for remuneration. But to maintain the indispensability of capital artificially by blocking alternate ways of achieving the same level of utility has the opposite effect on the economy as a whole by negating the true purpose of the maintenance of capital. Individual capitalists serve the interest of the whole economy best by applying their intelligence and foresight to the discovery of the most profitable investment opportunities. They assume a nefarious role when they invoke *state protection against technical progress* that threatens the value of their capital investments. And this is just as true when the state itself is the owner of the threatened capital asset. In fact, the danger becomes all the more acute when its alleged interest in protecting national wealth from depreciation leads it to suppress new technologies. As to the argument supporting so-called *regulation of automotive transportation of persons and freight*, we can state with certainty that the collective economic interest does not consist in the maintenance of capital and that a policy that aims to maintain individual capital assets in such cases will make a nation poorer rather than richer. It would of course be a different matter if Austria could prevent the introduction of an invention that displaced a natural resource that is sold abroad, such as magnesite.[7] In this case Austria would have the same interest as individual capitalists in thwarting such an invention, and from the point of view of the world as a whole it would be as socially irresponsible in its actions as capitalists in a similar situation. But it is obviously absurd to think that as a country we can somehow preserve our wealth by obstructing innovations and by compelling our fellow-citizens to make fuller use of existing facilities.

VII

There are a number of closely related cases in which it is widely believed that greater efficiency could be achieved in an analogous manner if only consumers could be compelled to make better use of existing facilities. This would be true, in particular, where consumers stubbornly insist on demanding *a great number of just slightly different products*. Let me address myself briefly to this question of product differentiation, in which in a certain sense technical development gives rise to underutilized productive capacity, an issue that has recently triggered interesting scholarly debate.

Here we are dealing with consequences of what is commonly called *imperfect competition*, such as that *between similar brand-name products* like different tooth

[7] [Magnesite, or anhydrous magnesium carbonate, is a mineral used in fertilizers, cement, steelmaking, and other applications. It is presently mined at several sites in eastern and southern Austria and has been an important Austrian export since before the First World War.—Ed.]

pastes. In contrast to the ideal case of perfect competition, in which nobody can ask more than anyone else for the same article, since he would immediately lose all his customers, under imperfect competition individual producers typically can ask for a slightly higher or slightly lower price than other producers of similar products without immediately losing or taking over the entire market. As you will realize at once, this imperfect competition is a much more common phenomenon than ideal perfect competition, on which theorists like to concentrate. One of the main reasons for the actual existence of imperfect competition is obviously that many industries require very large facilities for maximum efficiency, so that in some sectors of the economy there is room for only one or a few such facilities.

The most advantageous scale of production for any given facility is one in which average unit costs begin to rise when production expands. As long as average costs are falling, it is obviously cheaper to produce more with the same facilities than to spread production among several facilities of equal size. Conversely, as soon as average unit costs begin to rise, one can roughly say that production costs will be lower in a new facility and that it is therefore more advantageous to produce additional amounts in a new facility. It is easy to demonstrate that under perfect competition, each enterprise will expand its production to the point where average costs begin to rise.

The situation is different under imperfect competition. It may well happen that there is room for no more than one entrepreneur in a given industry because even before average costs have reached a minimum, the public's demand for the product will decline at an even greater rate. As long as we are dealing with a clearly defined commodity that is sharply differentiated from all other commodities, no competitor will be able to gain a foothold. It would be in the interest of each firm to increase its own production at lower unit costs rather than to allow entry to a competitor whose costs are greater as long as his volume of production remains low. But the situation is different when we are dealing with very similar but not exactly identical products, perhaps those whose brand names have been established within distinct groups of consumers. There are people who will stick to their usual brand even if they could buy the same product more cheaply. In that case, it will not be easy for any one producer to drive out the others completely.

But one might argue that in cases where demand for a group of very similar products is too small to allow more than one firm to operate under the most advantageous conditions, that is, at lowest cost, it would be in the public interest to limit production to one of the similar products and to concentrate it within a single firm. This firm would use its capacity to the fullest, while product differentiation and consumer stubbornness are responsible for the existence of many underutilized factories, each of which produces at too high a cost. *Compulsory standardization*, limiting consumer choice to a single one of the various products, would be advantageous to everyone, since all consumers would be able to get the product at a lower cost.

This argument has lately caused quite a stir and has triggered all sorts of *proposals for rationalization, in particular for the regulation of retail trade.* But is this a valid argument? It is open, in my opinion, to two serious objections. First of all, if it were really likely that consumers would prefer less choice and cheaper products, why don't entrepreneurs exploit this fact and induce consumers to buy only their products at a lower price? But secondly and more significantly: who is to decide whether the public's preference for a particular item or brand is really so unreasonable? Who is to say that it is irrational for consumers to refuse to respond to a slightly lower price and to stay loyal to a familiar brand rather than switch to a supposedly equivalent product? The standardization fanatics are on very dangerous ground here and I for one would not take kindly to the idea that someone else would decide what should or should not appeal or taste good to me.

To be sure, the points that I have raised in passing in my talk are in themselves an incomplete refutation of the above arguments. My reason for bringing them up is less their practical significance than the fact that this recent discussion focused on the relationship between excess capacity and waste and thus, for completeness' sake, deserved to be mentioned. At the very least, in this instance theoretical considerations about costs led to a less naïve interpretation of the concept of excess capacity and went beyond the purely technical one, which still tends to predominate. Unfortunately, as we shall see [in] short order, this theoretical development has not as yet had the least impact on empirical research.

VIII

The cases discussed so far now should have sufficed to show that *underutilized capacity is not always tantamount to wastefulness.* Much more, however, remains to be said about the extent to which the specter of excess capacity has influenced modern economic policy. I will therefore still turn briefly to a few related problems. While I have tried so far to explain the way excess capacity originates, I must now address myself to the influence exerted by the existence of unutilized capacity. In particular, I would like to discuss the relationship between the existence of underutilized facilities and how much can be produced, the demand for capital, and finally its influence on the prospects for further modernization of firms.

Even now it remains a deeply entrenched notion that for reasons of profitability, no new facilities should be constructed under any circumstances as long as existing ones are not fully utilized, and that if this is not the case the construction of new facilities cannot be profitable. For this reason it may be helpful to give a few examples where the intentional creation of excess capacity is rational (even under genuine competition and not because of the familiar cartel practices that tend to encourage it). A closer look at seemingly simple and self-evident cases will clarify certain connections that may later prove to be essential; it will demonstrate in particular what constitutes excess capacity in the economic as opposed to the technical sense.

It is of course easiest to prove that temporary idling of existing facilities does not constitute wasteful excess capacity in the case of *daily and seasonal fluctuations*. No sensible person would claim that it is always inefficient not to utilize existing production facilities twenty-four hours a day, although certain engineers obsessed with rationalization should, to be consistent, consider it wasteful that I do not use the bed I purchased twenty-four hours a day; in their view of efficiency, the number of available beds should not exceed one-third of the population. More instructive, however, are certain cases of seasonal fluctuations. It would undoubtedly be feasible in various industries to spread out work evenly throughout the year and accumulate supplies to satisfy demand concentrated over a few weeks of the year. This would minimize the size of fixed capital equipment and allow facilities to operate continuously, but it would not prove that this process is invariably more efficient. In many cases where this arrangement is perfectly feasible from a technical point of view, it is in fact not only more profitable for the owner but more rational for the economy as a whole to build facilities that are large enough to satisfy the seasonal demand within a time span equal to or only slightly longer than the seasonal demand and to keep the equipment idle the rest of the year. That will be the case whenever *raw materials or labor used in the process are so valuable that the loss of interest on the products kept in stock is greater than the interest (and amortization) cost for larger amounts of capital equipment.* This case is particularly instructive because it shows how scarcity of capital, by making it necessary to economize on circulating capital, can entail underutilization of fixed capital. Here we have a particularly simple case of the seeming paradox which plays such an important role in modern explanations of depressions: that existing capital equipment cannot be fully utilized for lack of capital, a phenomenon that may be wrongly interpreted as excess capital. I will have more to say in a moment about this relationship between underutilized productive capacity and the demand for capital.

IX

Let me first try to answer this general question: does the existence of productive capacity that is underutilized in a technical sense prove that production could be increased accordingly by utilizing this capacity? It is certainly feasible to increase production in any given industry to some extent. However, what may be technically feasible speaking for individual industries need not be feasible for the economy as a whole. Therein lies the difference between a technical and an economic perspective. One or two empirical *investigations*, supposedly conducted from an economic angle, were recently undertaken *in the United States*. Despite their good intentions, they were seriously flawed on that score. They were designed to *refute certain clearly exaggerated assertions by technocrats* and other engineers claiming that current output could be multiplied with existing productive facilities. These investigations, which yielded relatively modest estimates of potential increases in production, were vigorously applauded by sensible people on the one hand and just as vigorously attacked on the other by technocrats and their ilk. Upon closer examination, however, even the results of these investigations were revealed to be greatly overstated. In the method used, representatives of the individual industries were asked by how much they could increase their production with existing facilities if demand for the product were unlimited (nothing was said about the price). The results obtained for the individual industries in this manner were then summed as the potential increase in total volume of production for the economy as a whole. For *the more careful and thoroughgoing* of these two investigations, the estimated amount by which American industry could on average have raised its output *above the level of the boom period between 1925 and 1929 was 20%*. In the *second investigation*, estimates ranged *between 60% and 100%* in the most common replies to questionnaires sent out to topnotch entrepreneurs and engineers.

But how should we interpret these estimates of production volume increases attainable in all individual industries with existing capital equipment and unlimited demand? Do these numbers demonstrate in any way that existing facilities were poorly utilized or that all industries could simultaneously have produced so much more? It is obvious from the way the questions were worded that they referred to all technically utilizable facilities but did not even consider whether an increase in production could not have been attained more effectively by building new facilities for this purpose rather than by utilizing the old ones. Potential productive capacity presumably included not only *technically obsolete facilities* but also facilities that were not profitable either *because of other changed circumstances* (for instance a location that became less favorable) or because of an *original miscalculation*. We know that the reason why in all these cases available facilities have not been used is that the prices did not even cover the running costs of these facilities. The only explanation for such a situation in a true competitive economy is that there must have existed a greater demand elsewhere for the other factors of production required in conjunction with the existing facilities. Under these circumstances, the particular industry could be expanded only *at the expense of another product for which a greater demand had existed.*[8] I can only mention in passing that in today's economy the scarcity of other factors of production is often not a natural scarcity but a scarcity artificially created by price fixing, in particular by setting minimum prices for labor. In practice this means that the labor input cannot exceed the amount where the produce of the marginal unit of labor corresponds to an arbitrarily determined wage level.

X

We can show, accordingly, that the commonly made claim that there is *no potential for profitable investments as long as large quantities of underutilized equipment exist* is untenable. It is equally unwarranted to assert that after an economic crisis existing facilities must first be brought back into full use before investment activity can be revived. We have seen that on the one hand scarcity of capital itself may be one of the causes of underutilized capacity and that, once additional capital becomes available, fuller utilization will be encouraged. At the same time, what is often counted as underutilized capacity consists of obsolete or otherwise unprofitable facilities that are at most usable on a temporary basis and that should in no way prevent the construction of newer, more efficient facilities.

What should we think of the frequently raised argument that *the overabundance of equipment exerts such a downward pressure on the price that it interferes with* economically desirable *modernizations*? This is an issue that comes up often in current discussions of economic policy in England. With regard to the textile, shipping and coal industries the argument is invoked that the government should first help to get rid of the excessive facilities so that better prices make it possible to modernize. In some instances, this argument has already borne fruit. It is not obvious why modernization would be justified if it becomes profitable only when the same goods are produced at new, higher prices, and thus with higher costs, than those prevailing today. I am assuming that in specific instances technical experts, in their preference for modern equipment, would be right that it would be more efficient to build more modern facilities if no facilities yet existed at all. But this tells us nothing, as we have seen, as to whether it really is efficient to replace the existing old facilities with new ones. The *engineer's aesthetic pleasure in having the technically best facilities* and the whole concept of technical superiority of a given method of production which is unrelated to its efficiency, constitute at least as *serious* a *threat* to a firm's survival

[8] [In other words, the existence of "excess capacity" in plant and equipment is consistent with full employment of other inputs, and therefore does not imply that aggregate output is below potential output.—Ed.]

as technical backwardness. It is much to be desired that technical experts learn this lesson and that they try to understand the limitations imposed by profit calculations in a competitive economy. They should regard them as necessary economic constraints on the effectiveness of their actions rather than as nefarious restrictions.

You will probably think that my answers to the questions that I have raised are based on a *utopian laissez-faire ideal* that might have *theoretical advantages* but *cannot be implemented on a practical and political level.* And you may in a way be right. In individual cases and in our modern economy, as it is now constituted, it may often be either impossible or inappropriate to act in a way that would be correct under ideal conditions. "This is the curse of every evil deed; that, propagating still, it brings forth evil."[9] And I admit quite readily that if I were asked to give concrete advice on economic policy, I could probably not always adhere to the basic principles outlined here. I do consider it the task of academic economists, however, to represent the claims of reason, no matter what their short-run effectiveness. Public opinion, which today may in truth hamper a reasonable policy, is not set in stone, and I am afraid that our predecessors, the previous generation of economists, bear some blame for the current state of affairs. If all hope is forlorn, *one hope* still remains: that we academic teachers, through our influence on the thinking of the next generation, will undo at least in part the great harm inflicted by some of our predecessors.

[9] [Hayek here quotes from Friedrich Schiller's play *Die Piccolomini*, act 3, scene 1: "Das eben ist der Fluch der bösen Tat, dass sie, fortzeugend, Böses muß gebären." The present text uses Samuel Taylor Coleridge's translation, *The Piccolomini* (London: Longman and Rees, 1800), p. 134.—Ed.]

TEN

THE MAINTENANCE OF CAPITAL[1]

Contents: I—The Nature and Significance of the Problem. II—Professor Pigou's Treatment. III—The Rationale of Maintaining Capital Intact. IV—The Action of the Capitalist with Perfect Foresight. V—Obsolescence and Anticipated Risks. VI—The Reaction of the Capitalist on Unforeseen Changes. VII—The Impossibility of an Objective Standard with Different Degrees of Foresight. VIII—"Saving" and "Investing." IX—Capital Accounting and Monetary Policy.

I—The Nature and Significance of the Problem

It is not likely that in the whole field of economics there are many more concepts which are at the same time so generally used and so little analysed as that of a "constant amount of capital." But while in the investigation of the effects of nearly any change this is almost without exception treated as a given datum,[2] the question what this assumption exactly means is rarely asked. To most economists the answer to it has apparently seemed so simple and obvi-

[1] This article [*Economica*, n.s., vol. 2, no. 7, August 1935, pp. 241–76—Ed.] was sketched and most of it actually written a considerable time ago. I have delayed publication because I felt that a satisfactory treatment of the subject would require further investigation of some of the more general aspects of the theory of capital. But although I have since come to the conclusion that such a treatment, on the basis of re-examination of the whole complex of questions raised by capitalistic methods of production, would make some reformulation of the argument of this article necessary, I do still feel that a discussion, which starts from the more conventional approach, and which is, therefore, intelligible apart from the setting that a more complete treatment would require, may not be quite useless.

[2] [The most familiar use of the assumption of "holding capital constant" is the comparative-static analysis of the profit-maximizing response by a business firm to a change in the market price of its output or the market wage. In Alfred Marshall's approach the analytical "short run" is defined by "holding constant" the firm's capital equipment, while in the analytical "long run" the firm may vary its capital. But Hayek's subject matter here is constancy of capital at the aggregate level, not at the firm level. At the aggregate level, as Hayek notes below, the issue is constancy of the *value* of capital and not of the elements of the set of capital equipment.—Ed.]

ous that they have never attempted to state it. In consequence the difficulties involved have hardly ever been realised, still less have they been adequately investigated.

The difficulties of the problem would undoubtedly have been realised if economists had been more generally conscious of its importance. But although, even in the analysis of a stationary equilibrium, the inclusion of the "quantity of capital" among the determinants of that equilibrium means that something, which is the result of the equilibrating process, is treated as if it were a datum, this confusion was made relatively innocuous by the essential limitations of the static method, which while it describes the conditions of a state of equilibrium, does not explain how such a state is brought about.

It was only with the more modern attempts to make the descriptions of the conditions of equilibrium the basis of the analysis of the dynamic processes, that the exact meaning of this assumption became of serious consequence. But we need not go far beyond the description of one state of equilibrium to see why it matters. Even the very simplest "problem of variation" as the effect of a shift in demand can only be answered on the basis of a definite assumption as regards the "supply of capital," and the usual answer shows immediately how problematic is the assumption on which it rests.

The idea implicit in the discussion of problems of this sort is that there is a quantitatively determined fund of capital, which can be distributed and redistributed in any way between the different lines of production without changing its aggregate value.[3] But has this assumption of a perfectly mobile capital fund any definite meaning? And if so, what determines whether this value remains constant, what are the conditions under which it will remain constant, how is it measured, and by what is this constant magnitude represented? Certainly not by the concrete capital goods. It is the essential difference between them and factors like labour or land that they will not remain physically the same when prices change, but that the physical composition of the aggregate called capital will change in consequence of any change in the data. Any of the problems of variation with which we are concerned will involve what is commonly called a transformation of capital into other forms. It is not the list of the different pieces of individual capital goods which is assumed to remain unchanged, when we speak of a constant supply of capital, in the same way as

[3]This common assumption has recently been stated with particular emphasis by Professor Pigou in his latest article on the subject to be quoted later. He finds the basis of his deductions "in the concept of capital as an entity capable of maintaining its quantity while altering its form and by its nature always drawn to those forms on which, so to speak, the sun of profit is at the time shining." *Economic Journal*, June 1935, p. 239. [A. C. Pigou, "Net Income and Capital Depletion," *Economic Journal*, vol. 45, no. 178, June 1935, pp. 235–41. The same "quantitative fund" conception of capital is integral to Frank Knight's theory, which Hayek criticizes in "The Mythology of Capital" elsewhere in the present volume.—Ed.]

we assume that the total supply of labour or land is composed of elements of the same kind, when we regard its supply as unchanged.[4]

Even if a definite meaning can be attached to the statement that the value of the capital goods has an existence independent of the capital goods themselves, it does not help us in any way to explain why, or under what conditions, this aggregate value should remain constant, when conditions change. There can be no doubt that the value of at least some of the existing capital goods will be very materially affected by almost any conceivable change. The question then is why should the capitalists, in spite of this change in the value of their concrete capital goods, be able and willing, by an appropriate adjustment of their investment activity, to maintain the total value of their possessions at exactly the same figure as before the change. Is there any justification for considering this in any sense to be the "normal" behaviour of the entrepreneurs, or is it even conceivable that they can, under all circumstances, behave in such a way? Must we not rather assume that under some conditions it will be impossible for the capitalist to maintain the value of his capital constant, while under others it could hardly be considered in any sense "normal" if he did no more than this?

What, then, is that neutral state in which the owners of capital are supposed to take a merely passive attitude, performing no new saving or dissaving? This question, already of considerable importance when we try to trace the consequences of any other change, becomes of special importance when we turn to the autonomous changes which can be said to originate on the side of capital. Then already the initial problem, of what can be regarded as such an autonomous change on the side of capital, depends on our definition of that neutral state. In the usual discussions of this sort of problem, it seems to be generally implied that there is a clear line between the normal process of maintaining and replacing the existing capital, and any net addition to it. It is assumed that it is always possible to decide in an unequivocal way whether capital remains constant, increases, or decreases, and that there are typical phenomena connected with each of these processes which, at least conceptually, can be clearly separated. Indeed, so long as all the other data remain constant, no difficulty arises in this connection. But as soon as one tries to apply these categories to a world where things are changing, all these alluringly simple concepts become dependent in more than one way on exactly what is meant by a given stock of capital. It is impossible to define income (or "earnings") and therefore savings before one has separated from the gross produce those quantities which

[4] [Hayek's argument here implies that the pairing of capital K with labor L in an aggregate production function masks an important difference between capital and labor. Such a pairing has been common practice in growth theory since Robert Solow in 1957 wrote $Q = F(K, L; t)$. Robert Solow, "Technical Change and the Aggregate Production Function," *Review of Economics and Statistics*, 39, August 1957, pp. 312–20.—Ed.]

are required to "maintain" capital, and it is equally impossible to say what are additions to the stock of real capital before one has shown what capital goods are required to make up for current depreciation.

If it should prove that serious difficulties arise in this connection, this would be a matter of great importance for the theory of the trade cycle. In the course of the last generation theorists in that field have tended more and more to agree that industrial fluctuations consist essentially in alternating periods of accumulation and decumulation of capital with all their typical consequences. More recently there has seemed to be considerable unanimity in seeking for causes of these fluctuations in the accumulation of capital in conditions which make the movement of investment to a certain extent independent of that of saving.[5] But although the quantitative relationship between saving and investing, their correspondence or non-correspondence, has become the central point of attack, it seems that all the writers who have made use of that approach[6] have failed to make clear exactly what they meant either by saving or investing. This would have required a careful definition of that neutral

[5] [In particular, conditions of monetary expansion that enlarge the volume of loanable funds beyond the volume of planned saving.—Ed.]

[6] [Hayek refers to the economists who traced the business cycle boom to investment in excess of planned saving, following the lead of the Swedish economist Knut Wicksell, *Über Wert, Kapital, und Rente nach den neueren nationalökonomischen Theorien* (Jena, Ger.: Gustav Fischer, 1893); English translation, *Value, Capital, and Rent*, trans. S. H. Frowein (London: Allen and Unwin, 1834); and Wicksell, *Geldzins und Güterpreise* (Jena, Ger.: Gustav Fischer, 1898); English translation, *Interest and Prices*, trans. R. F. Kahn (London: Macmillan, 1936). The boom was associated with a market rate of interest below the equilibrium or "natural" rate, and was funded by a disequilibrating monetary expansion, which came either in response to an increased business demand for borrowing or at the central bank's initiative. Dennis H. Robertson, in *Banking Policy and the Price Level* (London: P. S. King, 1926), pp. 88–89, to name a leading example, wrote that the banking system can supply an excessive volume of funds for investment by "extorting it from the general public through the multiplication of currency." Besides himself and Robertson, other contemporary Wicksellians that Hayek may have had in mind include those named in his essay "A Note on the Development of the Doctrine of Forced Saving," *Quarterly Journal of Economics*, 47, November 1932, p. 133—namely, Ludwig von Mises, *Theorie des Geldes und der Umlaufsmittel* [*The Theory of Money and Credit*] (Munich, Ger.: Duncker and Humblot, 1912); Joseph Schumpeter, *Theorie der Wirtschaftlichen Entwicklung* [*The Theory of Economic Development*] (Leipzig, Ger.: Duncker and Humblot, 1912); Arthur C. Pigou, *Industrial Fluctuations* (London: Macmillan, 1927); and John Maynard Keynes, *A Treatise on Money*, 2 vols. (London: Macmillan, 1930). Another likely candidate is the Swedish economist Gunnar Myrdal, from whom Hayek included an essay in F. A. Hayek, ed., *Beiträge zur Geldtheorie* [*Contributions to monetary theory*] (Vienna: Springer, 1933). Axel Leijonhufvud, "The Wicksell Connection," in *Information and Coordination* (Oxford: Oxford University Press, 1981), groups the Wicksellians of the period into the Swedish, Austrian, and Cambridge Schools. Leijonhufvud adds the names Gustav Cassel, Bertil Ohlin, and Eric Lindahl to the Swedish School, and Ralph G. Hawtrey to the Cambridge School. Tyler Beck Goodspeed, *Rethinking the Keynesian Revolution: Keynes, Hayek, and the Wicksell Connection* (Oxford: Oxford Uniersity Press, 2012), p. 3, emphasizes the Wicksellian kinship of Hayek and (early) Keynes, which distinguishes them both from Walrasian general-equilibrium macrotheorists.—Ed.]

position in which neither positive nor negative saving were made, because all the income and no more than the income was consumed, and in which capital goods were produced in exactly that quantity and composition that is required to keep the stock of capital intact.

But while it cannot be denied that modern trade cycle theorists (including the present writer) have lamentably failed to provide a concept which is indeed indispensable if their deductions are to have a clear meaning, it seems that they are not the only group of economists who have been deceived by the apparent simplicity of the problem. Even more than this group one should expect the writers on the income concept to have provided a clear answer. And even if the general discussions of the income concept should prove disappointing, one would certainly feel entitled to expect a definite answer in the discussions of business profits, since profits of all things can evidently only be defined as the excess of the total business assets over the equivalent of the capital invested at the beginning of the period. But while we find in general discussions of the income concept, particularly in the writings of Professor Irving Fisher,[7] at least some references to our problem, the standard works on business profits, like Professor F. H. Knight's *Risk, Uncertainty, and Profits*, or Mr. Ch. O. Hardy's *Risk and Risk Bearing*, are almost bare of any reference to the problem.[8]

II—Professor Pigou's Treatment

In view of these circumstances the solitary attempt first made by Professor Pigou a few years ago in the third edition of his *Economics of Welfare* deserves far greater attention than it has actually received. Although Professor Pigou discusses the problem for a special purpose, the definition of a national dividend, he raises most of the problems that need investigation. And it is only an additional reason for gratitude to that distinguished author that he has apparently not felt satisfied with his first attempt towards an answer and that he has in the fourth edition of the same work given us an entirely new ver-

[7] By his definition of income, which identifies it with actual consumption, I. Fisher seems to avoid the problem altogether. [Irving Fisher, *The Nature of Capital and Income* (New York: Macmillan, 1906).—Ed.] But it recurs in connection with his concept of earnings, which corresponds to the ordinary income concept. And although he does not provide an explicit answer, the solution of the problem which seems to be implied in his discussion, or at least the only solution which seems to be consistent with it, appears to be very much the same as that attempted in this paper.

[8] [Frank H. Knight, *Risk, Uncertainty, and Profit* (Boston: Houghton Mifflin, 1921); Charles Oscar Hardy, *Risk and Risk Bearing*, rev. ed. (Chicago: University of Chicago Press, 1923).—Ed.]

sion of his solution.[9] In the third edition he had still considered that the problem could simply and only be answered by "employing money values in some way as our measuring rod," but that we cannot employ crude money values but must introduce "corrections."[10] Accordingly, he defined as constant quantities of capital collections of capital goods, whose aggregate money value, divided by an appropriate index number of general prices, remained constant. After making some further allowances for changes in this magnitude caused by changes in the rate of interest, which need not concern us here, he proceeded to apply this definition to cases where the value of capital goods "is destroyed through a failure of demand or through a new discovery which renders existing instruments obsolete,"[11] and suggests, consistently with the criterion adopted, that in such a case it is convenient, although arbitrary, to say that the stock of capital has decreased (or in the reverse case of an expansion of demand that it has increased).

In the fourth edition of the *Economics of Welfare* the entire chapter is rewritten. Although no explicit explanation is given why the former answer has been abandoned, it is fairly evident from the nature of the changes made, and the general shift of emphasis, that the aim has been to make the decision more dependent on the reasons why it is thought desirable to maintain capital intact. Considerations relating to the constancy of the money value of capital which formerly occupied the chief place are now relegated to a subordinate place, and mentioned only to show that if, all other things remaining the same, in consequence of a contraction in the supply of money, money values all round are substantially reduced, and the money value of capital contracts along with the rest, nobody would consider this as a decrease of capital. The second case mentioned is again that of the effects of a change in the rate of interest on the value of capital, and it is decided (apparently on the assumption that such a change will not affect the return from the existing capital goods) that such changes are not to be considered as changes in the quantity of capital, so far as the estimation of the national dividend is concerned. But then the effects of changes in demand and of inventions are taken up, and here the decision is now the reverse from what it was before. In Professor Pigou's opinion, "we may say quite generally that all contractions in the money value of any part of the capital stock that remains physically unaltered are irrelevant to the national dividend; and that their occurrence is perfectly compatible with the

[9] Since this paper has been completed a further study of this problem has been published by Professor Pigou under the title "Net Income and Capital Depletion" (*Economic Journal*, [vol. 45, no. 178,] June 1935 [pp. 235–41]). Some references to this paper will be made in further footnotes.

[10] *Economics of Welfare*, 3rd ed. ([London, Macmillan,] 1929), p. 45.

[11] *Ibid.*, 3rd ed., p. 47.

maintenance of capital intact."[12] The same applies to actual destruction of the capital goods by "acts of God or the King's enemy," where the distinguishing criterion is that they are not incidental to the use of them, or as I shall suggest instead, because and in so far as they cannot be foreseen.[13] But all other physical deterioration in the capital stock, such as the ordinary wear and tear of machinery and plant, destruction by accidents like fire and storm, in so far as these are, as in the case of ships, incidental to their use, ought to be made good by adding "to the capital stock something whose value is equal to that which the machine, had it remained physically intact, would have now."[14] By this are explicitly excluded all the losses in value, which are not due to physical deterioration, but are due to causes like the changes in demand or the new inventions mentioned before, to which Professor Pigou now adds foreign competition. This is expressly confirmed by the concluding sentence of the paragraph, in which, summarising the result, he says, "Maintenance of capital intact for our purposes means then, not replacement of all value losses (not due to acts of God and the King's enemies), but replacement of such value losses as are caused by physical losses other than the above."[15]

We shall have to discuss these cases in greater detail in the systematic part of this article. Here only one difficulty arising out of Professor Pigou's answer may be mentioned, since it opens up the vista on a set of problems which he has left untouched. What seems most surprising in his classification is that obsolescence, even where it is foreseen at the time a capital good is produced or acquired, and where accordingly the investment is made in the expectation that the product will cease to have value long before it has physically decayed, should not have to be made good in order to maintain capital intact. This means that gradually all existing capital may be squandered, in the ordinary sense, by erecting durable structures for very transient purposes, and replac-

[12] *Economics of Welfare*, 4th ed. ([London, Macmillan], 1932), p. 45. In his latest article on the subject Professor Pigou goes even further and suggests that also physical changes which, while leaving a capital good as productive as ever, bring nearer the day of sudden and final breakdown, should be disregarded in the same way as the nearer approach of the day that will make it obsolete (["Net Income and Capital Depletion,"] *Economic Journal*, p. 238).

[13] In his recent article ([*ibid.*], p. 240), Professor Pigou now suggests the same distinction.

[14] *Economics of Welfare*, 4th ed., , p. 47.

[15] *Ibid.* In the latest version of his views, to which reference has been made in the preceding footnotes, Professor Pigou now regards it as necessary in order to make good the depletion of capital implied in the discarding of a capital good, that a quantity of resources be engaged in the production of a new capital good which would suffice in actual current conditions of technique to reproduce the discarded element (*loc. cit.*, p. 239). Professor Pigou seems to overlook here the fact that "in actual current conditions of technique" it may be much more expensive to reproduce the identical capital good than it either was when it was first produced or than it would be to replace it by a much more up-to-date instrument. It would certainly be much more expensive to reproduce a new 1926 model of a car to replace one that is worn out, than to replace it by a 1935 model [that is, by a current model—Ed.].

ing them, when they become obsolete after a short time, only by capital goods of a value equal to that which they still possess after their temporary utility has passed. Surely there must be some cases where obsolescence, a decrease of usefulness of a capital good not connected with any change in its physical condition, has to be taken into account. And, apparently, the distinction must somehow be based on whether that change can be foreseen or not. But if this is so, does it not provide a criterion of much more general use than the casuistic distinctions drawn by Professor Pigou? This is the problem to which we have to turn.[16]

III—The Rationale of Maintaining Capital Intact

To "maintain capital intact" is not an aim in itself. It is only desired because of certain consequences which are known to follow from a failure to do so. And as we shall see, it is not even possible to attach a definite sense to this phrase if we try to apply it to a changing world, independently of why we want to do so. We are not interested in its magnitude because there is any inherent advantage in any particular absolute measurement of capital, but only because, *ceteris paribus*, a change in this magnitude would be a cause of a change in the income to be expected from it, and because in consequence *every* change in its magnitude may be a symptom for such a change in the really relevant magnitude, income. Professor Pigou has abandoned the attempt to define in terms of a value dimension of capital the position, in which the stock of capital undergoes no changes that need to be added to or deducted from the output of consumers' goods for the computation of the national dividend. He has thereby not only acknowledged the inherent difficulties of any value measurement, which in the present case indeed are particularly serious,[17] but

[16] Professor Pigou's views on the subject have recently been discussed in some detail in two Italian articles by A[ndrzej] M[arcin] Neuman ("Osservazioni sul concetto di 'capitale inalterato' e sulla recente formulazione del prof. Pigou" [Comments on the concept of "intact capital" and on the recent formulation of prof. Pigou]) and F. Vito ("La nozione di lunghezza media del processo produttivo" ["The notion of the average length of the production process]) in the *Rivista Internazionale di Scienze Sociale e Discipline Ausiliare*, Anno XLI, Serie III, September 1933 (vol. IV, fasc. V), [pp. 670–76 and 677–80,] and by R. F. Fowler, *The Depreciation of Capital, [Analytically Considered,]* London [P. S. King], 1934, pp. 14–21.

[17] In the case of the comparison of different money incomes of a person or a group of persons, the result of a computation of an index number can be given a definite meaning, if the index number is constructed in such a way as to show that the one income would buy all that could be bought with the other income *plus* something else, or that it will not buy all that can be obtained with the other income. (On all this cf. G. Haberler, *Der Sinn der Indexzahlen, passim*, and J. M. Keynes, *A Treatise on Money*, Book II.) [Gottfried Haberler, *Der Sinn der Indexzahlen: Eine Untersuchung über den Begriff des Preisniveaus und die Methoden seiner Messung* [The meaning of

he has apparently also recognised the much more fundamental fact that such constancy of the value dimension has no necessary connection with the reasons why we wish to "maintain capital intact," and that in consequence there is no reason to assume that people will in fact normally act in such a way as to keep the value of the stock of capital constant.[18]

What, then, are the reasons why we wish capital to behave in a particular way? In the first instance, this reason is evidently that the persons who draw an income from capital, want to avoid using up unintentionally parts of the source of this income, which must be preserved if income is to be kept at the present level. We want to avoid an unintentional temporary "splashing" or "stinting" which would have the effect of later reducing income below or raising it above the level at which we aim.[19] Capital accounting in this sense is simply a technical device, an abbreviated method of solving the complicated problems arising out of this task of avoiding involuntary infringements upon future income. Whatever the time shape of the future income stream derived from the capital in his possession at which an individual aims, there still remains the problem of deciding what is the required action with regard to the individual parts of his possessions. And although we have certainly no right to assume that every person will normally aim at a permanent constant stream of income from his capital, there is probably some justification for regarding this case as one of special interest. In any case, even when the capitalist aims at some other shape of the income stream, the problem remains the

index numbers: A study of the concept of the price level and the methods of its measurement] (Tübingen, Ger.: Mohr, 1927); John Maynard Keynes, *A Treatise on Money*, 2 vols. (London: Macmillan, 1930); reprinted as volumes 5 and 6 in *The Collected Writings of John Maynard Keynes* (London: Macmillan, 1971). In the first part of his review of Keynes' *Treatise*, Hayek commented that Book 2 offers "a highly interesting digression into the problem of the measurement of the value of money, and forms in itself a systematic and excellent treatise on that controversial subject. Here it must be sufficient to say that it deals with the problem in the most up-to-date manner, treating index-numbers on the lines developed chiefly by Dr. Haberler in his *Sinn der Indexzahlen*, as expressions of the changes in the price-sum of definite collections of commodities." Hayek, "Reflections on the Pure Theory of Money of Mr. J. M. Keynes," *Economica*, vol. 11, no. 33, August 1931, p. 272; reprinted in *Contra Keynes and Cambridge: Essays, Correspondence*, ed. Bruce Caldwell, vol. 9 of *The Collected Works of F. A. Hayek* (Chicago: University of Chicago Press, 1995), p. 123.—Ed.] But it must appear very doubtful whether there are any assumptions on which price levels, not only of consumers' goods, but of all goods composing the stock of capital, i.e. of all goods of any description, can be given a similar meaning.

[18] Professor Pigou's treatment of the problem in his recent article seems, however, to some extent rather a return to a much earlier materialist conception which sees in capital some physical substance whose magnitude is independent not only of its money value, but also of its serviceability.

[19] ["Splashing" (i.e., splurging) and its opposite "stinting" were terms respectively used by Dennis H. Robertson in *Banking Policy and the Price Level* to designate rates of consumption above and below one's permanently sustainable rate of consumption.—Ed.]

same, and the case of the constant income stream might simply be regarded as the standard with which the other cases are compared.

So long as we confine ourselves to the effects of the decisions of the capitalist on his own income stream, it may seem arbitrary to treat any one of the different sets of consistent decisions regarding his future income stream as in any way more "normal" than any other. It may even have a certain theoretical attraction simply to define whatever incomes he wants to have at different periods as equal incomes. We are, however, constrained by other reasons to abstain from such a pure subjectivism and to adopt a more objective standard. These other reasons are that we are interested in the maintenance of capital, not only because of the people who themselves deliberately distribute income over time and by so doing become capitalists, but also because of the effect of their activity on the income of other people. In the case of the workman, whose labour receives a greater remuneration because of the cooperation of capital, but who is not himself an owner of capital, we have no expression of his preference as regards the shape of his income stream, and we have to *assume* that he wants an income stream which does at least not decrease. Such a constant income stream in an objective sense might provisionally be defined as consisting at every successive moment of varying collections of commodities actually bought at an aggregate price, at which the collection of commodities actually bought at the beginning of the period might have been obtained.

IV—The Action of the Capitalist with Perfect Foresight

The next task, then, is to find out how the individual owner of capital goods will behave, if he wants to keep the income he derives from his possession constant, and if he has complete foresight of all relevant changes.[20] Complete

[20] It is, of course, not assumed that the capitalist under consideration has always possessed complete foresight, since in this case the problem of adaptation of his plans to an anticipated change would not arise. All that is assumed is that at a given moment all future changes relevant to his investments become known to him. The difficulties which any such assumption of foresight of all relevant changes involves are well known. The only way in which such foresight, not only of the real changes, but of all prices during the relevant period, is conceivable is that all these prices are actually fixed simultaneously in advance on some single market, where not only present but also all future commodities that will become available during the relevant period are traded. This introduces the further difficulty that to fulfil the condition it would be necessary that the periods for which people foresee are the same for all individuals, and that the changes that will happen in the more distant future are disclosed periodically and simultaneously to all people. However, it is not necessary here to go further into all the difficulties raised by this assumption, which will be dropped later, difficulties which are by no means exhausted by those mentioned. Attention had to be drawn to them only in order to make us realise how unreal the assumption of perfect foresight is (even for the limited periods relevant to our problem).

foresight in this sense need not refer to all the relevant future. It is sufficient for our purpose to assume that at any one moment he foresees all changes that will affect the return of the investment he then makes. His anticipation need only be correct for a period equal to that for which his investment runs, and if he makes investments in different fields, the extent of his foresight need only cover the relevant facts affecting the different investments during such different periods as these investments last. Beyond this, only some more general expectation as regards the rate of interest at which it will be possible to reinvest the capital recovered, will be necessary.

Within these periods, his anticipations must in the first instance cover the relevant price changes. But such foreknowledge is hardly conceivable without some foresight of the real changes, which bring about the changes in prices. The main types of changes, which he will have to foresee and the effects of which we shall have to discuss, will be changes in the demand for the products and the consequent changes, not only of the prices of the products, but also of the prices of the factors, changes in the quantities of the factors of production, and changes in their prices caused in this way (including, in particular, in both these cases, changes in the rate of interest), and finally, changes of technical knowledge or inventions. With respect to this last case the idea of foresight evidently presents some difficulty, since an invention which has been foreseen in all details would not be an invention. All we can here assume is that people anticipate that the process used now will at some definite date be superseded by some new process not yet known in detail. But this degree of knowledge may be sufficient to limit investments in the kind of equipment, which is bound to be made obsolete by the expected invention, in such a way that the old equipment wears out as the new invention can be introduced.

If we take first the case of an anticipated change in the demand, either away from or towards the product produced by our capitalist, his knowledge of this impending change, a full investment period in advance of its actual occurrence, will evidently put him in a position so to redistribute the earned amortisation quotas of his capital between the different industries, that he will derive the greatest return from them possible under the new conditions. But in what sense will these amortisation quotas represent a constant magnitude, and under what conditions can we assume that the capitalist will invest them and no more and no less, if he merely aims at keeping his income from capital from now onwards constant?

There is no reason to assume that, if he just continues to reinvest, after the change has become known, the amounts he used to invest, in what appears the most profitable way in the light of the new knowledge, this will have that effect. The shift in demand between different products, if the co-efficients of production in the different lines of industry are not exactly the same, is bound to change the relative prices of the factors, and these changes will occur gradually as all the entrepreneurs redirect their resources in anticipation of the impending change. If we take the simplest imaginable case where there is only one uniform scarce factor besides "capital," namely labour, it will depend on the relative quantities of labour required in the lines of industry, to and from which demand is expected to shift, whether the product of labour invested for longer periods will fall relatively to that of labour invested for shorter periods, or *vice versa*.

If we assume that the industry, whose product will be in stronger demand, is one where relatively more capital is required, the tendency will be for wages to fall, and prospective returns on capital to rise. The way in which this is brought about is that, out of the amortisation quotas shifted to the industry now more favoured by demand, the capitalist will be willing to pay only wages corresponding to the lower marginal productivity of labour there. And since the withdrawal of these amortisation quotas from the other industry will decrease demand for labour there, wages will gradually fall.

The position of the capitalist will thereby be affected in a double way. The gradual fall of wages will leave in his hands a greater amount of gross profits to be divided between investment and consumption. And the expected returns on the reinvestment of these receipts will be increased. How much of these gross receipts from capital will he have to reinvest, if he wants to obtain a constant income stream from that moment onwards? There are three main types of possible reactions of which only one corresponds to that criterion. Either he may go on, until the change has actually occurred, to consume only as much as before. In that case he will have invested during the period constantly increasing amounts of money, and will consequently find himself at the end of the period in possession of a greater stock of capital, which will probably give him a greater percentage return (on the assumption that all other entrepreneurs act in the same way, but that the consequent increase of capital will not lead to proportionally greater reduction of interest, i.e. that the elasticity of the demand for capital under the new conditions is greater than unity). In this case his net income would at the end of the transition period suddenly increase, a change which does not correspond to the postulate that income should remain constant from the moment when the impending change becomes known.

Or we may assume that during the transition period he continues to reinvest amortisation quotas of the same magnitude as before. In this case his expenditure on consumers' goods will gradually increase during the transition period as the rate of interest increases, his capital will remain the same in money value, and will give him from the moment the anticipated change has actually occurred onwards, a permanently higher income. This again clearly

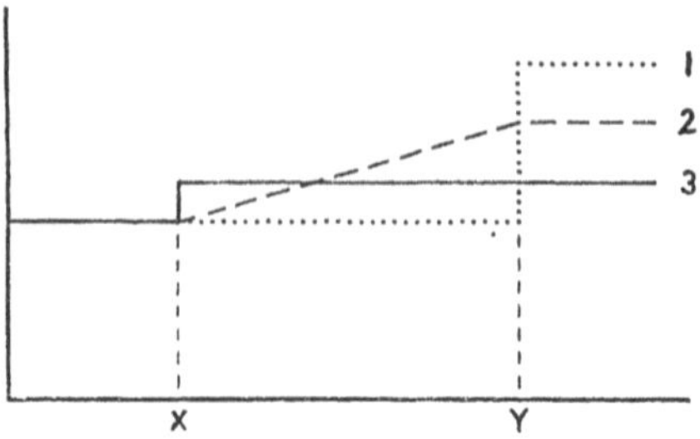

does not correspond to the assumption that he disposes of his resources in such a way, that in the light of his knowledge he may at every moment expect a constant income stream.

To do so he would have to raise his consumption, at the moment the impending change becomes known, to a level at which it can be permanently maintained. This implies that during the transition period he will increase his consumption and reduce his reinvestment to such a figure that at the end of the period he will be in possession of a quantity of capital which, although in every conceivable dimension it may be smaller than that he owned before, will at the higher rate of interest give him an income equal to that enjoyed during the transition period, and higher than that which he had before the change became known.

These alternative policies of the capitalist can easily be depicted by means of a diagram. The alternative income streams are here represented by the lines marked 1, 2, and 3 respectively. The ordinate for every point of the abscissa, on which time is measured, represents the magnitude of the income stream at that moment. The change is supposed to occur at Y, and to be first foreseen at X (which precedes Y by at least the maximum investment period). The line 1 then represents the income stream of the capitalist who goes on spending during the transition period XY as much as he did before, and thereby increases his capital in money terms, line 2 that of the capitalist who gradually increases his consumption and keeps his capital in money terms constant, and line 3 the income stream of the capitalist who immediately raises his consumptive expenditure to the level at which it can be permanently maintained (i.e. until some further change occurs), and thereby decreases the money value of his capital.

There is no difficulty in applying the same kind of analysis to the reverse case of an expected decrease of the return from capital, or to almost any other type of change that may be foreseen. If the shift of demand, instead of taking place from a less to a more capitalist line of industry, takes the reverse direction and the rate of interest is therefore due to fall, then a similar choice arises. Either the capitalist will anticipate the fall in his income and reduce it immedi-

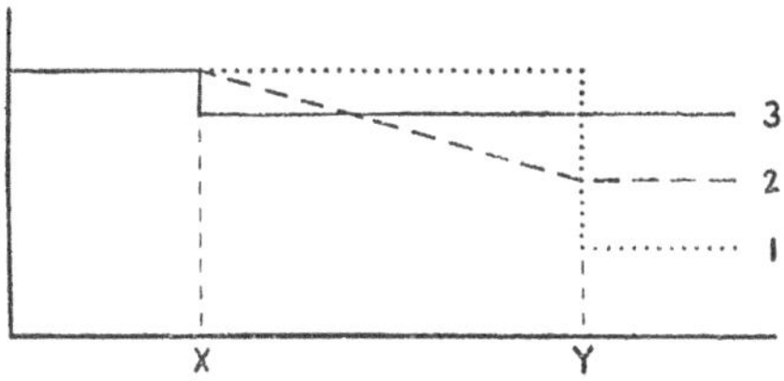

ately in order to avoid, by an increase of his capital in monetary terms, the full force of the later reduction which would otherwise be inevitable (case 3). Or he will only gradually reduce it as his gross receipts from capital fall (case 2). Or he will maintain his expenditure until the change actually takes place, and so reduce even the money value of his capital, from which henceforth he will draw a smaller percentage return (case 1).

Action of the type 3, which I suggest in both cases comes nearest to what is really aimed at by capital accounting, but does not imply the maintenance of, any dimension of capital as such, means in other words that the capitalist treats his gross receipts during the transition period as a terminable annuity of which he wants to consume no more than such a constant amount, that the sinking fund accumulated at the end of the period will secure him the same income in perpetuity. It is such action, which in my opinion best fulfils the purpose for which it is commonly desired to keep capital intact, from the point of view of the individual capitalist. It remains now to show what such action implies in the case of other types of changes, and what will be the effect of such action on the part of the capitalists on other incomes.

There is little more to be said about the effects of changes in the supply of factors, or—what is fundamentally the same thing—changes in technology. Since even an initial change in consumers' demand brings about changes in the relative scarcity of the different factors, there is really here no new problem beyond those already discussed. The anticipation of the forthcoming change will require the same kind of decision, and if the capitalist wants to keep his income stream constant after the impending change becomes known, he will have to redivide his changed gross receipts on the same principles as shown before. If, for instance, the supply of a factor of production is expected to decrease, or the production of a commodity in some other way to become more difficult,[21] or if on the other hand the discovery of new natural resources,

[21] Negative inventions, although apparently an absurd idea, are unfortunately by no means impossible. Losses of knowledge already possessed do occur, particularly in the field of economics, and the most glaring instance of this sort is, of course, the recrudescence of protectionism with its erection of negative railroads, to use Bastiat's very appropriate phrase. [Neoclassical "real business cycle theory" since the 1980s has reintroduced the concept of "negative inventions" or negative technology shocks. For an example, very much in the spirit of Hayek's example of pro-

or the invention of a new process facilitates the production of a commodity, this will again, as soon as the impending change becomes known, affect the decisions of the capital owners in a double way: it will affect the magnitude of the gross receipts from capital by way of the changes in the prices of the other factors that will occur in consequence of the adjustments to the expected change, and it will affect the return to be expected from the reinvestment of capital. The decision of the capitalists will accordingly depend in the same way on the effect of the change on the relative productivity of capital and the other factors, as was true in the former case. If the capitalist acts on the principle we have described as being most in accordance with what is the most obvious purpose of "maintaining capital intact," he will tend to let the money value of his capital decrease when in the future it promises to give a greater percentage return, because he will anticipate that greater future return; and he will attempt to increase the money value of his capital by reducing his expenditure immediately when he expects in the future a lower percentage return.

While in this way the capitalist will minimise the fluctuations of his own income, his action will rather tend to accentuate the effect of the change on other incomes. At least, if instead of acting in this way he would try to keep the money value of his capital constant (and still more if he acted according to the third alternative—case 1—i.e. if he kept his consumption constant until the expected change actually occurred), the incomes of the other factors would have to change to a much smaller degree than in the case where he aims at keeping the income from his capital constant. In the case where the marginal productivity of labour tends to fall and that of capital to rise, wages would have to fall less if the capitalists kept at least the money value of their capital constant and still less if they increased it. And in the reverse case wages would rise less if instead of maintaining or even raising the money value of their capital, capitalists allowed it to decrease. But there is little reason to assume that they will act in this way. Even where the capitalists do not want to keep their income constant under all circumstances but where, as will probably be the case to some extent, every increase of their expected income will induce them to plan for a gradually increasing consumption, i.e. to save, and perhaps an expected decrease in their income will in the same way induce them to plan for a decreasing consumption, i.e. to dissave, this is not very likely to result in a maintenance of the monetary value of capital (i.e. to make their action similar to case 2 above). One would have to assume a very pecu-

tectionism, consider the cartel-promoting policies of the early New Deal, which are identified as a negative technology shock, "defined as any exogenous factor that [reduces] the efficiency with which business enterprises transform inputs into output," by Harold L. Cole and Lee E. Ohanian, "The Great Depression in the United States from a Neoclassical Perspective," *Federal Reserve Bank Minneapolis Quarterly Review*, vol. 23, no. 1, Winter 1999, pp. 2–24.—Ed.]

liar shape of the indifference curves expressing the "willingness to save" of the capitalists in order to obtain such a result.

V—Obsolescence and Anticipated Risk

There remain two special cases to be considered before we abandon the assumption of correct foresight on the part of the capitalists. The first is obsolescence, as distinguished from wear and tear, as a cause of destruction of existing capital values. Although at first it may appear otherwise, this is a phenomenon which will occur even with perfect foresight. The second case on the other hand is somewhat intermediate between that of correct and incorrect foresight; it is the case where the probability of the occurrence of certain changes is correctly and equally foreseen and estimated by all members of the society. Since this case also raises the problem of obsolescence, it is convenient to treat the two cases together.

The first case would hardly require much discussion if Professor Pigou had not originally excluded obsolescence from the capital losses which have to be made up by new investment if capital is to be maintained intact. Obsolescence in this sense occurs everywhere where the usefulness of any piece of real capital diminishes faster than it decays in a physical sense.[22] There can be no doubt that many investments in actual life are made with complete awareness of the fact that the period, during which the instrument concerned will be useful, will be much shorter than its possible physical duration. In the case of most very durable constructions like the permanent way of a railroad, the prospective "economic life" ought to be regarded as considerably shorter than the possible "physical life." In many cases it lies in the very nature of the product that it must be made almost infinitely durable, although it is only needed for a very transient purpose. It is impossible to adjust the durability of a machine to the short period during which it may be needed, and in many other cases the strength needed from a construction while it is used necessitates it being made in a form which will last much longer than the period during which it is needed.

In all these cases it is known beforehand that the stream of receipts to be obtained from the investment is limited, not only to the period for which the

[22] [This properly general way of defining obsolescence includes the typical case where an outdated piece of equipment continues to provide services, albeit less valuable services. For example, previous-generation passenger jets shift from serving passengers of full-service airlines to those of low-cost airlines. In the text below Hayek sometimes speaks only of the limiting case of obsolescence in which the value of the equipment's services goes to zero. In his discussion of inventions, however, he considers the typical case in which outdated equipment is not scrapped but continues to be used.—Ed.]

good will last physically, but for the shorter period during which it can be used. The capitalist who aims at a constant income stream will have to take this into account in deciding about the division of his gross receipts between consumption and amortisation. He will again have to treat the gross receipts as a terminable annuity, and to consume no more than such an amount that the sinking fund accumulated at the end of the period will give him in the form of a perpetual income. This means that he will have to put aside amounts proportional, not to the physical wear and tear, but to the decrease in the value of the investment.

If, instead of acting in this way, he would, as Professor Pigou suggests, at the end of every accounting period put aside out of his gross receipts only such a part of the value of the instrument as is proportional to the physical deterioration that has taken place during the period, this would clearly mean that he would consume considerably more than he could expect to derive from the much smaller sinking fund accumulated when the instrument ceases to be useful.

The significance of such a decision on the part of the capitalist becomes particularly clear if we consider the case where the capitalist has to choose between two investments of equal cost, both represented by equally durable instruments, but one of the kind that is expected to remain useful so long as it lasts physically, while the other serves a very transient purpose. Under what conditions will he consider the two investments as equally attractive? The first answer is, of course, if they promise him the same permanent income. But under what conditions do they promise him the same permanent income? If the gross receipts from the investments while they flow were in both cases equal and just sufficient to provide the same income *plus* an allowance for depreciation proportional to the physical deterioration, the effect would clearly be that in the case where the instrument ceases to be useful long before it has worn out physically, only a fraction of the sum originally invested would have been recovered which would bring only a much lower income in the future. To decide for this alternative would mean that an income stream which starts at a given magnitude but decreases later on is treated as equal to an income stream which is permanently kept at the initial magnitude of the former. In order that investment in the instrument of only transitory usefulness may appear equally attractive as that of lasting usefulness, it would be necessary that, while the former remains in use, it would produce gross returns sufficiently large to allow for full amortisation of its original value. In other words, only if the expected returns cover, in addition to the same income, not only depreciation in the narrower sense but also obsolescence, can the two investments be regarded as equally attractive.

Thus, to neglect obsolescence, in deciding about the investments to be chosen, would in the same way frustrate the endeavour to keep the income stream at any definite level, as would a neglect of depreciation proper. In fact, from a purely economic point of view, there is no real difference between depreciation and obsolescence. Whether an instrument ceases to be useful because of physical decay, or for any other reason, makes no difference to the capitalist, when he has to decide whether it is worth while to invest in it or not.

That there could exist any doubt whatever about this point is probably due to the fact that, while the case where it is definitely foreseen that an instrument will become obsolescent at a certain date is by no means rare, it is not the case of which we think in the first instance when we speak of obsolescence. Of much greater practical importance than this case, where an instrument has for technical reasons to be made more durable than is really needed, is the case where it has been given a greater durability than turns out ultimately to have been necessary, because the period during which it would be needed was not known for certain. In so far as the effects of completely unforeseen and unforeseeable changes are here concerned, we shall consider them only in the following section of this paper. But, as has already been mentioned, there is an intermediate class between this case and that of complete foresight, the case where a definite probability exists and is generally known that a change will occur. And this case, as will be shown, is fundamentally similar to that just discussed, in the sense that here, too, the anticipated risk of obsolescence has to be taken into account if capital is to be maintained intact.

The capitalist who considers a number of different investment opportunities will usually find that they promise different returns with different degrees of probability. And while the degree of certainty with which he will be able to predict returns may be fairly high in so far as the immediate future is concerned, uncertainty will generally be much greater as regards the period during which he may hope to receive these or any returns. But while he will be unable to predict with certainty the periods during which he may expect returns in the different cases, he will have fairly definite ideas about the different degrees of probability that they will give returns for longer or shorter periods. In his choice between different investment opportunities, these estimates of the probable periods after which they will cease to give returns will play an important role. He will evidently consider an investment, where the risk, that it will soon cease to give any returns, is greater than in other cases, only if the gross returns are such that he can expect to amortise the capital sunk in it during a correspondingly shorter period. Only when he distributes his capital in such a way between the different investment opportunities, that the gross returns cover the probable rate of obsolescence, can he hope to obtain a constant income stream. If he acts in this way, and if his estimates of the probabilities were correct, even if in none of the individual cases he should have guessed quite correctly, his losses are likely to be balanced, so that on the whole he will succeed in maintaining his income stream constant.

This presupposes that his investments are sufficiently numerous and diverse to make such compensation possible, and that in the cases where he makes unexpected profits, i.e. where the investment continues to bring returns after its original value has been fully amortised, he does not treat these profits as net income, but he uses them to offset the losses suffered from other investments. Where the investments of the individual capitalists are not sufficiently numerous and diverse to make such internal compensation possible, the same results will follow for the capitalists as a class, provided again that those who make profit do not consume them but use them, or at least the greater part of them for new investment. Is there any reason to expect that in this case the capitalist, following the general principle we have regarded as normal, will behave in such a way? This brings us to the general question of how the capitalists will react on an entirely unforeseen change.

VI—The Reaction of the Capitalist on Unforeseen Changes

The changes whose effects we have now to study differ from those considered in the earlier parts of this paper by the fact that they are not foreseen but become known only when they actually occur (or at least some time after the investment affected by them has irrevocably been made). That is, we abandon at this point the assumption of more or less complete foresight on the part of the capitalist, and ask how he will have to act when an unexpected change affects the returns from an investment, to which he has already committed himself, if he wants to keep his income stream from that moment onwards constant.

The owner of any piece of real capital, who finds that in consequence of such an unforeseen change the gross returns which he may expect during the remaining "life" of that instrument will be either greater or smaller than he had anticipated, will have to choose between the same main types of action as those discussed in connection with a foreseen change. If we consider only the case where, in consequence of the change his gross receipts have decreased, he may in the first instance consume, during the remaining "life" of his investment as much as before (if the gross receipts are still as great as the amount he used to consume) and reduce only his depreciation allowance. The effect of this would be that when the returns from the investment cease he will only have accumulated a sinking fund considerably smaller than what would be necessary to give him an income equal to that enjoyed up to that moment. Or, in other words, he would have maintained his consumption after the change has occurred at the pre-existing level at the expense of an inevitable later reduction of his consumption, a reduction which would clearly have to be greater than if he had immediately reduced his consumption to a level at which it could be permanently maintained. To act in the latter way, i.e. again to treat the gross receipts to be expected during the remaining life of the investment as a terminable annuity, whose capital value is to be maintained constant, would evidently be the only course of action consistent with the aim of a constant income stream. The third possibility would be to continue, after the change has occurred, so far as possible the same allowances for depreciation and to reduce consumption to what remains beyond this, if anything does remain. In this way it would be possible in many cases to recover the full capital value originally invested. But could this properly be regarded as maintaining the capital constant? It would mean that the owner would have to reduce consumption for a period below the level at which it could be permanently maintained in order to increase it later above that level. It seems that this would have to be regarded in every sense as new saving, saving it is true to make up for a loss, but for a loss which has already occurred. This loss was irrevocably incurred when the investment was made in ignorance of the impending change.

The same applies, *mutatis mutandis*, to the case of profits due to an unexpected change. If, after a change which has increased the gross returns from his investment, the owner wants to keep his income permanently at the same higher level, this means that he must only consume so much of the gain as to leave an amount which, reinvested at the current rate of interest, would give him the same additional income in perpetuity.

If, for instance, his additional receipts after the change are £210, and the rate at which he can reinvest is 5 per cent., he must only consume £10, and invest the remaining £200, which at 5 per cent. will give him the same returns in every future year. Such "windfall profits" are, therefore, not income in the sense that their consumption is compatible with maintaining capital intact. Also consumption need not be reduced by the amount of "windfall losses" in order to maintain capital intact. In both cases only the current interest on the (positive or negative) capital gain ought to be counted as income.[23]

This principle applies, whether the change in question was completely foreseen, or whether it is a change, the probability of whose occurrence was anticipated, but which does not occur at the moment that was regarded as most probable. The difference between the two cases is that where the probability of the occurrence of the change was correctly anticipated, deviations of the individual cases from what was regarded as most probable are likely to balance in their effect, so that capitalists as a whole will succeed in keeping their income stream constant. But, where the changes were completely unforeseen,

[23] [Milton Friedman in *A Theory of the Consumption Function* (Princeton, NJ: Princeton University Press, 1957) would later famously distinguish *permanent* from *transitory* income. Hayek is in effect saying here that £10 per year is the gain in permanent income.—Ed.]

there is no reason to expect that gains and losses will balance in this way, so that at least total incomes from capital would remain constant. It is much more likely that in such a case, if the capitalists behave as described, it will have the effect of either permanently decreasing or permanently increasing the income from capital.

Of the different types of changes which would have to be considered in the exhaustive discussion we may confine ourselves here to that of an invention, which is in many ways the most interesting. The application to the case of a shift in demand between different types of consumers' goods, or of changes in the supply of factors, will present no difficulty. In so far as the invention is concerned, two kinds of effects have to be considered; on the one hand the possibility of a loss of capital invested in plant that is made obsolete by the invention, and on the other hand, the possible gains on plants and stock which, at least during a transition period, may bring higher returns than was expected. Although there is some reason to suppose that any unexpected change is much more likely to lead to considerable capital losses than to capital gains, it is not impossible that in the individual case the gains may be greater than the losses.

The conditions, which must be given, in order that it may be advantageous to introduce newly invented machinery for the production of a commodity, which up to the present has been produced by a different still existing plant, are too well known to need more than a short restatement.[24] In order that the invention should lead to the complete abandonment of the old machinery, it would be necessary that it should reduce the total cost of production below the prime cost of running the old plant (or, quite exactly, to such a figure that the difference between it and the prime cost is lower than the return to be expected from the investment of the scrap value of the old plant). In this case the capital value of the old plant would be completely destroyed (or reduced to the scrap value of the plant). Much more frequently will it be the case that, while the new invention does not result in a sufficient lowering of cost to drive the old plant out of business altogether, it will make an increase of sales at the reduced price possible. In this case only the additional output will be produced by the new process, and the value of the old plant will be reduced to a figure corresponding to the capitalised value of the lower surplus over running costs, which is henceforward to be expected. In all these cases capital losses will occur, which may be further increased by a rise in the

[24] Cf. Pigou, *Economics of Welfare*, 4th ed., p. 188, [Lionel] Robbins, *An Essay on the Nature and Significance of Economic Science* [London: Macmillan], 1932, pp. 50 *et seq.*, and my inaugural address "On the Trend of Economic Thinking," *Economica*, May 1933. [Hayek, "The Trend of Economic Thinking," *Economica*, no. 40, May 1933, pp. 121–27. It is reprinted in *The Trend of Economic Thinking: Essays on Political Economists and Economic History*, ed. W. W. Bartley II and Stephen Kresge, vol. 3 of *The Collected Works of F. A. Hayek* (Chicago: University of Chicago Press, 1991), pp. 17–34.—Ed.]

rate of interest, which may be the general effect of the increased demand for capital caused by the new invention. In so far as such a rise in the rate of interest takes place, the losses in capital values caused thereby are not inconsistent with maintaining capital (i.e. income from capital) constant in our sense.

Capital gains will occur in consequence of an invention—apart from the increases in capital values of natural resources, like mineral deposits and other non-reproduceable [*sic*] factors—mainly during such transition periods until it is possible to increase the supply of particular instruments, which are now also required in the newly invented process. If, e.g. the new machinery required can be produced only in a particular plant, which before was expected to be used up only very slowly over a long period, and if it takes a long time to erect an additional plant of the same sort, the owner of the existing plant will clearly be able to make considerable and unexpected profits during the interval. Since these profits will be of a temporary character, he ought not to regard them as ordinary income, but to reinvest so much of it as will secure him in perpetuity an additional income equal to that which he actually consumes during the transition period.[25]

VII—The Impossibility of an Objective Standard with Different Degrees of Foresight

So far the criterion, for what is to be understood as maintaining capital intact on the part of the individual entrepreneur or capitalist, is purely subjective, because it depends on the extent to which the individual capitalist foresees the future. Entirely different actions by two capitalists who hold different views on the future, but who are otherwise in exactly the same position, may satisfy our criterion. Both may, in the light of their different knowledge, do their best to obtain a constant income stream, and yet both will probably fail, earlier or later, and in different degrees. Are we to say that neither has been maintaining his capital, and ought we to reserve this term to the case of action with perfect foresight? In a world where very imperfect foresight is the rule this would clearly lead to absurd results. We should not only have to say that nobody ever succeeds in maintaining his capital intact—which in a sense of course would be true—but we should also be prevented from using this concept of maintaining capital intact as a description of the actual behaviour of the entrepreneurs, who want neither to decrease or to increase their income from their

[25] It is not possible here to enter into a discussion of the distinction between capital-saving and labour-saving inventions. But it should be clear that at least the older concept of capital-saving inventions[,] which was based on the idea that capital which in the past was used in the industry affected by the invention will in consequence become available for use elsewhere, assumed a kind of capital maintenance which will not occur in the real world. The part of the capital embodied in the now antiquated machinery will be lost at the same time as it becomes "superfluous."

possessions. Taking into account the fact that human foresight is of necessity very imperfect, and that all economic activity must be based on anticipations, which will partly prove incorrect, it would still seem desirable to find a criterion which would enable us to distinguish between losses—or rather missed opportunities of faster improvement—which are unavoidable in view of the unpredictability of the change, and capital losses due to what appear to be avoidable mistakes.

At first one might feel inclined to base the definition of what is to be regarded as adequate maintenance of capital on such a degree of foresight as the intelligent capitalist can reasonably be expected to possess. But closer examination of the problem soon reveals that any attempt to find an objective test of what can be regarded as maintenance of capital, short of the case of absolute foresight, must necessarily fail. It seems commonsense to say that if an entrepreneur expects a change in taste, e.g. because he hopes to interest the public in a novelty, but is disappointed in his expectations, and loses the capital invested in the venture, this is a loss of capital which must be made up out of new savings, if capital is to be kept intact. If this did not happen, and similar failures were frequently repeated, the capital available for the production of things which people want would be considerably reduced by conversion into equipment for making things which nobody wants. On the other hand, the loss of capital due to an unforeseen change in taste seems merely the incidental and unavoidable concomitant of a process leading to what is now a preferred income. Yet if entrepreneurs had correctly anticipated the change—and some entrepreneurs may have done so—the wants of the public would have been supplied even better. Is, therefore, the loss of the entrepreneurs, who did not foresee correctly, to be counted as a capital loss to be deducted from gross output? and does it already mean that they might have foreseen the change if a single happy speculator chanced to do so, who, according to all reasonable expectations should have proved to be a waster of capital?

It is not possible to base the distinction here on the concept of a change, and to say that to invest in anticipation of a change which does not occur is wasting capital, while to invest in the mistaken assumption that things will remain as they are is only a cause of unavoidable loss. In the first instance, it is by no means evident what is to be regarded as a change. If a temporary change is mistakenly considered as permanent, or if the expectation that the seasonal fluctuations of the past will be repeated is disappointed, are these to be regarded as mistaken expectations of a change, or as a mistaken expectation that things will remain constant? Clearly in economic life, and outside of a fictitious stationary state, the concept of a change itself has frequently no meaning except in the sense of a change relative to expectations. In the second place, and even more important, an approximately correct anticipation of the majority of "changes" in the usual sense is an indispensable condition of that degree of progress which is observed in actual life. One need only consider for a moment what would happen if entrepreneurs always acted as if things would remain forever as they are at present, and changed their plans only after a change in demand (or some other change) had actually occurred, in order to see what would necessarily be the effect on general productivity. Every change would mean an enormous loss, or rather, the adaptation of production to the change would become so expensive (not because the loss on existing investment would have to be counted as cost, but because the "free capital" required for the new production would be so scarce) as to make it in many cases impossible. How rich, on the other hand, should we now be if all past changes had been correctly foreseen from the beginning of things!

All this means simply that the mobility of capital, the degree to which it can be maintained in a changing world, will depend on the foresight of the entrepreneurs and capitalists. If this is a commonplace, it is at least a commonplace to which far too little regard is paid in usual reasoning. It means nothing less than that the amount of capital available at any moment in a dynamic society depends much more on the degree of foresight of the entrepreneurs than on current saving or on "time preference." This is simply a corollary to the equally obvious and neglected fact that "capital" is not a factor, the quantity of which is given independently of human action even in the comparatively short run. How great a contribution to the possibility of satisfying human wants a given stock of capital goods will still represent some time later, will depend largely on how correctly the entrepreneurs foresee the situation at this moment. Their anticipations in this respect are quite as important a "datum" for the explanation of the dynamic process as the "stock of capital," and the latter concept has in fact little meaning without the former. As an enumeration of individual capital goods existing at the beginning, the "stock of capital" is of course an important datum, but the form in which this capital will still exist some time afterwards, and how much of it will still exist, depends mainly on the foresight of the entrepreneurs and capitalists. It would probably be no exaggeration to say that to maintain his capital so as to receive the greatest lasting return, is the main function of the capitalist-entrepreneur.[26] But not only is in this sense the size of the productive equipment of society dependent on the success of the entrepreneur, it is also dependent in a world of uncertainty on his capitalising capital gains ("windfall profits"). It should be recognised that much of the new formation of capital equipment (which need not represent net additions to capital in the traditional terminology) does

[26] In this connection it is hardly possible to draw a sharp distinction between the entrepreneur and capitalist.

not arise out of savings proper, but out of those gains of individual capitalists which are part of the process of capital maintenance.[27] This process will, as shown above, always involve unforeseen profits on the part of some and unforeseen losses on the part of other entrepreneurs, changes on capital account, which are part of an ever-proceeding process of redistribution of wealth, not to be confused with the distribution of income. The entrepreneur who finds that a risky undertaking succeeds, and who for a time makes extraordinary profits because he has restricted the amount of investment so as to give him in case of success a margin of profit over cost which is proportionate to the risk, will not be justified if he regards the whole profit as income. If he aims at a constant income stream from his investment, he will have to reinvest such part of his profits as will be sufficient to give him an income equal to the part he has consumed, when the rate of profit in what has now proved to be a successful line of business falls to normal.[28] It is in such a way that, in case of changes in demand or technical progress, etc., capital is newly formed without new saving in place of that which is lost elsewhere. There is, of course, no reason to assume that the capital lost and that which is newly formed will correspond in any quantitative sense; and it is exactly for this reason that the usual concept of a net change in capital, which is supposed to correspond in some way to saving, is of little value. There has in this case been no abstention from consumption which could have been maintained at that level. If anybody can be said to have refrained from consumption which would be compatible with enjoying the same income permanently, it is not the entrepreneurs, but rather the consumers who for a time had to pay a price in excess of the cost which the production of the commodity entails after it has proved an assured success. But this "saving" is of course neither voluntary nor does it represent an abstention from consumption, which could have been regarded as permanently possible so long as the outcome of the venture was uncertain. It can hardly be questioned that in the actual world a great deal of the equipment which is made necessary by some change is financed out of these temporary differences between cost and price. But it may appear somewhat paradoxical that where it can be provided in this way this ought not to be classed as saving but as a capital gain, a kind of transfer of capital which means that not only new capital is formed in place of that lost elsewhere, but that it is formed exactly where it is most needed, and in the hands of those most qualified to use it; this follows, however, necessarily from the consistent use of the definition of maintaining capital and saving, which we have adopted. It will

[27] [That is, retained earnings that are productively reinvested.—Ed.]

[28] It is of course possible that he regards himself as so much more clever than his competitors that he will count on being able to make permanently supernormal profits of this sort. To this extent he would be quite justified in regarding them as income.

be shown in the next section that this use of the terms proves convenient in other directions also.

VIII –"Saving" and "Investing"

The upshot of the discussions of the last sections is that if changes in the data occur (such as new inventions, shifts in consumers' demand or changes in the supply of factors), the amount of capital (conceived as a multiple of the income of a given period, or—what amounts to the same thing—the result of a certain "average" waiting period,[29] or in any other conceivable quantitative sense), which is available and required to maintain income from then onwards at a constant level, will change also, and that in consequence there is no reason to expect that any of the conceivable dimensions of capital will remain constant. It remains true, of course, that *ceteris paribus* it is necessary to maintain or replenish a reservoir of goods of a constant size, in order to maintain a given output. But when conditions change so as to make a smaller or larger reservoir necessary for the same purpose, its contents will tend to change automatically in such a way as to preserve income constant from the moment when the change becomes known. The fact that an impending change is likely to become known to different people at different times will lead to capital gains and capital losses of individuals, with the effect that persons who have shown the greatest foresight will command the greatest amount of resources. But in a world of imperfect foresight not only the size of the capital stock, but also the income derived from it will inevitably be subject to unintended and unpredictable changes which depend on the extent and distribution of foresight, and there will be no possibility of distinguishing any particular movement of these magnitudes as normal.

These conclusions have rather far-reaching consequences with respect to the much used, or much abused, concepts of saving and investing. If the stock of capital required to keep income from any moment onwards constant cannot in any sense be defined as a constant magnitude, it becomes also impos-

[29] [The "average" waiting or investment period for inputs corresponds to the ratio of capital value to annual income assuming (as in Hayek's *Prices and Production*) a perfectly triangular structure of production (even continuous input, point output), with the value of the capital stock (regarded entirely as goods in process) represented by the area of the right triangle whose legs are final income per year and the investment periods for inputs in years. If the "average" investment period between input and final output is (say) 4 years, then the investment period leg is 8 years long, and the value of the capital stock = ½ (8 years)(income per year) = 4 times annual income. By the time he wrote *The Pure Theory of Capital*, Hayek no longer considered such a model of production to be generally satisfactory but instead considered it a special limiting case.—Ed.]

sible to state that any sacrifices of present income in order to increase future income (or the reverse) must lead to any net changes in the amount of capital. Saving and investment in the ordinary meaning of the terms are, of course, one of the causes, but by no means the only cause, which affect the magnitude of capital (in any conceivable quantitative sense), and the changes in the size of the capital stock cannot therefore be regarded as indications of what sacrifices of present income have been or are being made in the interest of future income. This idea, appropriately enough for the analysis of the effects of a change under otherwise stationary conditions, must be completely abandoned in the analysis of a dynamic process. If we want to retain the connection between the ideas of saving and investment, and that of a sacrifice of potential present income in the interest of future income (and it will be shown that it is this concept which is of importance in the connection in which those terms are commonly used), we cannot determine the size of either saving or investment by any references to changes in the quantity of capital. And with the abandonment of this basis of the distinction, there will, of course, have to fall the habitual practice of economists of separating out such part of general investment activity as happens to leave the capital stock in some sense constant, as something different from activities which add to it, a distinction which has no relationship to anything in the real world.[30]

To deny that the usual distinctions between new and merely renewed investment, and between new savings out of net income and merely maintained savings, as distinctions based on the idea of quantitative increases or decreases of capital, have any definite meaning, is not to deny that they aim at a distinction of real importance. There can be no doubt that the decision[s] of the consumers as to the distribution of consumption over time are something separate from the decisions of the entrepreneur-capitalist as regards what quantities of consumers' goods to provide for different moments of time, and that the two sets of decisions may or may not coincide. What I do want to deny is only that the correspondence or non-correspondence between these two sets of conditions can be adequately expressed in terms of a quantitative correspondence between (net) saving and (net) investment. But if this distinction is not to be formulated in this particular way, what are we to put in its place? In general terms the answer is not difficult. If we must no longer speak in

[30] The same applies, of course, in an even stronger degree to the assumption implied in this distinction that the activities which lead to such net increases of capital are in any way subject to a different set of determining influences from those which lead to a mere quantitative maintenance. This should always have been obvious from the mere fact that when additions in this sense are being made (i.e. if capital increases in the usual terminology) this will always affect the concrete form of the new capital goods by which the old ones are replaced. [Hayek's point here implies, in particular, a criticism of Frank Knight's conception of capital maintenance as automatic but capital accumulation as discretionary.—Ed.]

terms of absolute increases and decreases of capital we must attempt a more direct comparison of the time distribution of income. Capital accounting, as has been mentioned before, is itself only an abbreviated method of effecting this comparison in an indirect way, and when this indirect method fails it is only natural to go back to its *rationale*, and to carry out the comparison explicitly. Instead of comparing them each with the supposed standard case of capital remaining "constant," and so arriving at the concepts of net saving (net income *minus* consumption) and net investment, and then to juxtapose these derived concepts, we shall have to compare directly the intentions of the consumers and the intentions of the producers with regard to the income stream they want to consume and produce respectively.[31]

The question, then, is essentially whether the demand for consumers' goods tends to keep ahead of, to coincide with, or to fall behind the output of consumers' goods irrespective of whether either of the two magnitudes is increasing, remaining constant or decreasing in an absolute sense. But in order to give this question a clear meaning we have yet to settle in terms of what are the demand for and the supply of consumers' goods to be measured, in order to establish whether they coincide or whether the one exceeds the other. In a sense of course demand and supply are always equal, or made equal by the pricing process, and to speak of their relative magnitudes presupposes some unit in terms of which their magnitude is measured independently of the prices formed on the market.

Consider first the decision of the "savers," or the body of consumers as a whole. What we can assume of them is, not that they will under all conditions aim at an income stream of a particular shape, but that if they are offered a present income of a given magnitude, *plus* the sources of a future income of a certain magnitude, they will attach certain relative values to

[31] [Hayek's conception of intertemporal equilibrium here is a matching between the consumers' planned time-profile of consumption and the producers' planned time-profile of output. He had introduced that conception in "Das Intertemporale Gleichgewichtssystem der Presie und die Bewegungen des 'Geldwertes,'" *Weltwirtschaftliches Archiv*, no. 1, July 1928, pp. 33–76; translated as "Intertemporal Price Equilibrium and Movements in the Value of Money," in *Good Money, Part 1: The New World*, ed. Stephen Kresge, vol. 5 of *The Collected Works of F. A. Hayek* (Chicago: University of Chicago Press, 1999). When Hayek wrote, in n. 1 above, that he had sketched the present article (published 1935) "a considerable time ago," he may have meant as early as 1928. He applied the intertemporal-plan-matching concept to business cycle theory in "Preiserwartungen, Monetäre Störungen und Fehlinvestitionen," *Nationalökonomisk Tidsskrift*, 3rd series, no. 43, 1935, pp. 176–91; translated by Hayek as "Price Expectations, Monetary Disturbances, and Malinvestments" in Hayek, *Profits, Interest, and Investment* (London: George Routledge & Sons, 1939); and reprinted in Hayek, *Good Money, Part I, op. cit.*, pp. 186–227. He developed the concept's methodological implications further in "Economics and Knowledge," *Economica*, n.s., vol. 4, no. 13, February 1937, pp. 33–54; reprinted in Hayek, *Individualism and Economic Order* (Chicago: University of Chicago Press, 1948).—Ed.]

these incomes. For every such combination of a given present income and the sources of a certain future income we must assume these relative valuations to be determined.[32]

If the relative value consumers attach to the sources of future income, compared with present values, should be higher (or lower) than the cost (in terms of present income) of reproducing new sources of future income of the same magnitude, more (or less) such sources will be produced. And assuming that the relative valuations of the consumers do not change abruptly—which is least to be expected when in each successive period the available income is equal to that for which they have planned—then production will tend to provide in each successive period such amounts of present income and sources of future income, that their relative cost (in terms of each other) will approximately correspond to the relative values attached to them by the consumers.[33] But if for some reason—say because additional money has become available for investment purposes—the price[s] of the sources of future income have been raised out of correspondence with the valuation of consumers, more sources of future income and less current income will be provided for the next period than consumers will be then willing to take at prices corresponding to their relative cost. Consumers will find that they get less current real income, and in consequence will attach a greater value to it compared with the sources of future income—investment will have exceeded saving in the usual terminology.[34]

Under the assumption of otherwise constant conditions (i.e. unchanged knowledge, taste, etc.) this process can be described in the familiar way in terms of changes of the investment period, to which correspond changes in the quantity of capital (in terms of income of a period). We would say that, by increasing the waiting period and thereby accumulating more capital, producers have caused a temporary gap in the income stream which leads to a relative rise in the prices of consumers' goods. But as soon as we drop this *ceteris paribus* assumption this is no longer true. The correspondence between the value attached to the sources of future income and their cost is then no longer dependent on the cost of reproducing the same amount of capital, which under changed conditions will make it possible to produce the same future income.

[32] [That is to say, using Irving Fisher's now-standard apparatus, we assume an intertemporal indifference curve map.—Ed.]

[33] [In Fisherian terms, the consumers' intertemporal marginal rate of substitution will come into equality with the producers' intertemporal marginal rate of transformation.—Ed.]

[34] [Here Hayek succinctly characterizes the "over-investment" phase of his business cycle theory. Roger Garrison's later restatement of Hayekian cycle theory allows for a temporary bulge in the sum of investment plus consumption. Hayek, by contrast, does not here allow for simultaneous over-investment and over-consumption. Hayek's consumers must settle for less even in the short run.—Ed.]

Additional investment, in the sense that total output is reduced for a time in order to increase it at a later date, may take place, although at the same time the quantity of capital is reduced (and the "period of production" shortened).[35] Breaks in the even flow of consumers' goods, which make corresponding changes in the attitude of the consumers necessary if disturbances are to be avoided[,] will only occur when that quantity of capital is not maintained which under the conditions prevailing at any moment is required to provide such a constant flow.

The correspondence between the supply of current consumers' goods and the demand for them, which is what has been aimed at by the saving-investment equations, can only be stated adequately if we measure both supply and demand in terms of the alternatives open to consumers and producers under the circumstances existing at the moment.[36] To do this it seems necessary to abandon entirely the concepts of saving and investment as referring to something beyond and outside the normal process of maintaining capital quantitatively intact, and to substitute an analysis on the lines suggested, which does not try to separate "old" and "new" investment, and "new" and "maintained" saving as distinguishable phenomena. Or, if we want to retain the familiar terms and to use them without any reference to changes in the quantity of capital, we might say that "savings" correspond to "investment" when the value of the existing capital goods (in terms of consumers' goods) is such that it becomes profitable to replace them by the capital goods that are required to produce the income in the expectation of which people have decided currently to consume as much as they actually do. I believe that some theories, which used to be stated in terms of net saving and net investment, can be restated in terms of these concepts, and I have tried to sketch such a reformulation of my own views in another place.[37] But I am rather doubtful whether the same is possible with some other theories which seem more dependent on the concepts of saving and investing as absolute magnitudes.

[35] This does not, of course, affect the fundamental proposition that the additional saving is required to make an extension of the process of production possible compared with the time dimension that would be possible without this saving.

[36] All this might apparently have been explained in simpler fashion by comparing the cost of the output of consumers' goods coming on the market during a given period with the expenditure on this output (or by comparing the share of all factors of production which have contributed to the output of a given period with the share of their income which is spent on the output), if it were not for the fact that the concept of cost (and, of course, income) is itself dependent on the concept of maintaining capital intact. This way of stating the relation would be adequate only if we count the cost (in terms of present consumption) which is required, *not* to keep capital intact in some quantitative sense, but to provide sources of so much future income as consumers want to buy at prices covering cost.

[37] "Preiserwartungen, monetäre Störungen und Fehlinvestitionen," *Nationalökonomisk Tidsskrift*, vol. 34, 1935. ["Price Expectations, Monetary Disturbances, and Malinvestments," cited in n. 31 above.—Ed.]

All this is, of course, no reason for not using the concepts of absolute increases or decreases of capital under any circumstances. In the discussion of comparatively long-term changes it may sometimes be quite innocuous. And in the discussion of short-run changes it would be equally legitimate to speak of causes, which *ceteris paribus* would lead to increases or decreases of capital. But we must be very careful not to assume that they actually do, and not to base any distinctions on supposed net changes in the quantity of capital which do not actually take place. Particularly the phenomenon of the trade cycle is probably largely concerned with changes within that region of indeterminateness between clear increases and clear decreases of capital, inside which the concept of an absolute change has no meaning. But it remains probably true that net accumulations and decumulations of capital in the usual sense will present similar phenomena as booms and depressions—at least when real accumulation proceeds faster and real decumulation proceeds slower than saving and dissaving.[38]

IX—Capital Accounting and Monetary Policy

This discussion of the problems connected with the concept of the maintenance of capital has by no means been exhaustive. We have touched on many points which have not been cleared up, and there are many others equally important which have not even been mentioned. This is, however, unavoidable in an article which treats what is in many respects one of the central problems of economic dynamics. But there is one further problem of great importance on which some remarks must be added in this concluding section.

Up to this point we have been largely concerned with an attempt to derive the appropriate action from the *rationale* of "maintaining capital intact," but we have said little about the effects of the actual practice of the entrepreneur, that "abbreviated method" which consists in regarding capital as a money fund of definite magnitude, and on which actual capital accounting is based. This practice is, of course, largely due, and partly justified, by the fact that the

[38] Ricardo seems to have seen clearly the difficulties which exist in this connection when he wrote: "The distress which proceeds from a revulsion of trade is often mistaken for that which accompanies a diminution of the national capital and a retrograde state of society; and it would perhaps be difficult to point out any marks by which they may be accurately distinguished." *Principles*, ch. xix, *Works*, edition McCulloch, p. 160. [The passage quoted appears on p. 160 of David Ricardo, *Principles of Political Economy and Taxation* (first published 1817), in *The Works of David Ricardo*, ed. J. R. McCulloch, new ed. (London: John Murray, 1846). McCulloch's one-volume collection of Ricardo's works was republished many times with the same pagination, so Hayek may have had a later edition at hand. The 1888 edition is available online at http://oll.libertyfund.org/title/1395.—Ed.]

capital of the individual enterprise is to a great extent furnished in the form of money loans, and that in consequence the entrepreneur has in the first instance to provide for a repayment of the money loans.

It was also this practice of treating capital as a money fund which has given rise to the theoretical concept of capital as a quantitatively determined fund. But while the actual use of this concept in real life does not mean that we have to accept it as the basis of theoretical analysis, and does not relieve us from the duty of going back to the *rationale* of its use, the results of this theoretical investigation are little more than a starting point for a study of the effects of the actual practice.

A more exhaustive investigation would, therefore, have to proceed after this preliminary clearing up of the fundamental concepts to the main task of explaining what the effects are of the actual accounting methods used by capitalists, to what extent, and under what conditions, they fulfil their purpose, and when they fail. That there are cases where the rigid application of the money fund concept fails is, of course, generally recognised and to some extent taken account of in the distinction made between changes on income account and changes on capital account. It is also obvious that the results achieved by this method will be largely dependent on monetary policy. Of course, no monetary policy can make the money value of capital behave in such a way that a constant value will always correspond to a quantity of capital which will give the same real income, and that all attempts to increase the future output of consumers' goods at the expense of the present and *vice versa* will lead to corresponding changes in the money value of capital; and in consequence a policy of the capitalist-entrepreneur which aims at nothing but this, will always err to a considerable extent, i.e. will lead to positions where their distribution of resources between current consumption and the provision of future consumption is not in accord with consumers' preferences. But the degree to which capital accounting in terms of money will prove deceptive will depend on the particular monetary policy followed.

To realise these effects in different situations would require a fairly detailed analysis of a number of representative instances. It is only possible to discuss here in the most general way one case, probably the most important and the one which has received the greatest attention in recent discussion; that of a continued increase in output due to "technical progress." Now, in spite of all the complications discussed before, it still remains true that *in any given situation* the value of capital required to provide an income stream at a certain constant or increasing rate will have to stand in a definite proportion to the value of current income. This proportion will change with any change in the relevant data, but where we have to deal with a development from moment to moment it is still approximately true to say that in order that the replacement of capital be sufficient to maintain the income stream at least at a constant rate its value should maintain a constant proportion to that of income. With the money value of capital being kept constant this will evidently only be true if the money value of aggregate income be kept constant also. Any policy which increases the money value of current income and particularly a policy which stabilises the average prices of consumers' goods and therefore raises the aggregate value of income in proportion as real income rises would mean that the money value of capital has to be raised in the same proportion and to be maintained at this increased value if sufficient provision for the replacement of this income is to be made. Any use of the nominal profits of the money value of capital so made for consumption purposes, as would follow from a policy of maintaining money values constant, would lead to insufficient replacement or a consumption of capital in the usual sense.

There can be no doubt that this sort of "paper profits" has played an enormous role not only during the great inflations, but also during all major booms—even if no rise in the absolute level of the prices of consumers' goods has taken place. And even more important than the pseudo-profits computed by enterprises under such conditions are the gains on capital appreciation made on the Stock Exchange. Stock Exchange profits made during such periods of capital appreciation in terms of money, which do not correspond to any proportional increase of capital beyond the amount which is required to reproduce the equivalent of current income, are not income, and their use for consumption purposes must lead to a destruction of capital.[39] So long as the expansion of credit, which has caused this movement, continues at a sufficient rate, this tendency may be overcompensated and the money value of capital continue to grow. But the monetary demand for consumers' goods fed out of such pseudo-profits will prove too large to permit of a maintenance of capital at a proportional value without constant further expansion of credit. That the increasing money values of capital cannot be maintained without further inflation if the amount of appreciation is generally used for consumption purposes, is, of course, only another form of expressing the truism that capital values, which people in general try to convert into income, cannot be maintained beyond the time during which some outside cause operates in the direction of a further rise. But as soon as the cause of a further rise disappears the inherent tendency to "realise" the nominal profits, i.e. to convert part of the capital into income, will assert itself and lead to a fall even in the money value of capital.

But at this point we must stop. This final sketch of some of the conclusions that seem to arise was only meant to suggest some of the problems out of the wide field which opens up at the point where we left the main investigations. It

[39] It is in this way, and in this way only, that during a boom the Stock Exchange is likely to "absorb savings."

seems that the approach to which it leads may ultimately help much to judge the significance of actual business practices, particularly the practices of joint stock companies, the different methods of financing and the Stock Exchange. The students of these fields have in the past had little enough help from the theory of capital. The ultimate clearing up of the issues raised in this article should go far to provide them with better tools.

ELEVEN

MAINTAINING CAPITAL INTACT[1]

by A. C. Pigou

In a rough general way the concept "maintaining capital intact" is easy to grasp. Capital consists at any given moment of a definite inventory of physical things. What these are depends in part on how the general interplay of demand and supply has worked in the past. But at any given moment they are constituted by an unambiguous physical collection. In order that capital may be kept intact, if any object embraced in this collection becomes worn out or is thrown out (scrapped), it must be replaced by "equivalent" objects. When we have got hold of this notion we are able to develop a correlative notion, net real income. From the joint work of the whole mass of productive factors there comes an (annual) in-flowing stream of output.[2] This is gross real income. When what is required to maintain capital intact is subtracted from this there is left net real income. This is Marshall's way of approach.

In his book on *The Pure Theory of Capital*[3] Professor Hayek proposes to throw over the concept of maintaining capital intact and—necessarily—with it the concept of net real income, and to use only the concept gross real income. When he speaks of "the really relevant magnitude, income" (p. 298), it is gross real income that he has in mind. His reasons for this attitude are two-fold. On the one hand, except in a stationary state the notion of maintaining capital intact has no "strict meaning"; on the other hand, it is a concept of which the economist has no need. Thus, whereas I like to set out three identities: (1) net income = net investment plus consumption, (2) net income = gross income minus depreciation, (3) net investment = gross investment minus depreciation, Professor Hayek only cares to set out one, namely gross income = gross investment plus consumption. My identities, of course, imply Professor Hayek's,

[1] [*Economica*, n.s., vol. 8, no. 31, August 1941, pp. 271–75.—Ed.]

[2] There are, of course, depletions of capital other than those due to wear and tear and obsolescence, e.g., capital losses due to earthquake or war, which it is not customary to offset before reckoning net income. In what follows these will be ignored. They are discussed in my article on "Net Income and Capital Depletion" in the *Economic Journal* of June, 1935. [A. C. Pigou, "Net Income and Capital Depletion," *Economic Journal*, vol. 45, no. 178, June 1935, pp. 235–41.—Ed.]

[3] Macmillan & Co., 1940. [*Sic*—although Hayek dated his preface "June 1940," Macmillan published the book in 1941.—Ed.]

but his identities do not imply mine. He is satisfied with a part only of what I require. I shall begin with the first of his two reasons.

The gist of it, if I have not misunderstood, is as follows. If capital were perfectly homogeneous, consisting of a single type of article only, the quantity of capital would be something perfectly self-contained and unambiguous. What this quantity amounted to at any time would, of course, be a consequence of the interplay of demand and supply in the past. But at any given moment it would be a physical datum, independent of, prior to, affecting, not affected by, the equilibrating process. But in actual life capital is not homogeneous; it is heterogeneous, consisting of a great number of different sorts of things. It is still true that at any given moment the quantities of the several items included in it constitute an independent physical datum. But how exactly is an inventory of diverse items to be conceived as a "physical magnitude"? Clearly it can only be so conceived if we treat the given quantities of its several items as all *equivalent to* so many units of one item; and the only plausible way of doing this is to equate a unit of B to a unit of A when it is *worth* a unit of A. But the relative values of A and B and of all other things, so far from being independent of the equilibrating process, are determined through that process. For example, the relative current values of different types of machines are affected by the rate of interest, those promising a given yield in the distant future being more valuable relatively to those promising the same yield in the near future, the lower is the rate of interest.[4] Hence the quantity of capital expressed in the only way in which it is practicable to express it is not an unambiguous physical datum, as it would be if capital were an homogeneous entity. On the contrary, the quantity expressed in terms of any given component will be different at two times if the relative values of the components have changed, even though the physical constituents of the capital stock are identical at both times. It follows that the maintenance of these physical constituents unaltered need not entail that capital is maintained intact. That concept has no clear or sensible meaning.

The whole of this reasoning apart from the two last sentences I accept. I accept too the view that, if maintaining capital intact has to be defined in such a way that capital need not be maintained intact even though every item in its physical inventory is unaltered, the concept is worthless. But the inference I draw is, not that we should abandon the concept; rather that we should try to define it in such a way that, when the physical inventory of goods in the capital stock is unaltered, capital is maintained intact; more generally, in such a way that, not indeed the quantity of capital—which, with heterogeneous

[4] For, if machine A promises a yield x n years hence and machine B an equal yield m years hence (m being greater than n) the value of B = the value of A multiplied by $[1 / (1 + r)]^{m-n}$ where r is the annual rate of interest.

items, can only be a conventionalised number—is independent of the equilibrating process, but changes in its quantity are independent of changes in that process. Let us enquire whether and how this can be done.

Suppose that capital consists of two sorts of goods only, *A* and *B*, that at date 1 there are 500 units of each, and that one unit of *A* is worth 2 units of *B*. Then the stock of capital as a whole is "equivalent" either to 750 units of *A* or to 1,500 units of *B*. At date 2 one unit of *A* has become worth 4 units of *B*, so that at that date 500 units of *A* plus 500 units of *B* are equivalent to either 625 units of *A* or to 2,500 units of *B*. As between the two dates one unit of *A* has become worn out or has been discarded out of the capital stock (e.g., scrapped on account of obsolescence). How many additional units of *B* must have been created in order that capital as a whole may have remained intact between the two dates? *Prima facie* it seems that there is nothing to choose between two answers, first, 2 units (in accordance with the valuation of the first date), secondly, 4 units (in accordance with that of the second date). But let us seek guidance from the special case of homogeneous capital. The quantity of this is a physically given magnitude, and nothing that happens either to people's desire attitude towards capital or to the cost (in any sense of cost) of producing new units can affect it in any way. By analogy, with heterogeneous capital also it is proper so to define quantity change that, the physical constituents of the capital stock being given, no such change can be brought about by anything that happens either to desire attitudes or to cost of production. Hence, if between dates 1 and 2 a unit of *A* disappears, capital will be maintained intact provided that a new unit of *A* is introduced irrespective of what the relative values of *A* and *B* have become and irrespective of the cost of production of *A*. If it is decided for any reason not to provide a new unit of *A*, but to provide instead some units of *B*, the number of units of *B* required to make up for the loss of the unit of *A* must then clearly be the number that at date 2 is worth—which is equivalent to saying is expected to yield the same income as—one unit of *A*.[5]

This way of defining maintenance of capital intact is readily generalised when capital consists, not of two, but of many kinds of goods. Moreover, if we suppose wearing out or discarding on the one side and replacement on the other to be a continuous balanced process, it is unambiguous. In practice, indeed, we have to do with finite time intervals. That being so, the quantity of *B* that is deemed equivalent to a given quantity of *A* over any period may be different if replacement of decayed or discarded capital takes place once a week, once a month, once a quarter or once a year; for the relative values of *A*

[5] We must not say "which has the same cost of production as one unit of *A* would have," for that would give absurd results if *A* had become impossible to produce, i.e., had come to have infinite cost of production.

and *B* may undergo frequent variations. Hence the precise meaning of maintaining capital intact is relative to the length of the accounting period with which we are accustomed to work. It will be agreed, however, I think, that in normal conditions this is not an important matter. In a rough general way then this definition will serve. It is not necessary to my purpose, nor do I wish, to claim that it is the best possible one. The possibility or, if we will, the high probability, that a better one could be found only strengthens my case.

Turn then to Professor Hayek's second reason for proposing to abandon the concept maintaining capital intact, namely that it is not needed. Against this I have two considerations to offer. First, as we have seen, and as is indeed obvious, to abandon this concept entails abandoning also that of net real income. In spite, however, of Professor Hayek's claim (p. 336) that the distinction between gross and net investment—which is, of course, the same as that between gross and net income—"has no relationship to anything in the real world," it cannot be denied that both business men and the income tax authorities seek after and make practical use of this distinction—or the best approach to it that they can find. It is net income, not gross income, upon which income tax is assessed. If a Chancellor of the Exchequer were to attempt to assess it upon gross income, what an outcry there would be! Surely it is proper for economists to take cognizance of this fact and, while admitting that perfect definitions cannot be found, to try to make them as little imperfect as they can.

Secondly, real income is of interest to economists largely because of its relevance to what Professor Irving Fisher calls psychic income—income of satisfaction or utility. Of course the relationship between these things is highly intricate—a matter not to be discussed here. But gross and net income are not on a par. We can easily imagine two situations in one of which the production of a given gross real income entails the wearing out or using up of a much larger mass of capital elements than it does in the other. Hence net real income is, or at all events may be, a great deal more relevant to psychic income than gross real income. This is, so far as it goes, a second good reason for economists to try to disentangle it.

No doubt, if it could be shown that the disentanglement is, from the nature of the case, utterly and for ever impossible, it would be the part of wisdom to abandon the attempt. We do not want to spend our lives in squaring the circle or inventing perpetual motion machines. But that is not the situation with which we are faced. We cannot, indeed, in this field evolve concepts which are perfectly clean cut. There are bound to be rough edges. Some of us, myself among the number, have tried our hand at smoothing these down. No doubt we have in some degree failed. But we have not, I suggest, failed so grievously that others, instead of giving our baby another wash, should empty both it and the bath away.

TWELVE

MAINTAINING CAPITAL INTACT: A REPLY[1]

Professor Pigou's defence of the conception of "maintaining capital intact" consists essentially of two parts. The first is a restatement of his own attempt to define its meaning. The second is a plea that, even if this particular attempt should not be regarded as successful, economists ought still to continue to seek for the definite and unique sense which he believes must be behind the admittedly vague meaning that this concept has in practice. I shall try briefly to answer each point in turn.

1. Professor Pigou's answer to the question of what is meant by "maintaining capital intact" consists in effect of the suggestion that for this purpose we should disregard obsolescence and require merely that such losses of value of the existing stock of capital goods be made good as are due to physical wear and tear. Once this proposition is accepted and the concept is defined so that in all instances "when the physical inventory of goods in the capital stock is unaltered, capital is maintained intact," the rest of his argument necessarily follows. I am unable to accept this basis of his solution.

If Professor Pigou's criterion is to be of any help, it would have to mean that we have to disregard *all* obsolescence, whether it is due to foreseen or foreseeable causes, or whether it is brought about by entirely unpredictable causes, such as the "acts of God or the King's enemy," which alone he wanted to exclude in an earlier discussion of this problem.[2] Now this seems to me to be neither useful for theoretical purposes nor in conformity with actual practice. The consequences of using this concept of "maintaining capital intact" can best be shown by considering an imaginary case. Assume three entrepreneurs, *X*, *Y*, and *Z*, to invest at the same time in equipment of different kinds but of the same cost and the same potential physical duration, say ten years. *X* expects to be able to use his machine continuously throughout the period of

[1] [*Economica*, n.s., vol. 8, no. 31, August 1941, pp. 276–80.—Ed.]

[2] See [A. C. Pigou,] *Economics of Welfare*, 4th ed., [London, Macmillan,] 1932, p. 46, and my discussion of the various stages in the evolution of Professor Pigou's theory of "maintaining capital intact" in this journal, August, 1935, particularly pp. 245–248. [Hayek, "The Maintenance of Capital," *Economica*, n.s., vol. 2, no. 7, August 1935, pp. 241–76; included in the present volume.—Ed.]

its physical "life." *Y*, who produces some fashion article, knows that at the end of one year his machine will have no more than its scrap value. *Z* undertakes a very risky venture in which the chances of employing the machine continuously so long as it lasts and having to scrap it almost as soon as it starts to produce are about even. According to Professor Pigou the three entrepreneurs will have to order their investments in such a way that during the first year they can expect to earn the same gross receipts: since the wear and tear of their respective machines during the first year will be the same, the amount they will have to put aside during the first year to "maintain their capital intact" will also be the same, and this procedure will therefore lead to their earning during that year the same "net" income from the same amount of capital.[3] Yet it is clear that the foreseen result of such dispositions would be that at the end of the year *X* would still possess the original capital, *Y* one tenth of it, while *Z* would have an even chance of either having lost it all or just having preserved it.

I find it difficult to conceive that this procedure could have any practical value or any theoretical significance. That entrepreneur *Y*, acting in this manner, would to all intents and purposes throw his capital away, i.e. would plan to lose it, hardly needs pointing out. But take the case where a clear concept of net income is most wanted, namely, direct taxation. To treat all receipts except what is required to make good physical wear and tear as net income for income tax purposes would evidently discriminate heavily against industries where the rate of obsolescence is high and reduce investment in these industries below what is desirable. The manufacturer of wireless sets, e.g., who expects this year's model to be superseded in a year's time by technical improvements, would certainly have to restrict investment and output so as to keep prices high enough to enable him to write off obsolescing equipment in the course of the year. But if his allowance for obsolescence were treated as income, this would in effect amount to a special capital turnover tax and force him further to reduce his investment. Such a system would therefore discriminate heavily against all industries with rapid technological progress (or new and experimental industries) and thus slow down technological advance.

Analytically the use of this concept of "maintaining capital intact" would be no less misleading. One of the purposes for which we want a definition of net income is to know what are the long run costs on which an adequate profit must be made in order that investment in that particular industry should appear profitable. It is immediately clear that all foreseeable obsolescence (whether it can be predicted with certainty or only with a certain degree of probability) must here be taken into account. No entrepreneur would regard the three alternatives mentioned before as equally profitable, if the gross

[3] For our present purposes we can disregard any differences in the cost of operating the three machines.

returns to be expected were the same—although if he accepted Professor Pigou's conception of "maintaining capital intact" he would have to do so. But in that case he would not long remain an entrepreneur.

But while I feel that it is impossible simply to disregard obsolescence in this connection, it is not difficult to see why Professor Pigou is reluctant to admit it among the factors which have to be taken into account in "maintaining capital intact": because, once one admits it, one is on the path which leads inevitably to complete scepticism concerning the possibility of any objective criterion of what "maintaining capital intact" means. Most people will agree with Professor Pigou that not *all* obsolescence has to be made good before we can consider any income as being "net." To demand that all capital losses due to unforeseen and unforeseeable changes should be made good before any income can be described as net income might mean that not only certain individuals, but, in certain circumstances, even whole communities, might have no net income for years on end—although they might be in a position permanently to maintain their consumption at their accustomed level or even to raise it. I entirely agree with Professor Pigou's implied contention that in many such cases the making good of past losses should be regarded as new saving rather than as mere maintenance of capital. But this applies only to losses due to causes which had not been foreseen. And the real problem of maintaining capital intact arises not after such losses have been made, but when the entrepreneur plans his investment. The question is, what allowance for amortisation he ought to make in his calculations so that, in view of all the circumstances known to him, he can expect to be able to earn the same income in the future.[4] But the knowledge on the basis of which he has to make this decision will necessarily change as time goes on, and with it will change the provision he has to make in order to achieve his aim. No watching of the "quantity" of his capital from the outside, that is, without knowing all the information he possesses at different dates, can tell us whether he has done his best to avoid involuntary encroachments upon his sources of income or the opposite. And if we know what information he commands at the different successive dates, the action which we should think most appropriate on his part is not likely to be one which would keep any measurement of his capital constant. In a changing world, where different people, and even the same people at different times, will possess different knowledge, there can be no objective standards by which we can measure whether a person has done as well in this effort as he might have done. In such a world there is no reason to expect

[4] [An allowance for amortization of a machine (or other capital asset) is a periodic sum that the owner sets aside from gross earnings and accumulates (or uses to pay down the IOU with which he financed the asset), so that he can replace the asset when its income-earning ability declines or ends.—Ed.]

that the quantity of capital, in whatever sense this term be meant, will ever be kept constant, even though every individual owner of capital might do all in his power to avoid that involuntary "splashing" or "stinting" which capital accounting seeks to prevent.[5] This is a conclusion of some importance, since much of present economic theory is based on the contrary assumption, so well expressed by Professor Pigou when he wrote of "the concept of capital as an entity capable of maintaining its quantity while altering its form and by its nature always drawn to those forms on which, so to speak, the sun of profit is at the time shining."[6]

There is one more point in this connection where I am anxious to correct a wrong impression which seems to have been left by what I said on this question. I hope I nowhere did say, and I certainly ought not to have said, that with the concept of "maintaining capital intact" the concept of net income should also disappear. All that I meant to argue was that we cannot hope to define the latter by any reference to the "quantity" of capital and its changes. For an explanation of the alternative procedure I must refer to my *Pure Theory of Capital*, particularly pp. 336 *et seq.*

2. It is unlikely that Professor Pigou would have been led to advocate a solution of the puzzle which is so obviously imperfect if it were not for the fact that among the various solutions yet suggested it seemed to be the least imperfect, and if he had not been convinced that there must be a solution. His argument is that business men and legislators constantly use the concept of maintaining capital intact and seek after a clear distinction, and that the economist ought to help them to approach as closely as possible to the ideal solution which has not yet been found. Nobody denies, of course, that the practices actually followed in this connection are of the greatest importance for the economist and that he ought to know as much about them as possible. Nor do I want to deny that these practices aim at some purpose and that the economist ought to try to help as much as he can in achieving it. The question is, however, whether this ultimate purpose of the practices ostensibly aiming at "maintaining capital intact" is adequately defined by these words. I personally have come to the conclusion that while the ordinary practice of trying to keep the money value of capital constant is in most circumstances a fairly good approximation to the real purpose of capital accounting, this is not true in all circumstances. I have tried to show that this ultimate purpose has no direct or necessary connection with changes in the quantity of capital, however measured, and that therefore no policy which aims at maintaining a particular

[5] ["Splashing" and its opposite "stinting" were terms respectively used by Dennis H. Robertson in *Banking Policy and the Price Level* (London: P. S. King, 1926) to designate rates of consumption above and below one's permanently sustainable rate of consumption.—Ed.]

[6] *Economic Journal*, June, 1935, p. 239. [A. C. Pigou, "Net Income and Capital Depletion," *Economic Journal*, vol. 45, no. 178, June 1935, pp. 235–41.—Ed.]

measurement of capital constant can fully achieve that purpose in all circumstances. If this conclusion is essentially negative, it need for that reason be no less useful. If the usefulness of the practices aiming at "maintaining capital intact" have definite limitations, the important thing is that these limitations be recognised. The fact that practical men try to apply to all cases a formula which has served them well in a great many cases does not prove that in these attempts the formula must necessarily have any meaning at all. The problem which the accountant and the income tax inspector face is not what constitutes in any real sense "maintaining capital intact" in these cases—although they may have to interpret provisions which use such or similar phrases—but what are the most appropriate practices which will achieve the same end which in the more ordinary situations is adequately achieved by keeping the money value of capital constant.

INDEX

abstinence theory, 133
Adler, Solomon, 3, 93
amortization quotas, 56–57, 65, 98, 166–67
Ashley, William J., 53, 56, 108
assets: business, 160; physical, 115, 115n21, 196; values of, 103
assumptions: concrete, 30; realistic, 40, 132
Austria, xx, 15, 20, 48, 61, 63, 103, 149; capital consumption in, xx
Austrian business cycle theory. *See* business cycle theory
Austrian capital theory. *See* capital

Bentham, Jeremy, 95n30
Boettke, Peter J., xxviii
Böhm-Bawerk, Eugen von, ix, xviii–xxiv, 5–7, 10, 15–18, 20–24, 33–34, 56, 77, 103, 119; capital theory, 22, 29–30, 102–3, 108n15, 111, 118; imputation, 6, 6n11; influence on Hayek, ix, xviii–xxiv; value theory, xviii, 21, 21n4, 27; against wages fund, 103
business cycles, xix–xxxi, 21, 53, 56, 62, 91, 103–5, 115–16, 121, 125, 127–28
business cycle theory, Austrian, xxi, xxvi, 45, 183, 184

Caldwell, Bruce J., x n3, xii n7, xiv n10, xvi n16, 143n4, 164n17
capacity: excess, xxix–xxxi, 55–61, 72–73, 141–45–155, 154n8, 159–60, 180; productive, 14, 55, 74, 109, 132, 133, 150, 153; underutilized, xxxii, 151, 154
capital: additions to stock of, 59, 71–72, 104, 121, 127–29, 154; amortization of, 56, 131, 131n29, 139n40; Austrian capital theory, xx, xxiii, xxx, 100, 119n2; available capital, 49, 57; Cambridge capital controversy, 82n17; circulating, 56, 152; constant amount of, 156; consumption of (*see* capital consumption); conversion of, 49, 59, 60; creation of, 69, 70; demand for, 138, 151; destruction of, 55, 58, 64, 188; fixed, 51, 60–61, 87, 15; fund, concept of, 119, 120, 130, 131–36, 133n34, 140, 159; general theory of capital, 102; good will, 110n16; horizontal expansion of, 122n16; invested, 56, 65, 140; joint-stock, 62, 64; maintaining, xxix, xxx, 69, 121n7, 132, 148–49, 156–57, 175–78, 180–85, 190–97; maintaining intact, xxix, xxx, 98, 113n20, 132, 156, 163–64, 170, 186–90, 194–98; maintaining intact, rationale of, 156, 163, measuring, xxx; mobility of, 96–97, 112–15, 140, 179; mythology of, 118, 135; old, 64, 65, 147, 148; original, 103, 195; particular, xxiii, xxviii, 137; permanence of, 138; perpetual, xxiv, 120, 130, 132; provision of, 51, 51n10, 65; quantity of, xxiii, 60, 64, 72, 82, 86, 91, 100–105, 113, 120, 131–33, 148, 179, 181–87, 191, 195, 197; real, 51, 64, 97–99, 159, 174; reproduction of, 68, 108, 120, 130, 137, 138, 184; role of, xxiv, 111;

capital (*continued*)
scarcity of, 65, 152; shortage of, 61, 65, 66; total, 113, 124; transfer of, 114, 128, 180; transformation of, 133, 157; working, 57, 61
capital accounting, 130, 164, 169, 183, 187, 197; and monetary policy, 156, 186
capital accumulation, xix, xxviii, 48, 48n4, 70, 77n4, 137, 159, 182
capital and fluctuations, x, 1, 20, 47, 141
capital and interest income, 15, 16, 20, 21, 140
capital and interest of capital, xviii, 20–33, 28n15, 37, 114, 120
capital constancy, 156, 156nn1–2, 158, 164, 170, 175, 196, 197, 198
capital consumption, xx, xxi, xxvii, 48n5, 47–66, 54n15, 76, 97, 106, 106n12, 188; actual, 62; Austria's, xx, 106n13; capital consumption and saving, xx; persistent, 49, 51
capital costs, 146–47
capital depletion, 157, 161–62, 190, 197
capital discounting, 77n4
capital disposal, 56, 56n17, 135; invested, 57
capital formation, xx, xxii, 56, 65, 68, 69; in Germany, 66, 66n22
capital gains, 176–77, 181
capital goods, xxii, xxiii, xxv, xxvi, xxviii, xxix, 52, 53, 58, 116, 131, 135, 137, 158, 161; additional, 58; capital equipment, 50, 58, 60, 64, 111, 144, 152, 156, 179; changes to, xxi, 53; concrete, 97, 140, 157, 158; decline of, 54; durable, 87, 97, 129n27; existing, 55, 58, 76, 95–99, 125, 134–35, 140, 152, 153158, 161, 185; existing production facilities, 58, 61, 152; existing productive resources, 122, 126; free capital, 57, 65, 69, 76, 92, 97, 179; given stock of, 133, 139, 179; heterogeneous, xxvi, 147, 147n6, 191–92; homogeneous, xxvi, xxviii; impermanent, xxv, 122; increment of, 106; individual, 99, 157, 179; industries, 116; inherited, xxv, 79; nature of capital and income, 160; neglect of impermanent, xxv; neglect of inherited, xxv; new, 131, 135, 139, 182; obsolescence of, xxx–xxxi, 93, 162–63, 171–73, 190–96; particular, xxxii, 137; physical deterioration of, 162, 172; producing, 58; production of, 69, 107; reallocation of, xxiv; reduction of, 59, 99; replacement of, 121, 133, 187; stock of, xxx, 52, 54, 76, 96, 131, 134, 139, 179, 194
capital investments, xxxii, 60, 112, 149; additional, 59; old, 147
capitalisation, 63, 109
capitalist-entrepreneurs, 132, 179, 187
capitalistic production, xxiv, 49, 51, 54, 77, 100, 119
capitalists or capital owners, 56, 156, 158, 165–69, 170–79; individual, xxxii, 149, 169, 174, 177, 180
capitalist system, 55, 65
capital levies, 49, 63
capital limits, 122, 136
capital losses, xxxi, 55–56, 57, 60, 145, 171, 176, 178, 181, 190, 196
capital per head, 60
capital problem, 139
capital saving, 177
capital shrinkage, xxviii
capital stock, xx, xxiii, xxix, 52, 63–65, 69, 75, 95, 160–64, 167, 179–82, 191–94; economy's, 62; supply of capital, xxvii, 42, 59, 66, 68, 122–24, 130, 135, 140, 157; supply of free capital, 69, 92
capital structure, xxi, xxix, 106, 116
capital values, 103, 110, 148, 171, 175–77, 181, 188
Cassel, Gustav, xxiv, 57n17, 77, 100, 117, 119, 135, 136; on capital disposal, 57n17
central planning, xi, xiv, xvii, 3, 23; Hayek and Mises on, xvi, xvii n16; Hayek and Wieser on, ix n1; opponents of Mises

and Hayek, xiii; socialist calculation problem, ix, xi–xiv, xvii, 3, 23
ceteris paribus assumption, 184
Clark, John Bates, 91; Clarkian doctrine, 138; distribution of rent, 105n10; marginal productivity theory, 119n3
Cohen, Avi J., xxiv, xxv, xxvi, 119n3
competition, xiv, xxvi, xxxi, 11, 44, 51, 62, 144–48, 152; imperfect, 149, 150
competitive economy, 141–48, 155
complementary goods, xiv, 1, 6–7, 13, 15, 19
construction period, 101–8, 111–13
consumer goods, xxix, 2–7, 12–15, 17, 24, 50–54; industries, 62; per capita, xxi, 52; prices of, xiii, 52; production of, 51, 52, 57
consumers, xii, xiii, xviii, 69, 71, 72, 81, 82, 94, 134, 151, 183–88; satisfaction of, xxxii
consumption, xxi–xxvi, 54, 64, 67, 72, 106, 168, 174–75, 180; current, xxii–xxiv, 51–52, 107, 121, 187; marginal, xviii, xix; purposes of, 49, 63, 64, 70, 188; real per capita, xxv, 52
cooperation, 11–12, 165
"cost goods," 8, 9
costs, 50, 71, 72, 94, 102, 108, 145, 148, 150, 176, 180, 184–85, 192, 195; average, 150; law of, 7–8, 15–18; reductions in, 72, 146; relative, 40, 184; total, xxxi, 51, 147, 176
credit expansion, xxi, xxii, 71–73, 188

depreciation, 101–3, 109, 149, 172–73, 175
depressions, xxvi, 49n6, 58, 71–72, 114–16, 152, 186. *See also* business cycles
Dickinson, H. D., xii
disinvestment, 104–8, 113
durability, 76–78, 87–88, 92–93, 101, 104, 113–16, 127–29, 171, 173. *See also* capital goods: durable
dynamic processes, xxvii, 76, 98, 98n37, 157, 179, 182
economic dictator construct, xxxi, 143, 146
"Economics and Knowledge" (Hayek), xvi, 183n31
economics of decline, 48
Economics of Welfare (Pigou), 160–61, 162n12, 176n24, 194n2
economic system, xiv, 14, 19, 112, 125, 143
economic theory, xvi, 2–4, 7, 10–11, 18, 27, 97, 104, 120
economic value, 3, 6, 7, 14, 109, 110
economists, xii–xiii, xvii, xx–xxii, xxix, 47–51, 120, 193, 197; academic, xxxii, 141, 142, 155
Edelberg, V., 77n6
Edgeworth-Bowley box, xiii
entrepreneur, xxxi, 51, 52, 70, 90, 143, 144, 145, 146, 147, 148, 177, 178, 179–80, 195; classes, 65
entrepreneur-capitalist, xxix, 182
equilibrating process, xxvi, xxix, 157, 191, 192
equilibrium: concept of, xiv, xviii, xix, 24–26, 50, 75, 81–82, 91–94, 157–15; level, 50–51; prices, xiii
exchange, xiii, 2, 10, 12, 30, 70, 125; exchange economy, xii, xv, 3, 11
expectations, 90, 162, 178, 185

factors of production, xii, xiii, xxv, 2–5, 8–18, 34, 51, 72, 92, 116, 124, 126, 133, 136–39, 147, 153–54, 170, 190; marginal product of, 90–93; original, 51, 79, 79n10; permanent, 38, 126, 134; pricing of, xiv, xv, xvi, xxvi; produced, xxiv; quantity of, 71–72, 86, 124; supply of, 169, 176, 181
Fetter, Frank, 11, 21, 45
Fisher, Franklin, xiv, xv n11, 9
Fisher, Irving, xviii, xxxi, 32, 45, 46, 160; diagrams, 37n3; Knight on Fisherian interest theory, 44n11; stock vs. flow, concept of, 109n15; *The Theory of Interest* (Fisher), xviii, 37n3

forced saving, xxi–xxii, 69, 72, 73, 159
foresight, xxxi–xxxii, 113, 143, 149, 156, 165; imperfect, 138, 177, 181; perfect or complete, 138n39, 139–40, 165, 171–74, 177
free society, 109
Friedman, Milton, xxvi, 175n23
frontier, consumption-investment, xxi

Garrison, Roger, xxi–xxii, 52n11, 184n34
general equilibrium: approach, xiv, xv; model, xiii, xiv
goods: durability of, 78, 111, 137; economic, 1, 6–8, 13–16, 20–24, 29, 71–73, 93, 101, 129, 134, 185; free, 137; intermediate, xxiii, xxv, 96n33; permanent, 137, 138; physical inventory of, 191, 194; production of, 8, 22, 145; replaceable, 6; supply of, 26–31
goods-in-process, xxiii, 75, 75n1
gross receipts, 167–70, 172–75, 195
growth: of capital, 52, 60; economic, xxi, xxvi–xxviii, 70, 107, 109, 125

Hansen, Alvin H., 45n13
Hardy, Charles O., *Risk and Risk Bearing* (Hardy), 160, 160n8
Hayek, Friedrich A., x, xi, xii, xiii–1, 15, 22, 47, 79, 100–101, 106–7, 136, 159, 164, 183, 190; Hayek-Knight capital controversy, xxiv, xxv
Hicks, J. R., xxx, xxx n57; *Theory of Wages* (Hicks), 97n35
hoarding, 70–72
Hobson, John A., 105n10

identities, mathematical, 131, 134, 190–91
immobility of production factors, 114–17
imputation, x–xiii, xvii, 1–7, 10, 13, 16, 18; principle of, in jurisprudence, 2, 2n5; problem of, xi–xiv, xvii, xii n61, 2–5, 7, 9, 11, 13, 15–19, 84n21; theory of, x, 2–7, 11–17, 28
income, 38–44, 46, 72, 74, 130, 160, 163–65, 170, 175, 180, 181–85, 188, 196; additional, 175, 177; annual, 43, 181; concept of, 160; constant, xxix–xxx, 38–39, 165–70, 172–75, 177, 180–81; current 94, 184, 187, 188; gross, xxix, xxx, 190, 193; income period, 42, 43; income stream, xxx, 44, 125, 134, 164, 165, 168, 172, 174, 183, 184, 187; permanent, 38, 125; real, 50, 187–90, 193; total, 38, 43, 94, 101, 111
index numbers, 163–64
indifference curves, 38–44, 171; indifference map, 36
industrial fluctuations, 53, 77, 139, 159. *See also* business cycles
industrial revolution, 70
industries, 57–62, 64, 79–80, 90–92, 123–28, 166–68, 188, 195
inflation, xx n30, xxvi, 63, 188; effects on accounting profits, xx n30; effects on stock market, 63; inflationists, 188
input curve, 126n23
inputs, xii, xiii, xviii, xxi, xxiii, xxvi–xxvii, xxxii, 4, 78, 79–84, 181
instruments, 67, 122, 128, 130, 139, 162, 171–74
interest, xviii, xxii, xxx, 15, 16, 20–22, 26, 31, 34, 82, 86, 93, 109, 149, 182; changes in rate of, 88; compound rate of, 83, 85; dynamic conception of, 31, 31n21; existence of, 20, 33, 46; function of, 86, 136; interest income, 56, 58; interest surface, 83, 87, 88; market rate of vs. natural rate of, 159n6; positive rate of, 41, 44–45, 73; rate of, 31, 40, 44–45, 74, 82–83, 86, 91–94, 137–38, 166
intermediate products, 52, 53, 79, 83, 94, 95–98, 126–27; quantity of, 71, 80, 81, 82; stock of, 53, 95, 98. *See also* goods-in-process
intertemporal choices, 21
inventions, 45, 143, 144–46, 149, 161, 166, 170–71, 176–77; capital-saving,

177; labour-saving, 73, 177; negative, 169n21; new, 123, 144, 146, 147, 162, 166, 176, 177, 181
investment, xxii–xxiv, xxxi, 40, 42, 44, 45, 72–73, 101, 110–15, 125, 134–35, 166, 172, 174, 182, 195; additional investment, 34, 71, 185; amount of, 42; capitalistic, xxi, 52; current, xxvi, 52, 90, 95–99, 134–36; fixed, 61, 146; investment activity, 52, 68, 154, 158; investment and output, xxiii, xxvii, 100, 117, 123, 129, 136; investment and saving in business cycle theory, 45; investment boom, xix, xxx; investment curve, 78, 80, 86, 89, 90, 91, 93, 126; investment figures, 80, 82; investment function, 78–94, 98–99, 126–27; investment goods, 115; investment item, 110, 113; investment purposes, 71, 184; investment structure, 80, 94–102, 116, 124–29; net, 183, 185, 190, 193; new, 51, 57, 61, 69, 71, 72, 101, 108, 132, 171, 174; period of, 112, 119, 123; productivity of investment, 40, 41, 44, 45, 125; profitable, 70, 138, 154; quantity of, 111; renewed, 133, 182; self-liquidation of, 131n29; structure of, 100, 111; successive, 39, 39n5, 41, 42; time dimension of, 121, 122, 127, 129; total, xxii, 86, 90, 111
investment opportunities, 41, 74, 173; profitable, xxxii, 149
investment periods, xxvi, xxvii, 42, 86–93, 98, 118, 124–29, 181, 184; average period of, 51, 71, 124, 135–36, 138n39, 181; maximum, 84, 168; possible, 37, 39

Jevons, William Stanley, 77, 104n10, 119; investment figures, 78–79

Kaldor, N., xx, xxviii
Kelsen, Hans, x n3
Keynes, John Maynard: on crises, 51n9, 115n21; *Treatise on Money* (Keynes), xxi, 51, 159, 163–64; on underconsumption, 51
Kirzner, Israel M., xiv, xvi
Knight, Frank H., xxiii, xxiv, xxviii, xxix, 100–103, 107–9, 119–23, 127, 131, 136; Crusonia plant, xxii–xxviii; *Risk, Uncertainty, and Profit* (Knight), 102n8; theory of capital and interest, xxi–xxiii, xxv–xxvii, xxx
knowledge, xii–xv, xxxi, 3, 47, 59, 107, 143, 166–69, 177, 196
Kydland, Finn E., xxviii

labor, xxii, xxiii, xxv, 51, 53, 54, 59–60, 75, 79, 124, 128–30, 136, 137, 154, 158; current use of, 76, 97, 98, 99; disutility of, 19; frozen vs. new, 54; productive, 108; total quantity of, 79
labor-capital ratio, 59n19; labor-plus-capital, 104
laborers, 103, 104; support of, 104, 105
land, xi, xxv, xxxii, 4, 51, 79, 95, 97, 103–5, 136, 157, 158
Lange, Oskar, xiii, xiv, xxviii
Leijonhufvud, Axel, 159n6
Lerner, Abba, xiii, xiv, xxvi
liquidation of capital investment, 106–7, 112–13, 115n21
liquidity, 115n21
liquidity preference, 45n14
living standards, 48n3
London School of Economics, xx, 77
losses, 6, 16, 28, 55, 58–61, 145, 148, 175–79, 196

machines, xxii, xxx–xxxii, 54–55, 105–6, 110, 114, 146–47, 191–95
Machlup, Fritz, xx, xxviii, 48n5, 57, 57n17; contra Knight, 119n2
malinvestment, 183n31, 185; economy-wide cluster of, xxviii, xxx
Mankiw, N. Gregory, xxvi n47
marginal product, 51, 90, 91, 104, 124; of capital, xxviii; of labor, 91, 91n27, 124n19

marginal productivity, 10, 12, 60, 122, 137, 170; theorists, xv; theory of, 10–13, 119
marginal utility, 1, 7–9, 15–16, 20, 24–25, 23–29, 29n17, 32–34, 36; school, 5, 9, 12, 13–15; Wieser's conception of, 9, 9n14
margins of growth, 125
market, xii, xiv, xvi, 3, 50, 54, 72, 94, 145, 150, 183, 185; prices, xvii, 156; process, xiv, xv; value, xxix, 63–64
Marshall, Alfred, 75n2, 190; on capital, 77, 77n4, 97, 190; short run, 156n2
Mayer, Hans, xin4, 9n14, 22n7, 22–23, 27–28, 31
Menger, Carl, xxix, 1, 5–7, 104n10
methods of production: capitalistic, 31, 122; efficient, 3
Mill, John Stuart, 53, 53n12, 56, 106, 108
mind, xv, 13, 26, 45, 50–53, 59, 61–63, 117, 120, 142–47
Mises, Ludwig von, x–xvii, xx–xxii, 3n6, 47n2, 47–48, 56, 159n6
Monetarism, xxvi, xxvi n47
monetary disturbances, xxx, 183–85
monetary policy, xxvi, 156, 186, 187
money, x, xi, xxi, xxxi, xxxii, 1, 51–54, 68–70, 114–15, 159, 164; costs, 50; incomes, 50, 163; loans, 187; value, 115, 161, 164, 167, 168, 169, 170, 183, 188; value of capital, 161, 187–88, 197–98
Montgomery, Michael R., xxviii
Morgenstern, Oskar, 63n20
"Mythology of Capital" (Hayek), xxiii–xxvi, 79n10, 118; Hayek's response to Knight, 119–40

national dividend, 160–63
net income, 69, 94, 167, 174, 182, 190–97; and capital depletion, 157, 162, 190, 197; capitalised perpetual, 105
net return, 38–39, 44
new capital, 68, 70, 73, 128–29, 138, 147–48, 162, 180; formation of, 49, 65
new facilities, 147, 148, 150, 151–53
New Keynesianism, xxvi, xxvi n47
non-permanent means of production, 97n36
non-permanent resources, 127–33

original factors, 39, 41, 54, 72, 79, 80, 82, 95–98, 125–27
output: constant, 88–90; current, 72, 94, 153; function, 77–81, 84–92, 98, 101; given, 87, 88; integral, 98; quantity of, 80, 92, 108, 137; stream, 76, 80, 84–89, 94, 98
over-investment, 73, 116, 184
owners, xxxi; of capital, xxx, 49, 56, 65, 106, 158, 165, 170; of factors, 69–70, 106–10, 144–49, 152, 174–77

patents, 144–45, 144–45n5
perfect foresight, assumption of, 138, 139, 165
period of production, xxiv–xxviii, 78–81, 94–95, 105, 108, 111, 117, 119, 123, 125–27; analysis, 130, 138; average, xxv, 80, 86, 119, 124, 136; change in, 53, 83–84, 91–92, 103, 123, 127, 129, 167, 172–73; and industrial fluctuations, 53, 77
physical productivity, 31, 92
Pigou, Arthur C., xxix, xxx; on capital goods, 157–63, 171–72, 190–97
political economy, xx–xxii, xxiv, xxix, 1, 48, 53, 56, 87, 93, 108–9, 186
Positive Theory of Capital, The (Bohm-Bawerk), 15n17, 20–21n3, 27, 103n9
Prescott, Edward C., xxviii
present income, xix, 38n4, 38–39, 42, 44, 46, 183–84; sacrifice of, 38, 39, 125, 182
preservation: of capital, 38, 131; of natural resources, 139
price level, 72, 159, 164, 197; in Hayek's review of Keynes, 164n17
prices, xii–xxvi, 2–3, 50, 52, 60, 94, 153–54, 165–66, 184; changes in relative,

xxvi, xxxii, 54, 107, 146, 150, 151; expected, xxx, 183, 185; of factors of production, xvi, 3; formation of, 11, 12, 17
Prices and Production (Hayek), xx, xxiii–xxiv, xxv, 23, 49, 78, 91
probability, 11, 171–75, 195
producer goods, 2, 8, 19, 22–29, 31, 52; complementary, 17; irreplaceable, 6; specific, 8–9; value of, 2–4, 7–19
producers, 2, 4, 6, 9, 11–14, 19, 24–25, 29, 51, 53, 150, 183–85
product differentiation, 149–50
production, xxiv, xxvii, 3, 8–20, 24, 52, 57, 81, 90–97, 107, 108, 129–30, 150, 152–54; average period of, xxv, 51, 72, 117, 119, 124, 126 (*see also* period of production); capitalistic methods of, 54, 60, 156; concept of, xxvii, xxviii; costs of, 49, 50, 52, 55, 62, 72, 94, 113, 144, 146, 150, 192; curves, 25, 37, 39, 42–44, 80–89; expansion of, 22, 101; factors of (*see* factors of production); improved method of, 146, 147; lengthening, 23, 24, 26, 80, 80n14, 94, 100, 101, 104, 121, 127–30, 137; methods of, xix, xxviii, 23, 80, 93, 95, 122; new, 129, 179; particular line of, 14, 82, 128; period of, xxv, 100, 104, 111, 112–13, 116; possibilities frontier, 52n11; produced means of, 97, 127; roundabout, xix, xxv, xxvi, 23, 26, 124, 124n19; stage of, 57, 96; structure of, xviii, xix, 18, 22, 91; technique of, xii, xv, 123; wages and, 77
productive capacity, 98, 102, 109, 110, 148, 152; underutilized, 58, 149, 152
productive equipment, 63, 95, 122, 179; new, 70, 73
productive organization, 106, 108
productive processes, 24, 25, 124
productive resources, xxi, 52, 116, 117, 126, 146
productivity, xviii, xix–xx, 4, 23, 26, 31, 34, 44, 50, 54, 59, 120, 125; constant, 41; relative, 4, 170; of roundabout production processes, 21, 23
products, 8–20, 24–26, 29, 33, 81, 83–85, 92, 130, 148, 150; demand for, xxi, 50–54, 72, 73, 152, 153–54, 161, 166–67, 183–85; final, 52, 58, 79, 81, 83, 102, 103, 130; larger, 23, 24; satisfaction, xiv, 19
profits, xxx–xxxii, 65–70, 102–3, 144–45, 160, 174–75, 180; on capital investments, 57–60, 63; normal, 51
psychological factors, 27, 28, 40, 65, 72, 145n5
purchasing power, 53, 72
Pure Theory of Capital, The (Hayek), ix n2, xv, xviii, xix–xx, xxiv–xxv, xxx, 76–78, 86–87, 126, 181, 190, 197

rationalization, 59, 151–52
real capital, 51, 64, 97–99, 174; stock of, 99, 159
real income, 50, 187–90, 193; gross, 190, 193
reinvestment, 51, 57, 61, 69–70, 86, 106, 124, 131, 167, 168, 170
relative values, 40n6, 40–41, 82, 84, 91, 99, 103, 183–84, 191–92
rent-goods, 97–98
reproduction: of capital, 68, 108, 130, 137, 138; reproducing capital, 120, 184
resources: available, 51, 52, 148; productive, 33–34, 67–73, 116, 122, 126–30, 134, 162, 167–68, 181
return, xix, 42n9, 42–45, 59, 119–20, 125, 164–70; rate of, 43–44, 98, 105
Ricardo, David, xxv, 2, 4, 186; rent theory, 4n7
Road to Serfdom (Hayek), 143n4
Robbins, Lionel, xvii, 77, 176
Robertson, Dennis H., 71, 159, 164, 197
roundabout production processes, xix, 21–25, 31
running costs, xxxi, 55, 144–47, 153, 176

saving, xx–xxii, 34, 40, 44–45, 67–74, 147, 159, 180–82, 185; individual, 68–70; new, 51, 52, 56, 57, 65, 67, 71, 137, 158, 175, 178, 180, 182, 196; path of, 40, 41, 43, 44, 45; planned, 159; rate of, xix, 34, 45, 46, 72; supply of, 69, 74
Schönfeld, L., 10, 27, 29, 30
Schumpeter, Joseph A., xii, xv, xvi, 10, 18, 21, 32, 33, 34, 45, 136n36, 159
Schwartz, Anna J., xxvi, xxvi n47
scrap value, 146, 176, 195
seasonal demand, 152
Sennholz, Hans F., 6, 15, 16, 20, 47
service life, 104–5, 108, 112, 115
services, 87–90, 108–9, 126–27, 131–34, 137–39, 171; capacity to render, 132, 133; consumable, 131; consumed, 109, 111; permanent, 133; productive, 4, 96, 102
simple economy, xv, xvi, 2, 8, 12
Smith, Adam, 51n10, 103, 105n10
socialism, xi–xvii, xxviii–xxix, 3, 56, 65–66, 142n2; economic calculation under, xi–xvii
Socialism (Mises), xi
society, xi, xii, 45–46, 66, 68, 100–103, 109–13, 116–17
Sozialpolitik, 9–10, 20, 23, 27, 33, 56, 78
"splashing," 164, 197
Staatswissenschaften, x–xi, 9, 11, 22–23, 27, 136
stages of production, xxiii, xxv, 57; earlier, 70, 91, 96, 101, 136
static analysis, 21, 25, 30–31, 35, 38, 122, 138n39, 140, 157
stationarity, xxviii, 46, 49, 105–6, 121, 122; stationary conditions, 33, 37, 42, 44, 80, 86, 94, 95, 98, 107, 122, 182; stationary state, xxvi, xxvii, xxix, 32, 34, 44, 190
Stigler, George, xxviii, xxviii n52
stinting, 164, 197
stock exchange, 62, 188–89
structure of production, 120, 140. *See also* capital structure
subjective value, xi, xiii, xvii, 1, 2, 3, 10, 17; distinction from utility, 1n2; theory, xi–xv, 1n1, 2–7, 10, 17, 19
subsistence fund, 95, 134, 135

tastes, xiii, xiv, 33, 34, 151, 178, 184; constant, 32–36, 38, 45
taxes: capital, 63–64; inheritance, 49; payroll, 58
technical change, 123, 158, 166
technical progress, xxix, xxxii, 47, 50, 141–55; and excess capacity, xxxi, 141
technocrats, 142, 153
technology, 4, 10, 52; advancing, 73; changes in, 101, 169; negative shocks to, 169n21; new, xxxi, 101, 149; shifts in, xxix
theory: of capital, xxiv–xxviii, xxxi, 77–78, 96, 111, 114, 119, 124–26, 133, 139, 156; of distribution, 2, 17; of investment, xxiv, 100–119, 136; of wages, 97, 104
Thünen, H. v., 4, 5, 10
time: consuming production processes, 20, 23–26; shape of input and output streams, 76, 125, 134; structure of production, 23, 23n8–9, 75, 98–101, 123, 133, 135. *See also* capital structure
time-preference, xix, 41, 41n7, 44, 45; rate of, 43–45
"Time Preference and Productivity" (Hayek), xix–xx
"time-to-build" models, xxviii, xxviii n53
Tomo, Shigeki, x n3
Tout, Herbert, 45
trend of economic thinking, 176

underconsumption theory, xxi, 51n9
undervaluation of future needs, 20–22, 26, 29n17
unemployment, 51, 54, 58–64, 74, 116; benefits, 58–60
units of analysis: individual, 8, 75, 80, 81, 82, 83, 87, 91, 92; marginal, 12, 15, 91, 93, 154

utility, 1–2, 6–8, 18, 26–29, 32–36, 148–49; choice-theoretic, xvii; comparison of, 27–29, 36, 101, 125, 163, 183; dependent, 5, 7, 16; individual, 25–30; isolated comparisons, 25–27; loss of, 6, 28; maximizing, 18; present, 28, 36; relative, 23, 33, 36, 40, 73; total, 6, 26
utility analysis, 32–37, 39, 41, 43, 45
utility curves, 25–26, 33n2, 33–35

value: aggregate, 157, 158, 188; dimension of capital, 132, 163; discounted present, 90, 184; formation, 26, 28, 30; imputation of, xv, 7–8, 12, 13, 17, 127n24; losses, 162; measurement of capital in terms of, 82, 103, 163, 17; money (*see* money: value); relations, 14, 22; theory of, 3, 12, 20, 27, 31
Vaughn, Karen, xxviii
Veblen, Thorstein, 142n2
Vienna, 64, 159; University of, ix–xx

wages, 49n6, 51, 54–60, 91, 97, 104, 116, 124, 167, 170; equilibrium, 50; high, 58, 59, 60, 63; higher, 50, 57, 59, 60, 122; theory, 97, 104
wages fund, 103, 104, 133
Warburton, Clark, xxvi, xxvi n47
waste, xxxii; related to technical progress, 143–45; related to underutilized technology, 151
wealth, 55, 68–69, 101, 108–11, 121, 132, 136, 149, 180; concentration of, 69, 70; stock of, 136n35
welfare, 160–62, 176, 194
Welter, Erich, 66
Wicksell, Knut, ix, 11, 14, 21, 45, 93, 97; on business cycles, 159n6; on capital theory, 77; on durable capital goods, 87, 87n24, 97; on time preference, 45
Wicksteed, P., 11, 105n10
Wieser, Friederich von, x–xii, xv, xvi, xvii, 1, 2, 7–10; influence on Hayek, x–xii, xv, xvi, xvii; partitioning concept, 16; on producer goods, 17, 22

Yeager, Leland B., xx, xxvi

For Product Safety Concerns and Information please contact our EU representative GPSR@taylorandfrancis.com Taylor & Francis Verlag GmbH, Kaufingerstraße 24, 80331 München, Germany